Blockchain
Data Analytics

A Wiley Brand

MAR   2021

Blockchain Data Analytics

by Michael Solomon

A Wiley Brand

Blockchain Data Analytics For Dummies®

Published by: **John Wiley & Sons, Inc.**, 111 River Street, Hoboken, NJ 07030-5774, www.wiley.com

Copyright © 2020 by John Wiley & Sons, Inc., Hoboken, New Jersey

Published simultaneously in Canada

For general information on our other products and services, please contact our Customer Care Department within the U.S. at 877-762-2974, outside the U.S. at 317-572-3993, or fax 317-572-4002. For technical support, please visit https://hub.wiley.com/community/support/dummies.

Wiley publishes in a variety of print and electronic formats and by print-on-demand. Some material included with standard print versions of this book may not be included in e-books or in print-on-demand. If this book refers to media such as a CD or DVD that is not included in the version you purchased, you may download this material at http://booksupport.wiley.com. For more information about Wiley products, visit www.wiley.com.

Library of Congress Control Number: 2020937204

ISBN 978-1-119-65177-2 (pbk); ISBN 978-1-119-65175-8 (ebk); ISBN 978-1-119-65178-9 (ebk)

Manufactured in the United States of America

SKY10020899_090120

Contents at a Glance

Table of Contents

Introduction

Data is the driver of today's organizations. Ignore the vast amounts of data available to you about your products, services, customers, and even competitors, and you'll quickly fall behind. But if you embrace data and mine it like it contains valuable jewels, you could find the edge to stay ahead of your competition and keep your customers happy.

And the potential value you can find in data gets even more enticing when you incorporate blockchain technology into your organization. Blockchain is a fast-growing innovation that maintains untold pieces of information you could use to decrease costs and increase revenue. Realizing blockchain data value depends on understanding how blockchain stores data and how to get to it.

Blockchain Data Analytics For Dummies introduces readers to blockchain technology, how it stores data, how to identify and get to interesting data, and how to analyze that data to find meaningful information. You learn how to set up your own blockchain analytics lab and local blockchain to learn and practice blockchain analytics techniques. After you set up your analytics lab, you find out how to extract blockchain data and build popular analytics models to uncover your data's hidden information.

About This Book

Blockchain technology is often described as the most important and disruptive technology of our generation. At its core, blockchain technology provides a novel way to add data to a ledger of transactions that is shared by other users whom you do not trust. Blockchain technology has the potential to change the way we conduct business at every level. And, while managing transactions between any two or more parties, any data related to the transaction gets stored on the shared ledger that can never be changed or deleted. The availability of unmodified history of transactions can be a huge advantage for organizations of all types.

Unlocking the trends or lessons in these blockchain transactions is the focus of this book. *Blockchain Data Analytics For Dummies* gives you the foundation of blockchain technology data storage and techniques to analyze blockchain-based data. You learn — in clear language — how to build analytics models and populate them with blockchain data.

Foolish Assumptions

I don't make many assumptions about your experience with blockchain technology, application programming, or cryptography, but I do assume the following:

>> You have a computer and access to the Internet.

>> You know the basics of using your computer and the Internet, as well as how to download and install programs.

>> You know how to find files on your computer's disk and how to create folders.

>> You're new to blockchain and you aren't an experienced software developer.

>> You're new to building data analytics models.

Icons Used in This Book

TIP

The Tip icon marks tips (duh!) and shortcuts you can use to extract blockchain data and build analytics models.

REMEMBER

Remember icons mark the information that's especially important to know.

TECHNICAL STUFF

The Technical Stuff icon marks information of a highly technical nature that you can normally skip over.

WARNING

The Warning icon tells you to watch out! It marks important information that may save you headaches when writing your own blockchain applications.

Beyond the Book

In addition to the material in the print or e-book you're reading right now, this product also comes with some access-anywhere goodies on the web. Check out the free cheat sheet for more on blockchain technology and data analytics at www.dummies.com/cheatsheet/blockchaindataanalyticsfd.

You'll find summary information about blockchain technology, data analytics models, and extracting blockchain data. The cheat sheet is a reference to use over and over as you gain experience in extracting blockchain data and building data analytics models.

In addition, if you'd rather download the code you see in this book instead of typing it, go to http://www.dummies.com/go/blockchaindataanalyticsfd. You can download zip files for each of the projects you'll create to develop and test data access and analytics scripts.

Where to Go from Here

The *Dummies* series tells you what you need to know and how to do the things you need to do to get the results you want. Readers don't have to read the entire book to just learn about some topics. For example, if you just want to learn about extracting blockchain data, you can jump right to Chapters 5 and 6. On the other hand, if you need to set up your own blockchain analytics lab, read Chapter 4, which tells you how to do that with clear, step-by-step instructions.

1

Intro to Analytics and Blockchain

Chapter **1**

Driving Business with Data and Analytics

I n the twenty-first century, personalization is king — and data makes personalization possible. A good friend can pick out a much more personal gift for you than a stranger because that friend knows what you like and dislike. Marketers have known for decades that establishing a connection with someone can dramatically increase the chances that the person will become a customer. Organizations' desire to attract customers and increase sales drives the pursuit of meeting consumers' needs.

Consumers demand personal attention and have come to expect a high level of individualized customer service, online or when physically shopping in a bricks-and-mortar store. Due to advances in consumer interaction sophistication, the bar is high for all types of organizations. For example, it isn't good enough for web searches to return a general list of responses. Consumers expect their searches to be personalized and filtered based on their preferences. Today's search engines, and most shopping sites, suggest responses before you even finish typing. It's almost as if the search function knows you and what you're about to ask.

The capability to guess what a user is likely to ask or find interesting is based on data. Humans are creatures of habit and most processes (and even natural events) tend to be cyclic. The repetitive nature of behavior means that if you have enough historical data, you should be able to predict what comes next. Expending effort to collect, maintain, and analyze data related to your organization's operation can help to reduce costs, limit exposure to fines and lawsuits, and lead to increased revenue.

In short, learning how to use your data helps you learn how to make your organization more profitable. In this chapter, you learn about ways that data can provide value to organizations.

Deriving Value from Data

The increased trend toward personalized offerings both depends on data and exposes data's importance to business operations. Data is no longer simply a consequence of engaging in transactions — data is necessary to increase the volume of transactions. Organizations are learning how valuable data is to their capability to conduct and expand operations. If you want to stay competitive in today's economy, you'll have to provide an experience that's responsive and personal. Data from previous transactions makes it possible to anticipate subsequent activity and tailor offerings to customer and partner preferences.

For example, the items you've bought online in the past give online shopping sites such as Amazon.com enough of your background to be able to make suggestions for additional purchases. Using past data to recommend future purchase or actions is a common way to derive value from data. In this section, I introduce three ways organizations can identify data with the greatest potential value.

Monetizing data

Over the past two decades, many organizations have come to view data as the primary fuel of the information age. Since the dawn of the twenty-first century, many organizations with data as their central business driver either started or expanded rapidly. Amazon relies on customer data to make additional purchase suggestions, while companies such as Facebook and Google rely on data as their primary product to drive advertising revenue. All these organizations found ways to turn data into revenue.

As data becomes more directly associated with revenue, data giants Google, Facebook, and Amazon control a growing demand for access to that data. Users have long been encouraged to share their personal data and activities, with little or no compensation. In the beginning, the perception was that sharing personal data was harmless and had little value.

However, a growing number of consumers and business partners realize that their data has value. Legislative bodies have recognized the importance of personal data and are passing new levels of privacy protection legislation each year. Data not only has value in and of itself but, when linked to other related personal data, can also provide valuable insight into personal behavior.

The realization that personal data has value has resulted in a game of sorts. Organizations that value consumer data attempt to acquire as much data as possible, while consumers are becoming more willing to deny free access to their personal data or demand compensation. Compensation often takes the form not of a direct monetary payment but of other perks or discounts.

Exchanging data

As organizations realize the increasing value of consumer and partner data, the more they explore ways to leverage that value. When consumers interact with any organization, or organizations interact with partners, a trail of data artifacts is left behind. Artifacts that document transaction timing and contents, as well as any changes to data, describe how entities interact with organizations. As more interactions with all types of organizations become more automated, the quantity and frequency of data artifacts increases.

Organizations that collect data artifacts find that not all are useful — at least not to that organization. However, as data becomes more and more valuable, many organizations have expanded the scope of data they collect with the intention of selling that data to other organizations. As data becomes a source of both direct and indirect revenue, data collection and management moves from a supporting role to a strategic planning concern.

For example, political campaigns routinely spend large sums of money to purchase demographic information on customers who have purchased specific types of products. Political candidates who strongly support environmental issues find value in identifying people who purchase green products because these customers are likely potential supporters. The identities can then be used to solicit campaign donations.

TIP

The overuse of data selling has led to concern and frustration over personal privacy. Most people come to the eventual realization that online activity has consequences. Every time you provide your email address or telephone number to anyone, your data will likely end up being used by some other organization (or probably multiple organizations). Always be careful about what data you allow others to use.

Sharing and exchanging data isn't always bad. In some cases, you want your data to be shared among businesses and organizations. For example, sharing the complete service history for your car could make getting service easier and more reliable. With shared service data, you could take your car to any service provider and not have to remember the last time you had the oil changed or tires rotated. Techniques that support beneficial and responsible data sharing among organizations can be valuable to business and consumers.

Verifying data

One of the obstacles to realizing the full value of data is the dependence on its quality. Quality data is valuable, while incomplete or untrusted data is often worthless. What's worse, low-quality data may require more budget to clean than it will potentially generate in revenue. The only way to realize data's true value is to ensure that the data is valid and represents entities in the real world.

Verifying data has long been one of the highest costs associated with collecting and using data. Campaigns that depend on physical or email addresses will have little effect if the target addresses are largely incorrect. Bad data can come from many sources, including mischievous data submission, sloppy data collection, or even malicious data modification. An important aspect of relying on data is putting controls in place that verify the source of any collected data, along with that data's adherence to collection requirements.

A simple approach to verifying data in a distributed environment is to carry out a simple validation at the source and again at the server as the data is stored in a repository. While validating data at least twice may seem excessive, the practice makes user errors easier to catch and ensures that data received by the server is clean.

TIP

Validating data twice makes it possible for client applications to quickly catch errors, such as too many digits in a phone number or a missing field, while the server handles more complex validation tasks. A server may need access to other related data to ensure that data is valid before storing it in a repository. Server validation could include things such as verifying that order quantities are available in a warehouse and that data wasn't changed by a malicious agent during transmission from the client.

One of the reasons data verification is so important is that organizations are relying more and more on their data to direct business efforts. Aligning business activities with expectations based on faulty data leads to undesirable results. In other words, decisions are only as good as the data on which those decisions are based. The "garbage in, garbage out" adage still holds true.

Understanding and Satisfying Regulatory Requirements

The information age offers many new opportunities and just as many (if not more) challenges. The vast amount of data available to organizations of all types empowers advanced decision-making and raises new questions of privacy and ethics. Consumer protection groups have long been voicing concerns about how personal data is being used. In response to discovered abuses and the recognition of potential future abuses, governing bodies around the world have passed regulations and legislation to limit how data is collected and used.

Although collecting a few pieces of information about a customer may seem innocent, it doesn't take long for accumulated data to paint a picture of an individual's personal characteristics and behavior. Knowing the past behavior of someone makes it relatively easy to predict the person's future actions and choices. Predicting actions has value for marketing but also poses a danger to an individual's privacy.

Classifying individuals

The concern is that personal data has been, and will continue to be, used to classify individuals based on their past behavior. Classifying individuals can be great for marketing and sales purposes. For example, any retailer that can identify engaged couples can target them with ads and coupons for wedding-related items. This type of targeted advertising is generally more productive than general marketing. Advertising budget can be focused on target markets that provide the greatest ROI.

On the other hand, knowing too much about individuals may violate a person's privacy. One instance of a privacy violation was a result of the Target Corporation's astute data analysis. Target's analysts were able to identify expectant mothers early in their pregnancy based on their changing purchasing habits. When a new expectant mother was identified, Target would send unsolicited coupons for baby-related items. In one case, the coupons arrived in the mail before the mother had shared that she was pregnant; her family found out about the pregnancy from a retailer. Privacy is such a difficult issue because legitimate actions can violate a person's privacy.

Identifying criminals

Another aspect of privacy is when criminals, or other individuals who deliberately want to operate anonymously, hide their identities from exposure. Privacy may be important to the general population, but it's a necessity for criminal activity. The ability to deny, or repudiate, some action is crucial in avoiding discovery and capture, and to any subsequent defense. Money laundering and fraud are two activities in which privacy and anonymity are desired to obfuscate illegal activity.

On the other hand, law enforcement needs the ability to associate actions with individuals. That's why laws exist that protect the general public but allow law enforcement to conduct investigations and identify alleged perpetrators.

Protecting the privacy of law-abiding individuals while identifying criminals has become important across a spectrum of organizations. To enable law enforcement to deal with online privacy issues, legislative bodies have passed various laws to address those issues directly.

Examining common privacy laws

Here are a few of the most important privacy-related laws you'll likely encounter and may be compelled to satisfy:

>> **Children's Online Privacy Protection Act (COPPA):** Passed in 1998, COPPA requires parental or guardian consent before collecting or using private information about children under the age of 13.

>> **Health Insurance Portability and Accountability Act (HIPAA):** Passed in 1996, HIPAA modernized the flow of healthcare information and contains specific stipulations on protecting the privacy of personal health information (PHI).

>> **Family Educational Rights and Privacy Act (FERPA):** Passed in 1974, FERPA protects access to educational information, including protection for the privacy of student records.

>> **General Data Protection Regulation (GDPR):** Passed in 2016 (and implemented in 2018), GDPR is a comprehensive regulation from the European Union (EU) protecting the private data of EU citizens. Every organization, regardless of location, must comply with GDPR to conduct business with EU citizens. The EU citizen must retain control over his or her own data, its collection, and its use.

>> **California Consumer Protection Act (CCPA):** Passed in 2018, CCPA has been called "GDPR lite" to imply that it includes many of the requirements of GDPR. CCPA requires any organization that conducts business to protect consumer data privacy.

>> **Anti-Money Laundering Act (AML):** AML is a set of laws and regulations that assists law enforcement investigations by requiring financial transactions to be associated with validated identities. AML imposes requirements and

procedures on financial institutions that essentially make it very difficult to transfer money without leaving a clear audit trail.

>> **Know Your Customer (KYC):** KYC laws and regulations work with AML to ensure that businesses expend reasonable effort to verify the identity of each customer and business partner. KYC helps to discourage money laundering, bribery, and other financial-based criminal activities that rely on anonymity.

Predicting Future Outcomes with Data

Data can unlock lots of secrets. Data you collect through regular interactions with your customers and business partners can help you understand them and better meet their needs and wants. Assuming you have taken measures to protect individual privacy and have permission to collect and use the data, analyzing that data can benefit your organization and your customers (and partners, too).

A common way to use data is to build analytics models that help to explain the data, uncover hidden information, and even predict future behavior. Data analytics is all about using formal methods to unlock secrets that your data is hiding. These secrets aren't hidden on purpose — they just get lost in the mountains of data you collect. Without a structured approach to examining your data, you might miss some of its value that can lead to increased revenue.

Classifying entities

An *entity* is any object that your data describes, such as a customer, a vendor, a product, an order, or anything else that has characteristics data items can describe. In traditional database terms, an entity would correspond to a record or a row. The concept of a row maps to a spreadsheet concept as well. Think of a spreadsheet of customers. Each row would contain all the data that describes a single customer. Figure 1-1 shows a collection of customers in a table format.

TECHNICAL STUFF

These customers are stored in a comma-separated value (CSV) text file named `customer.csv`, and displayed in Visual Studio Code using the Edit as CSV extension. To learn more about Visual Studio Code and its extensions, see Chapter 4.

Note that each customer has a set of characteristics, such as name, address, and contact, stored in separate columns. Data analytics models use these different characteristics, also called *features*, to examine how different entities are related.

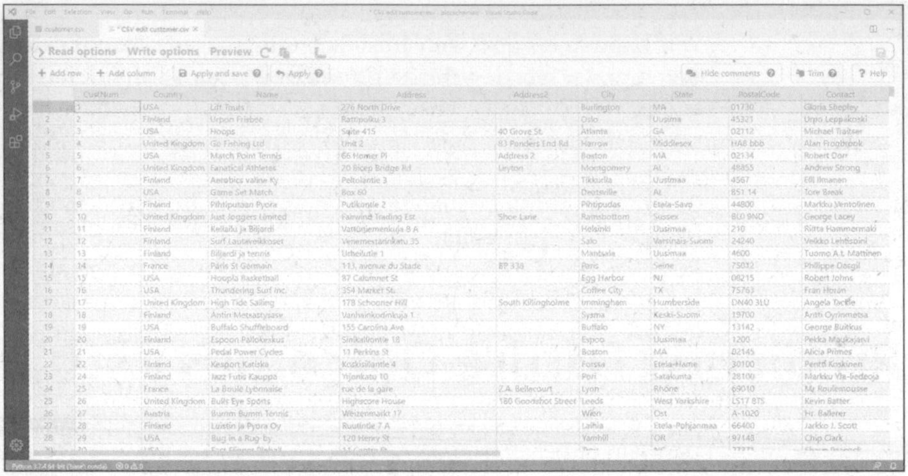

FIGURE 1-1:
Customer entities presented as a table.

One type of analysis is to examine the features of different entities to see if some features can help group entities or imply some relationship. For example, suppose you asked a group of people to name their favorite baseball team. You would expect that most people who answered "the Colorado Rockies" most likely live near Colorado. However, you can't always make such simple associations. If you asked the same question in the 1990s, not everyone who answered "the Atlanta Braves" lived in Georgia. During the 1990s, cable TV was becoming popular and Turner Broadcasting System, whose owner also owned the Braves, broadcast all Braves games nationally. Many people who didn't live in Georgia became Braves fans.

The Braves example shows that analytics models cannot be trusted unconditionally. Data analytics can provide tremendous value but also requires care and diligence to build models that return results that hold true over time.

Assuming that you invest sufficiently to build good models, classification models can help to identify entities that are similar. Similarity information helps organizations develop targeted marketing campaigns and services to give customers and partners the sense of being treated individually. You learn about several classification models in Chapter 7 and build a few in Chapter 10.

Predicting behavior

Although the capability to classify entities to identify groups of similarity can be valuable, analytics can also make predictions. Past behavior is a strong indication of future behavior. Humans tend to repeat actions and decisions, so you can use models that identify patterns to predict future actions. The capability to predict future actions can have tremendous value to organizations. If an organization can determine items that tend to be purchased together frequently, it can use that information to make additional purchase suggestions.

You've undoubtedly seen frequent item analysis results when you shop online. When your favorite website recommends that you purchase an additional item, and that item makes sense, it's because other people have bought that same item set in the past. How does the website know that? It used analytics.

One of the common analytics models you learn about in Chapter 7 and build in Chapter 11 is regression. Don't worry about the name right now (or the math). Regression is kind of like calculating the slope of a line on steroids. A *regression model* basically examines your data and figures out a line (or a curve) that matches the data you've seen. After you can graph your data, you can use that graph to guess what will happen based on new input data.

Let's see how that can help. Figure 1-2 shows a linear regression model built on audition data and resulting score data. This example comes from an example you use to build this model in Chapter 11.

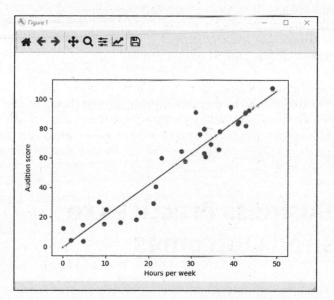

FIGURE 1-2: Linear regression model using hours practiced and audition scores data.

Here's the explanation you see again in Chapter 11: Suppose you're helping student musicians prepare for honor band tryouts. You've collected historical data on how many hours a week each student practiced, whether the student was accepted in the honor band, and what audition score each student earned. As you would expect, a linear correlation exists between hours of practice and audition score: The more a student practiced each week, the better score that student earned at his or her audition. A linear regression model can predict any student's audition score if you know how many hours that student practices each week. If you have a student who practices 30 hours per week, you could expect that student to earn a score of about 60 on the audition.

Regression models can help to accurately predict future actions. Using data to know what's next can be worth its weight in gold when making business decisions. (Yeah, I know data doesn't have weight, but you get the point.)

Making decisions based on models

Analytics models can help organizations make astounding decisions and gain lots of money. They can also lead organizations to make dumb decisions and lose lots of money. The trick is in knowing how good your models are.

This book is about building analytics models using blockchain data. You learn about blockchain technology and data in Chapters 2 and 3, but don't forget that although the quality of your data is important, building the right model is crucial to getting quality output. Never rely on your first choice of a model or on a single model. Always compare model types and configurations to find the right combination to return the highest quality results.

REMEMBER

If you take only one thing away from this book, I hope that it is to demand measurable verification from every model you build. You should be able to provide metrics for each model indicating its accuracy and that it actually works. Never release a model to your business unit without exhaustive verification. Your organization will use your models to make big decisions. Do your best to give it good tools.

Changing Business Practices to Create Desired Outcomes

Classifying your customers or building models to predict what comes next can help your organization be more responsive to needs. You can use analytics to help plan better and be ready for whatever comes next. But with some additional work, you can do far more with analytics results. Instead of just getting ready for what might happen next, you can use analytics results to alter today's activities and affect future outcome.

Predictive analytics predicts what future results may be. The next step in analytics maturity is prescriptive analytics. With *prescriptive analytics,* the model identifies changes you can make now to achieve a desired outcome. For example, prescriptive analytics can tell you how many tables to set out in a restaurant or which register lanes to open in a grocery store to meet sales goals. Prescriptive analytics gives organizations the leverage to make operational changes based on their understanding of data that leads to satisfying their goals.

Defining the desired outcome

In the preceding section, you learned about using analytics models to make predictions of future outcomes. There can be tremendous value in prediction, but you can use analytics also to set the outcome and tell you how to get there. Think about it. It's one thing to predict next week's sales, but wouldn't it be cool to set your next week's sales goals and let your analytics models tell you how to get there? With good analytics models, it's possible.

Predictive analytics basically gives you an equation: $y = mx + b$ (yes, that's a simple one and the same as the point-slope form of a line). Your model provides values for m and b. Your data provides a value for x and you solve for y. Simple algebra.

Prescriptive analytics is a little different. Prescriptive analytics ask the question: "If I choose a value of y, what value of x will get me there?" In other words, you choose a value of y (maybe your goal for next week's sales), and then solve for x. After you know x (perhaps x represents the number of prospect calls you need to make), you know what it will take to reach y (your sales goal). At its core, it's still simple algebra.

Even though the algebra is simple, putting prescriptive analytics into practice can be tricky. In algebra, equality is reflexive, which means you can read left-to-right or right-to-left. Technically, models should work the same way, but they don't always work that simply. Prescriptive analytics can provide some guidance on reaching goals, but you always have to take that guidance with a grain of salt. Try your model's recommendations, and then evaluate the results. Fine-tune your changes, and then try it again. The best use of prescriptive analytics is as a good suggestion, not a surefire approach to reaching goals.

Building models for simulation

One of the challenges in prescriptive analytics is the iterative and flexible nature of using models this way. Predictive analytics is pretty straightforward. You can determine future outcomes within a known range of error. When turning that model around and using it for prescriptive purposes, you can never be sure that your model is taking into account all the influences that affect outcome. The outcomes your predictive model measures may include unsampled features (characteristics) that happen even though you don't measure them. If this is the case, just changing one feature may not have the effect you expect.

Because prescriptive analytics is more than just turning a predictive model backwards, you'll have to run your model multiple times over your dataset, changing a single feature at a time. Building a model that is flexible enough to respond to multiple feature changes is the basis of simulation. You're simulating the nature of reality, which encompasses multiple features that change and some level of unmeasured uncertainty.

Investing the effort to build a good simulation can more than pay for itself. A solid simulation is flexible enough to change as new input shows different trends and still provide output that you can trust. A simulation that tells you how to reach your goals is even better than knowing the future.

Aligning operations and assessing results

The best response to having good analytics models is to change operations based on your model output. Whether your focus is understanding your business, predicting tomorrow's environment, or using your models to direct decisions, analytics will add value only if you make changes based on what you learn.

Using analytics models, especially those built on data from a blockchain, is the purpose of this book. As you work through each chapter, you should gain an appreciation of the rich data available to you, and how you can use that data to enhance your organization. Enjoy the journey.

Chapter **2**

Digging into Blockchain Technology

B lockchain is one of the most discussed technologies of our time. It's commonly described in many ways, including "a disruptive and game-changing technology," a "distributed ledger of transactions," and a "new kind of database." Although these short descriptions are different, there's some truth in each one, but none captures what blockchain is all about. In short, *blockchain technology* is a radical new approach to delivering trust and confidence over exchanges of value without relying on a trusted third party.

Wow, that's a mouthful! You've probably heard that blockchain supports transactions between participants in a trustless environment. Most of the time, when you transfer something of value from one party to another, you use a trusted third party (someone you trust to handle the money or whatever you're transferring). For example, when you pay a vendor, you use a bank (writing a check) or a payment card processor (using plastic). Both the seller and buyer trust the bank or card processor, so you can trust that the transaction will be completed as you expect. Of course, you can also pay with cash, but even cash transactions depend on a government to guarantee the value of the cash you use. Blockchain technology makes it possible for you to buy something from someone you don't know (or trust) and still trust that the transaction will complete as you expect without having to rely on a third party.

Blockchain does a lot more than just handle payments — it can manage the transfer of any asset from one owner to another. That asset can be cryptocurrency, real estate, cars, premium olive oil, or anything of value in the real or virtual world. And the great thing is that all information on how those ownership transfers take place stays on the blockchain for later review.

In this chapter, you learn what blockchain technology is all about, some of the different options available, and how to best use blockchain to solve business problems.

Exploring the Blockchain Landscape

From what you read in books and articles, blockchain technology disrupts everything and fixes every business problem — and both at the same time! This view of blockchain's omnipotence gives a little too much power to what blockchain can actually do. Blockchain can disrupt the way many business transactions are carried out, but it won't change everything. Likewise, this new technology can solve some business problems that have been around for a long time, but it doesn't fit everywhere. The trick is to understand what blockchain can do, and what it can do very well.

Managing ownership transfer

When something of value passes from one owner to another, it's referred to as an *ownership transfer.* One of the things blockchain can do well is manage ownership transfer for items of value without relying on middlemen, or intermediaries, to manage the transfer. You can transfer ownership by giving or selling something to someone. When you sell something, you exchange the thing you sold for some type of payment. Being able to transfer ownership without a middleman can disrupt lots of business models. For example, when you ride with a rideshare service and pay for it with a credit or debit card, the rideshare company normally pays a per transaction fee, but you can be sure it passes that cost along to you! Bypassing the payment card processor means your rides could be cheaper.

Without getting into the details quite yet, blockchain technology makes it possible for you and the rideshare provider to trust the transfer of payment for the ride without having to trust one another. The ability to pay for a ride without the driver or rider trusting one another can be disruptive to payment card processors.

Many intermediaries, such as banks, payment processors, brokers, international money transfer companies, and even music distributors, could lose revenue to blockchain. All these middlemen charge a fee by managing transfers that blockchain technology could simplify.

Doing more with blockchain

Blockchain started off as an approach to managing cryptocurrency transactions in a trustless environment. Since then it has matured to handle value transfers of many types and has grown into a viable component of an integrated enterprise infrastructure. Enterprises rely on many software and hardware components that work together to provide services to their customers and partners. Blockchain technology is no longer just a cool idea — now it has the power to improve business processes. You'll likely see more and more businesses relying on blockchain to help run their operations. Before you look into leveraging blockchain and its new way of handling data, it helps to explore the existing blockchain landscape to get a feel of where blockchain may be beneficial.

Understanding blockchain technology

At its most basic level, a *blockchain* is a list of blocks connected to one another, where copies of the entire list are distributed among a set of participants, called *network nodes*. Each block contains a set of transactions and is connected to the block that immediately precedes it. Each transaction describes the transfer of some amount from one owner to another owner. Each transaction may have more information, but the focus is the transfer of value.

The way in which new blocks are added to the chain ensures that all copies of the chain of blocks (that's why it's called a blockchain) are the same. Distributing copies of data to different locations has always been difficult. Sending copies of data to multiple recipients isn't hard, but keeping all those copies the same is very hard. Keeping distributed data in sync is another thing that blockchain technology does very well.

Comparing blockchain to something you know

One way to think of a blockchain is as a big spreadsheet that is shared among many nodes. Each row in the spreadsheet represents a transaction that records amount, from owner, and to owner columns, and sometimes contains columns with additional data. Periodically, a group of rows, called a *block of rows*, is added to the bottom of each copy of the spreadsheet. You can't go back and edit any rows in the spreadsheet, but you can add new rows. That analogy is simple, but it gives you an idea of how blockchain transactions are similar to the familiar spreadsheet.

One of the first difficulties in maintaining copies of spreadsheets is how to control adding new rows and protecting existing rows from changes. A full discussion of blockchain integrity is beyond the scope of this book, but following is a high-level overview of how blockchains ensure integrity.

Using cryptography with blockchain

Blockchain technology is based on the concept of linking blocks together using a cryptographic hash. A *cryptographic hash* function takes any characters as input and creates a fixed-length output that represents the input. Calculating a hash value is easy, but finding the original input from the hash is extremely difficult. If the input changes at all, the hash function will calculate a different hash value.

Blockchain nodes calculate the hash value of a block and store that value in the next block on the chain. That process links the blocks and also detects changes in blocks. If any data in any block gets changed, the hash value of the block changes and makes the next block's link (remember it was the original block's hash value) invalid. Any change breaks the chain.

Achieving consensus among network nodes

Blockchain network nodes submit transactions, and then special nodes called *miners* assemble the transactions into blocks and then compete with other miners to be the first to solve a mathematical puzzle that makes a block easy to verify by all other nodes. The first miner to solve the puzzle gets a small reward for the work.

Each blockchain can define a different method its nodes use to verify blocks, but all the nodes in a specific blockchain network use the same block verification method. Methods that blockchains use to verify the validity of new blocks are called *consensus algorithms.* A common consensus algorithm is the *Proof of Work (PoW)* algorithm, which asks miners to expend energy to solve mathematical puzzles in exchange for a prize.

Regardless of the type of consensus a blockchain uses, more than 50 percent of the nodes must agree that a new submitted block is the so-called truth. When a majority agrees, all nodes add the new block to their blockchain. Through consensus and guarantees that no previous data has changed, blockchain technology ensures that all copies of the blockchain are identical and can be trusted.

Reviewing blockchain's family tree

Blockchain technology is only a decade old, but its effect is already being felt across many types of businesses. In just a few short years, blockchain implementations have matured through three generations. Classifying blockchain development by generation helps to uncover blockchain's short history, and where it may be headed. Note, however, that some developments overlap and others may fit in more than one category.

Introducing blockchain's first generation

Blockchain technology was introduced with the release of Satoshi Nakamoto's paper, "Bitcoin: A Peer-to-Peer Electronic Cash System" in 2008. The paper proposed a completely new approach to handling electronic currency. It described a structured data repository that consisted of a chain of special blocks, called a block chain. This new approach made it possible for many nodes that do not trust one another to exchange currency without relying on a central authority. Blockchain's first-generation goals focused on managing transactions between nodes that do not trust one another. Trust, not performance, was the central issue.

Adding blockchain features in the second generation

Bitcoin did just what it was supposed to do and provided a new way to exchange value. With Bitcoin, many individuals and small business could interact directly with customers or one another without involving banks or payment processors. It didn't take long for other blockchain implementations to emerge, each with its own cryptocurrency. As blockchain become more popular, developers and researchers started looking for other ways to use the new technology. They found that with just a few changes, blockchain technology could do far more than just trade cryptocurrency.

Just five short years after Nakamoto's paper was released, Vitalik Buterin, the cofounder of *Bitcoin Magazine,* published a whitepaper that proposed the use of Ethereum, a new, more functional blockchain implementation that could do much more than just exchange cryptocurrency. Buterin had a plan for Ethereum and built a base of interest and financial support for this new generation of blockchain. The Ethereum Foundation, a Swiss non-profit organization, was founded and Buterin became the primary developer of Ethereum.

Ethereum was designed to be different than previous blockchain implementations. The two primary differences are Ethereum's smart contract and native cryptocurrency, ether. In Ethereum, you can access blockchain data only by executing a smart contract. Smart contracts provide rich functionality and blockchain data integrity, and make it possible for blockchain technology to do much more than first-generation implementations. With the release of Ethereum, blockchains could carry out a wide range of business transactions beyond just handling payments, such as automating many business decisions or even carrying out entire transactions automatically. Imagine a ridesharing app that sends an autonomous (driverless) car to transport you to your destination and then automatically transfers payment for the ride from your account into its own account — all automatically! That's just one example of what is possible in Ethereum.

Scaling to the enterprise in blockchain's third generation

Ethereum was an important blockchain advance toward general business acceptance. Despite blockchain's broader appeal and potential applications, the core technology still lacked many enterprise features. Most blockchain implementations assumed open access, no authentication, and a focus on trust. Enterprises rely on limiting access to sensitive information, integration with existing applications, and meeting performance goals.

Enterprise IT infrastructures can be extremely complex and cannot quickly change to accommodate radically new technology. To integrate well into an enterprise, new technology must be flexible enough to "play nice" with legacy applications and components. First- and second-generation blockchain implementations tended to be inflexible and difficult to modify. For instance, most blockchains do not make it easy to replace the consensus algorithm. Some older blockchain implementations allow you to use only the consensus algorithm that developers built into the blockchain. For example, the PoW algorithm may be popular in public blockchain implementations, but it's not a good fit for enterprise blockchains. PoW has a very high computing resource requirement to address the trustless environment, but enterprises generally have some trust among participants. When limited trust exists in an enterprise blockchain environment, other consensus algorithms may be a better fit. However, older blockchains may not provide an easy way to switch to a better-fit consensus algorithm.

The third generation of blockchains have all tried to address the problems of performance, scalability, and integration with other blockchains and legacy application and data. The third blockchain generation didn't start with any single paper or new implementation. It came into being slowly as multiple vendors began to address enterprise and integrations needs. These blockchain implementations include Cardano, Nano, IOTA, Hyperledger Fabric, and Enterprise Ethereum.

Looking to the future

The next generation of blockchain, the fourth generation, is fast approaching. Many blockchain experts agree that the next step for blockchain growth is coupling it with *artificial intelligence (AI)*. Because organizations of all sizes are beginning to utilize blockchain for transactions and value exchange storage, a growing cache of largely unexplored data exists. That data contains valuable traces of transactional activity. The next big move for blockchain is to leverage the value in data stored on the chain, which is the focus of this book.

Fitting blockchain into today's businesses

Blockchain technology is viewed as a disruptive technology due to the promise of removing intermediaries and changing the way business is conducted. That promise is a big one, but it is possible. Removing even some of the intermediaries in existing business processes has the potential of streamlining and economizing workflows at all levels.

On the other hand, changing a business process to blockchain technology is not a simple switch. For widespread implementation of blockchain technology, new business and software products that integrate with existing software and data are required. The challenge of moving from concept to deployment poses the greatest current difficulty for blockchain adoption.

Finding a good fit

The first step in successfully implementing blockchain technology in any environment is finding a good-fit use case. It doesn't make any sense to jump into blockchain just because it's new and cool. It has to make sense for you and your organization. That statement sounds obvious, but you'd be surprised how many organizations want to chase the shiny object that is blockchain.

Blockchain has many benefits, but three of the most common are data transparency, process disintermediation (removing middlemen), and persistent transaction history. The best-fit use cases for blockchain generally focus on one of these benefits. If you have to look hard at how blockchain technology can meet the needs of your organization, it may be best to wait until there is a clear need.

I find that the most successful blockchain implementations are those that start with clear goals that align with blockchain. For example, suppose a seafood supplier wants to be able to trace its seafood back to the source to determine if it were caught or harvested in the wild using humane and sustainable methods. A blockchain app would make it possible to manage seafood from the point of collection all the way to the consumer's purchase. Any participant along the way, including the consumer, can scan a tag on the seafood and find out when and where it was originally caught.

To increase the probability of a successful blockchain project, start with a clear description of how the technology aligns with project goals. Trying to fit blockchain to an ill-suited use case leads to frustration and ultimate failure.

Integrating with legacy artifacts

After you determine that blockchain is a good fit for your environment, the next step is to determine where it fits in the workflow. Unless you're building a new app and workflow, you'll have to integrate with existing software and infrastructure.

If you are creating something new, the only considerations revolve around how your app stores the data it needs. Will you store everything on the blockchain? It may not make sense to do that. For example, blockchain does a great job at handling transactional data and keeping permanent audit trails of changes to data. Do you need that for customer information?

You may find that only part of your app data should be stored on the blockchain. It may make more sense to store supporting data in off-chain data repositories. (Now that we're in the blockchain era, legacy databases are called *off-chain repositories*.) If this is the case, your app will have to integrate with the blockchain and the off-chain repository.

In many cases, people are integrating new blockchain functionality with legacy applications and data. This integration effort could include introducing both new blockchain functionality and moving existing functionality to a blockchain environment. Although this task may sound straightforward, integrating with legacy systems involves many subtle implications.

Legacy systems define notions of identity, transaction scoping (defining how much work is accomplished in a single transaction), and performance expectations. How will your new app associate legacy identities with blockchain accounts? How will you adhere to your existing application's notion of traditional transactions? If your application supports rolling back a transaction, how will your blockchain do this? And lastly, will the integration of blockchain maintain sufficient performance or will it slow down the legacy application? Will the legacy application's users have to wait for blockchain transactions, or will they be able to carry out work like they did before the blockchain implementation?

Scaling to the enterprise

The last question in the preceding section leads well into one of the biggest current obstacles to blockchain adoption. Scaling performance to an enterprise scale is an ongoing pursuit that hasn't been completely resolved. Most enterprise applications use legacy database management systems to store and retrieve data. These data repositories have been around for decades and have become efficient at handling vast amounts of data.

According to Chengpeng Zhao (CEO of the cryptocurrency exchange Binance), a blockchain implementation must be able to support 40,000 transactions per second to be viable as a core technology in a global cryptocurrency exchange. Currently, only four popular blockchain implementations claim to be capable of more than 1,000 transactions per second (Futurepia, EOS, Ripple, and NEO). The most popular public blockchain, Ethereum, currently can handle about 25 transactions per second. Future releases of Ethereum, however, are focusing on raising the transaction throughput substantially. The technology is getting better but has a long way to go to be ready for the volume that enterprises require.

Performance isn't the only limiting factor when assessing blockchain for the enterprise. Integration with legacy artifacts and the ease with which the blockchain infrastructure fits into the existing enterprise IT infrastructure are concerns as well. Do all blockchain nodes require new virtual or physical hardware? Can the new nodes run on existing servers? What about network connectivity? Will existing network infrastructure support the new blockchain network? These are only a few of the many questions that enterprises must answer before deploying a blockchain integration project.

Understanding Primary Blockchain Types

In 2008, Bitcoin was the only blockchain implementation. At that time, Bitcoin and blockchain were synonymous. Now hundreds of different blockchain implementations exist. Each new blockchain implementation emerges to address a particular need and each one is unique. However, blockchains tend to share many features with other blockchains. Before examining blockchain applications and data, it helps to look at their similarities.

Categorizing blockchain implementations

One of the most common ways to evaluate blockchains is to consider the underlying *data visibility,* that is, who can see and access the blockchain data. And just as important, who can participate in the decision (consensus) to add new blocks to the blockchain? The three primary blockchain models are public, private, and hybrid.

Opening blockchain to everyone

Nakamoto's original blockchain proposal described a public blockchain. After all, blockchain technology is all about providing trusted transactions among untrusted participants. Sharing a ledger of transactions among nodes in a public network provides a classic untrusted network. If anyone can join the network, you have no criteria on which to base your trust. It's almost like throwing a $20 bill out your window and trusting that only the person you intend to pick it up will do so.

Public blockchain implementations, including Bitcoin and Ethereum, depend on a consensus algorithm that makes it hard to mine blocks but easy to validate them. PoW is the most common consensus algorithm in use today for public blockchains, but that may change. Ethereum is in the process of transitioning to the *Proof of Stake (PoS)* consensus algorithm, which requires less computation and depends on how much blockchain currency a node holds. The idea is that a node with more blockchain currency would be affected negatively if it participates in unethical behavior. The higher the stake you have in something, the greater the chance that you'll care about its integrity.

Because public blockchains are open to anyone (anyone can become a node on the network), no permission is needed to join. For this reason, a public blockchain is also called a *permissionless blockchain.* Public (permissionless) blockchains are most often used for new apps that interact with the public in general. A public blockchain is like a retail store, in that anyone can walk into the store and shop.

Limiting blockchain access

The opposite of a public blockchain is a private blockchain, such as Hyperledger Fabric. In a *private blockchain,* also called a *permissioned blockchain,* the entity that owns and controls the blockchain grants and revokes access to the blockchain data. Because most enterprises manage sensitive or private data, private blockchains are commonly used because they can limit access to that data.

The blockchain data is still transparent and readily available but is subject to the owning entity's access requirements. Some have argued that private blockchains violate data transparency, the original intent of blockchain technology. Although private blockchains can limit data access (and go against the philosophy of the original blockchain in Bitcoin), limited transparency also allows enterprises to consider blockchain technology for new apps in a private environment. Without the private blockchain option, the technology likely would never be considered for most enterprise applications.

Combining the best of both worlds

A classic blockchain use case is a supply chain app, which manages a product from its production all the way through its consumption. The beginning of the supply chain is when a product is manufactured, harvested, caught, or otherwise provisioned to send to an eventual customer. The supply chain app then tracks and manages each transfer of ownership as the product makes its way to the physical location where the consumer purchases it.

Supply chain apps manage product movement, process payment at each stage in the movement life cycle, and create an audit trail that can be used to investigate the actions of each owner along the supply chain. Blockchain technology is well suited to support the transfer of ownership and maintain an indelible record of each step in the process.

Many supply chains are complex and consist of multiple organizations. In such cases, data suffers as it is exported from one participant, transmitted to the next participant, and then imported into their data system. A single blockchain would simplify the export/transport/import cycle and auditing. An additional benefit of blockchain technology in supply chain apps is the ease with which a product's *provenance* (a trace of owners back to its origin) is readily available.

Many of today's supply chains are made up of several enterprises that enter into agreements to work together for mutual benefit. Although the participants in a supply chain are business partners, they do not fully trust one another. A block-chain can provide the level of transactional and data trust that the enterprises need. The best solution is a semi-private blockchain — that is, the blockchain is public for supply chain participants but not to anyone else. This type of blockchain (one that is owned by a group of entities) is called a *hybrid*, or *consortium*, *blockchain*. The participants jointly own the blockchain and agree on policies to govern access.

Describing basic blockchain type features

Each type of blockchain has specific strengths and weaknesses. Which one to use depends on the goals and target environment. You have to know why you need blockchain and what you expect to get from it before you can make an informed decision as to what type of blockchain would be best. The best solution for one organization may not be the best solution for another. Table 2-1 shows how blockchain types compare and why you might choose one over the other.

The primary differences between each type of blockchain are the consensus algorithm used and whether participants are known or anonymous. These two concepts are related. An unknown (and therefore completely untrusted) participant will require an environment with a more rigorous consensus algorithm. On the other hand, if you know the transaction participants, you can use a less rigorous consensus algorithm.

TABLE 2-1   ## Differences in Blockchain Types

Feature	Public	Private	Hybrid
Permission	Permissionless	Permissioned (limited to organization members)	Permissioned (limited to consortium members)
Consensus	PoW, PoS, and so on	Authorized participants	Varies; can use any method
Performance	Slow (due to consensus)	Fast (relatively)	Generally fast
Identity	Virtually anonymous	Validated identity	Validated identity

Contrasting popular enterprise blockchain implementations

Dozens of blockchain implementations are available today, and soon there will be hundreds. Each new blockchain implementation targets a specific market and offers unique features. There isn't room in the book to cover even a fair number of blockchain implementations, but you should be aware of some of the most popular.

Remember that you'll be learning about blockchain analytics in this book. Although organizations of all sizes are starting to leverage the power of analytics, enterprises were early adopters and have the most mature approach to extracting value from data.

TECHNICAL STUFF

The What Matrix website provides a comprehensive comparison of top enterprise blockchains. Visit www.whatmatrix.com/comparison/Blockchain-for-Enterprise for up-to-date blockchain information.

Following are the top enterprise blockchain implementations and some of their strengths and weaknesses (ranking is based on the What Matrix website):

» **Hyperledger Fabric:** The flagship blockchain implementation from the Linux Foundation. Hyperledger is an open-source project backed by a diverse consortium of large corporations. Hyperledger's modular-based architecture and rich support make it the highest rated enterprise blockchain.

» **VeChain:** Currently more popular that Hyperledger, having the highest number of enterprise use cases among products reviewed by What Matrix. VeChain includes support for two native cryptocurrencies and states that its focus is on efficient enterprise collaboration.

>> **Ripple Transaction Protocol:** A blockchain that focuses on financial markets. Instead of appealing to general use cases, Ripple caters to organizations that want to implement financial transaction blockchain apps. Ripple was the first commercially available blockchain focused on financial solutions.

>> **Ethereum:** The most popular general-purpose, public blockchain implementation. Although Ethereum is not technically an enterprise solution, it's in use in multiple proof of concept projects.

The preceding list is just a brief overview of a small sample of blockchain implementations. If you're just beginning to learn about blockchain technology in general, start out with Ethereum, which is one of the easier blockchain implementations to learn. After that, you can progress to another blockchain that may be better aligned with your organization.

Aligning Blockchain Features with Business Requirements

Blockchain technology is revolutionary because it provides features not found in other technologies. It doesn't solve all your computing problems and shouldn't be part of every application. In fact, blockchain's unique features address only a small subset of the many problems most enterprises face. Unfortunately, too many organizations choose to adopt blockchain technology and then try to find a place to put it. A far better approach is to understand what blockchain does well and then identify unsolved enterprise problems for which blockchain technology would be a good fit.

Reviewing blockchain core features

In this section, you look at some features that blockchain offers.

Transferring value without trust

One of the unique strengths of blockchain technology is that it supports transferring items of value between entities that do not trust one another. In fact, that's the big pull for blockchain. You have to trust only the consensus protocol, not any other user. Your transactions are carried out in a verifiable and stable manner, so you can trust that they are being handled properly and securely. This capability eliminates the need for a third party to act as a transaction broker. In today's economy, most transfers of value include at least one intermediary, such as a bank, to handle transfer details.

Reducing transaction costs by eliminating middlemen

Because blockchain allows entities that don't trust each other to interact directly, it eliminates most middlemen. Whether you're considering transferring money from one party to another or providing a product for payment, nearly all transactions need a middleman. Middlemen are entities such as bankers, importers, wholesalers, or even media publishers.

Blockchain makes it possible for producers to interact directly with consumers. For instance, artists can offer their art directly to buyers, without needing a broker or publisher. Eliminating middlemen either eliminates the fees paid for their services or replaces the fees with automated processes that greatly reduce costs, and these savings can be passed on directly to the consumer. Although blockchain transaction handling does incur a small cost, it's generally much less than what middlemen charge. That's good for producers and consumers.

Increasing efficiency through direct interaction

Lower fees aren't the only benefit of eliminating middlemen. Any time you can remove one or more steps in a process, you increase efficiency. Greater efficiency generally means reduced time required for a process to complete. For example, suppose a musician decides to release her latest single directly to her fans by using a blockchain delivery model. Her fans can consume the new single the moment it drops. With a publisher, the content must be delivered, approved, packaged, and then finally released. Although the delay for digital media may be minimal, blockchain can eliminate any delays introduced by middlemen.

The contrast becomes even clearer when looking at delivering physical goods by using blockchain. If you buy strawberries from California, have you ever thought how many times they were handled before you got them? Lots of processors stand between you and the grower. Blockchain can reduce the number of people who participate in the supply chain for pretty much anything.

Maintaining a complete transaction history

Another design feature of blockchain is its immutability. Because you can't change any data, anything written to the blockchain stays there always. "What happens in blockchain, stays in blockchain." Good news for any application that would benefit from a readily available transaction history.

Let's revisit the strawberries example. You might go to the grocery store today and buy strawberries with a label that says "Fresh from CA." You really have no idea whether the strawberries came from CA or perhaps Spain (the second leading exporter of strawberries). But with blockchain, you could trace a pint of strawberries all the way back to the grower. You'd know exactly where your strawberries came from and when they were picked. This level of transaction history exists for every transaction in blockchain. You can always find any transaction's complete history.

Increasing resilience through replication

Every full node in a blockchain network must maintain a copy of the entire blockchain. Therefore, all data on the blockchain is replicated to every full node, and no node depends on data that another node stores. If several nodes crash or are otherwise unavailable, other users of the application are unaffected. This resilience means that fault tolerance is built into the blockchain architecture. In addition, by distributing the entire blockchain to many nodes, which are owned by different organizations, you practically eliminate the possibility of one organization controlling the data.

Any application that benefits from high availability and freedom of ownership may be a good fit for blockchain. Many database applications go to great lengths to replicate their data to provide fault tolerance, and blockchain has it built right in!

Providing transparency

The last main category of blockchain features is directly related to the fact that the entire blockchain is replicated to every full blockchain node. Every full node can see the entire blockchain, providing unparalleled transparency. Although data stored in blocks is commonly encrypted, the data itself is available to any user of any node. If the data is unencrypted, anyone with access to a node can see it. If it is encrypted, a user with the proper decryption key(s) can access blockchain data from any node and then be able to decrypt it.

Blockchain transparency makes it possible to trust the integrity of the data. Any node can (and does) routinely verify the integrity of each block and, therefore, the entire blockchain. Any modifications to the "immutable" blockchain data become immediately evident and easy to fix.

Examining primary common business requirements

Now that you know some of blockchain's core features, it's important to also have a clear picture of your primary business requirements. The only appropriate blockchain use is when a blockchain feature aligns with a business requirement.

Although many business requirements differ from one enterprise to another, some common requirements exist:

>> **Controlling and recording transactions:** This requirement is the process of using applications and data systems to promote, control, and record the activities required to carry out a business operation. The act of recording activities documents some actions that change the state of the enterprise's stored data.

>> **Reducing or eliminating excessive cost:** Ongoing pursuits of enterprises that want to stay in business are to monitor the costs of operation and to identify and reduce (or eliminate) waste.

>> **Pursuing efficiency:** Process efficiency can deliver the dual result of reducing cost and increasing quality. Both results are desirable to a profitable business operation.

>> **Preserving artifacts for analysis:** Compliance, incident investigations, and analytics require the existence of historical transaction data. Collecting, managing, and archiving this type of data requires planning and ongoing resources.

>> **Protecting availability through redundancy:** An enterprise's information system assets have value only if they're accessible on demand by authorized individuals. The organization must enact plans to store and maintain redundant copies of critical data for when the primary data become inaccessible.

>> **Exposing data without compromising privacy:** This business requirement is often the most problematic. Most enterprises place a high value on their data, whether it's regulated sensitive data or intellectual property. Sharing an enterprise's data has value but is also risky. Sharing data in a manner that benefits the organization and its users is often a delicate balancing act.

Matching blockchain features to business requirements

As you read through the list in the preceding section, you may have noticed how nicely each of the business requirements maps to the earlier blockchain features list. That correlation was intentional. You also likely thought of several business requirements that weren't in the list. That's okay. The point of the previous two lists was to show that some business requirements align well with blockchain features.

Table 2-2 combines the previous lists and shows how blockchain technology can solve some common issues that enterprises encounter.

TABLE 2-2   **Business Requirements and Blockchain Features**

Business Requirement	Blockchain Feature
Controlling and recording transactions	Blockchain excels in transferring value in untrusted environments.
Reducing or eliminating excessive cost	By eliminating middlemen, blockchain can reduce overall, and incremental, transaction-processing costs.
Pursuing efficiency	Blockchain increases direct interaction among transaction participants and automates many steps in transactions, decreasing settlement time and reducing inefficient waiting time.
Preserving artifacts for analysis	Because existing blockchain data can't be changed, a historical transaction record is guaranteed.
Protecting availability through redundancy	Each node of the blockchain network maintains a copy of the blockchain, so the failure of any node has no effect on the overall network's capability to access blockchain data.
Exposing data without compromising privacy	Blockchain technology promotes data transparency. Because all nodes maintain copies of the ledger, the data is available to any authorized user.

Examining Blockchain Use Cases

Many good examples of use cases for blockchain technology exist. In this section, you look at just a few. See if you can think of a good blockchain use case in your own organization.

Managing physical items in cyberspace

One of the earliest large-scale blockchain use cases was the management of supply chains. The process of managing products from the original producer all the way to the consumer is expensive and time consuming. With today's product-tracking applications, it can be difficult for consumers to know much about the products they consume. Some products, such as electronics and appliances, may have descriptive tags that identify places and times of manufacture, but most products we consume don't provide that type of information.

Implementing supply chain management provides multiple benefits. The first is transparency. Producers, consumers, and anyone in-between can see how each product traveled from the place it was manufactured or acquired to where it was finally purchased and the time it took to get there. Inspectors and regulatory auditors can ensure that each participant in the supply chain met required standards.

This increased transparency occurs while eliminating unnecessary middlemen. Each transfer in the process occurs between active participants, not brokers.

TIP

Proper tracking of physical products in the blockchain depends on accurately associating the physical product with the digital identifier. For example, I recently checked my bag when I flew on a commercial airline. The agent was busily engaged in a conversation with another agent, and swapped my tags with those of another traveler. His tag was attached to my bag, and vice versa. When I arrived, the airline discovered that my bag, with the other person's tag attached, had flown to Mexico. Always remember that the blockchain only *represents* the physical world — it isn't the physical world.

Handling sensitive information

Healthcare has become one of the most popular topics of conversations ranging from politics to research to spending. It seems that everyone is interested in increasing the quality of healthcare while reducing its cost. The availability of large amounts of digital data have made advances in healthcare possible.

Researchers can analyze large amounts of data to explore new treatment plans, increase the overall effectiveness of existing drugs and procedures, and identify cost-saving opportunities. This type of analysis is possible only with access to vast amounts of patient medical history. The main problem for researchers is that a patient's *electronic health record (EHR)* is likely stored as fragments across multiple practices and databases. Although ongoing efforts to combine these records exist, privacy is a growing concern (we're back to the trust problem) and progress is slow.

EHR management is a good fit for a blockchain app. Storing a patient's EHR in an Ethereum blockchain can remove the silos of fragmented data without having to trust each entity that provides or modified parts of the EHR. Storing the EHR in this way also helps clarify the billing and payment for medical services. With comprehensive medical procedure history all in one place, medical service providers and insurance companies can see the same view of a patient's treatment. Full history makes it easier to figure out what should be billed.

Another advantage that blockchain apps can provide in the healthcare domain is in managing pharmaceuticals. Blockchain EHRs provide the information for medical practitioners to see a full history and current snapshot of a patient's prescription medications. It also allows researchers, auditors, and even pharmaceutical manufacturers to examine the effect and possible real side effects of their products. Having EHRs available, yet protected, can provide valuable information to increase the quality of healthcare services.

Conducting financial transactions

Financial services are interactions that involve some exchange of currency. The currency can be legal tender, also called *fiat* currency, or it can be cryptocurrency, such as Bitcoin or Ethereum's default currency, ether (ETH). Blockchain apps do a great job of handling pure currency exchanges, or exchanging some currency for a product or service. Financial services may center on handling payments, but there are more nuances to the many transactions that involve money.

Another rich field for blockchain in the financial services domain is real estate transactions. As with banking transactions, Ethereum makes it possible to conduct transactions without a broker. Buyers and sellers can exchange currency for legal title directly. Smart contracts can validate all aspects of the transaction as it occurs. The steps that normally require an attorney or a loan processor can happen automatically. A buyer can transfer funds to purchase a property after legal requirements are met, such as validating the title's availability, and filing required government documents. The seller receives payment for the property at the same time the title transfers to the buyer.

Chapter **3**

Identifying Blockchain Data with Value

M any descriptions of blockchain technology relate it to well-known data storage techniques. One of the more popular descriptions states that a blockchain is essentially a distributed ledger of transactions. This description is somewhat true but overly simplified. A blockchain does store transactions like a ledger and is distributed, but it contains far more interesting information. If a blockchain only stored transactions it wouldn't be very interesting because it would be little more than a distributed spreadsheet.

A blockchain is far more than just a distributed spreadsheet — it contains an indelible record of the data's current state (current values) and a complete historical record of how the data came to the current state. Traditional data repositories generally store only the final state of data. As you make changes, those changes overwrite any previous values. More sophisticated data repositories maintain audit records, which are generally external notes that record changes to data values.

Additionally, blockchain apps can create logging entries that document events that occur as smart contracts execute. The ability to record activities can provide a view of how data changes, not just the fact that it did change. And finally, each block in a blockchain stores information about the functions — and input parameters — in a smart contract that an application calls.

In this chapter, you learn about the different types of data available to you in a blockchain environment and how you can identify data that might be useful for analysis.

Exploring Blockchain Data

In this section, you discover what data gets stored in blocks on a blockchain. Although each blockchain implementation differs in its low-level details, the concepts are generally consistent across blockchain types.

Because the purpose of this book is to introduce you to the most important concepts of blockchain analytics, I won't cover the specific technical details of every blockchain. Instead, you learn about the specific features of the most popular public blockchain implementation, Ethereum. If you don't use Ethereum, don't worry — the concepts you learn here will apply easily to any other blockchain implementation.

TECHNICAL STUFF

The main difference between the most popular types of blockchain is the way in which they handle transactions. Bitcoin uses the *Unspent Transaction Output (UTXO) model,* in which each transaction spends some of what was leftover from a previous transaction, and then creates new output that is the remaining (unspent) balance after processing a transaction. The other main approach to handling transactions is the *Account/Balance model,* which Ethereum uses. In the Account/Balance model, each account has a recorded balance, and transactions add to, or subtract from, that balance. The Account/Balance model is similar to a traditional ledger. I focus on Ethereum and the Account/Balance model in this book.

Understanding what's stored in blockchain blocks

As mentioned in Chapter 2, blockchain is just a specially constructed group of blocks that are linked, or chained, to one another. Each block header contains the hash of the previous block, forming the link that creates the chain. From many descriptions, it sounds like the blocks in a blockchain are pretty much the same as the data in a database or other data repository. However, that view isn't accurate. Blockchain stores a lot more than just values of data items, which is why blockchain analytics is so interesting. A lot of information is in a blockchain, but you need to know how to get to it.

Each block consists of some header information and a collection of transactions. In most blockchain implementations, miners select the transactions they want to include in blocks. In Ethereum, if a miner is the first to mine that block, he or she selects transactions based on the potential payoff. Other blockchain implementations use different methods to create blocks. Hyperledger Fabric, for example, uses order nodes instead of miners. Because Hyperledger Fabric uses a different consensus mechanism, it doesn't rely on competing miners to create valid blocks. *Hyperledger Fabric* is built on a modular design that makes replacing components, including the consensus mechanism, easy. Hyperledger Fabric uses a consensus mechanism called Kafka by default, but that can be changed if desired. Kafka depends on current nodes electing a leader, and that leader has the authority to build blocks of transactions.

Recording transaction data

Regardless of the approach used to create new blocks, blocks generally contain transactions or smart contract code. Because blockchain technology was introduced to manage cryptocurrency, it stands to reason that transaction data focuses on transferring ownership from one address to another. In this section, you look at a block to see its header information and a list of transactions.

Etherscan is a popular website that allows you to examine the live Ethereum network, *mainnet*. Figure 3-1 shows a portion of Etherscan's block header view. The block we will examine is block number 8976776. Note that this block contains 95 transactions.

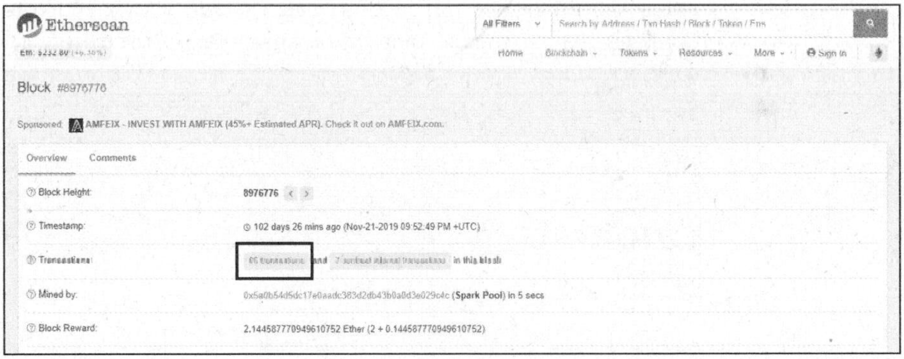

![Etherscan block header view showing Block #8976776 with Overview and Comments tabs. Block Height: 8976776. Timestamp: 102 days 26 mins ago (Nov-21-2019 09:52:49 PM +UTC). Transactions: 95 transactions and 7 contract internal transactions in this block. Mined by: 0x5a0b54d5dc17e0aadc383d2db43b0a8d3e029c4c (Spark Pool) in 5 secs. Block Reward: 2.144587770949610752 Ether (2 + 0.144587770949610752).]

FIGURE 3-1: Viewing block header information in Etherscan.

To find block 8976776 in Etherscan, go to `https://etherscan.io/` and enter the block number in the All Filters field. Then click or tap the search icon (magnifying glass).

TECHNICAL STUFF

Etherscan does much more than provide a way to peek at data on Ethereum's mainnet. You can examine and retrieve data from mainnet; popular testnets including Ropsten, Kovan, Rinkeby, and Goerli; and the Energy Web Foundation (EWF) chain. If you create an account and request a free API key, you can use the key to extract blockchain data.

To see a list of transactions in block 8976776, click or tap the 95 Transactions link. Figure 3-2 shows the first 5 transactions in block 8976776. You can see that each transaction has a From account, a To account, and an amount. In simplest terms, each transaction records an amount in the Value column being transferred from one Ethereum account to another.

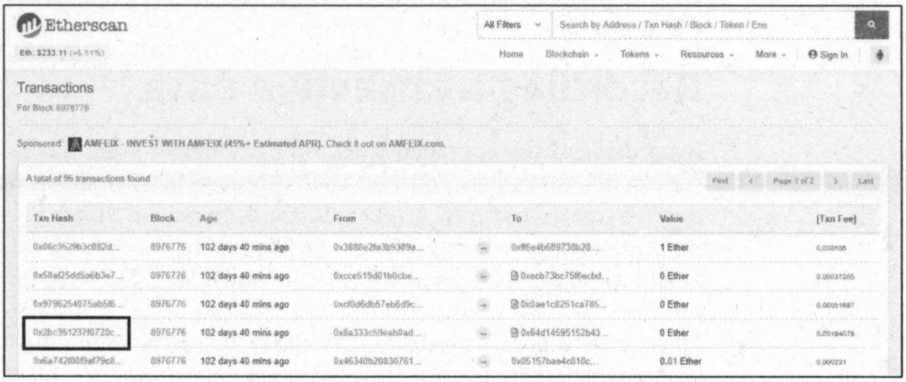

FIGURE 3-2:
Listing transactions in a block in Etherscan.

Click or tap the fourth transaction in Figure 3-2 to open the Etherscan transaction details page shown in Figure 3-3. This initial page shows general information about the Ethereum transaction. The To field shows that the target address is Contract, which means that this transaction is the result of a call to a smart contract.

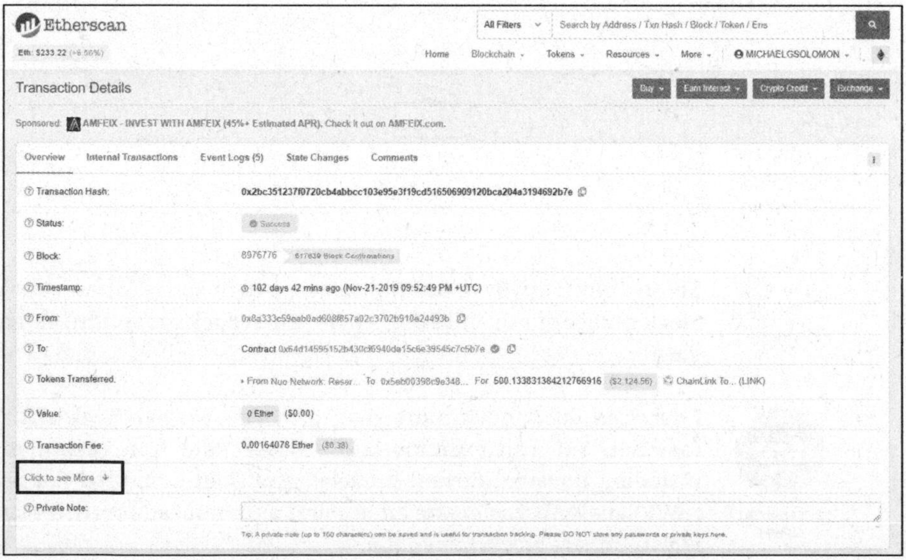

FIGURE 3-3:
Examining a transaction in Etherscan.

TIP

In Ethereum, the only way you can access data stored in the blockchain is through a smart contract. You use the smart contract's address (where the smart contract code is stored in the blockchain) to run, or invoke, one of its functions. Smart contract functions contain the instructions for accessing blockchain data.

Click or tap Click to See More, in the bottom left, to display the expanded transaction details page with additional information about the smart contract function call shown in Figure 3-4. You can see that this transaction is the result of invoking this smart contract's `cancelOrder()` function. You'll learn more about smart contracts and transaction details in later chapters, but for now, be aware that blockchain technology keeps a record of every change to blockchain data, which provides a great place to get analytics data.

FIGURE 3-4:
Exploring
additional
transaction
details in
Etherscan.

⑦ Transaction Fee:	0.00164078 Ether (10.10)
⑦ Gas Limit:	196,893
⑦ Gas Used by Transaction:	164,078 (83.33%)
⑦ Gas Price:	0.00000001 Ether (10 Gwei)
⑦ Nonce Position	7647 #1
⑦ Input Data:	Function: cancelOrder(bytes32 _orderHash, bytes _signature) MethodID: 0x7713fb18 [0]: 98dde4af9705d02529ebb41cb865e99ecdbd3d230f6f40ec0792290d1ca7edd [1]: 0000000000000000000000000000000000000000000000000000000000000040 [2]: 0000000000000000000000000000000000000000000000000000000000000041 [3]: cd506ac54f288bb29196b0b3676832efc0d8c534b3b02d3bf0c7381a476426bd [4]: 4f9e2bdeb18e9c4ba26b585a221fea76f92344db99fec711fa61229a7dad5560 [5]: 0100000000000000000000000000000000000000000000000000000000000000 View Input As ▾ Decode Input Data
Click to see Less ↑	
⑦ Private Note:	
	Tip: A private note (up to 100 characters) can be saved and is useful for transaction tracking. Please DO NOT store any passwords or private keys here.

Dissecting the parts of a block

Before you can start extracting data from a blockchain for analysis, you need to learn a little more about how the data you want is stored. Most of that data is stored in blocks, so that's what I discuss next.

TIP

Yes, that's right! Most but not all data you'll want for analytics is stored in blocks. Some blockchains, including Ethereum, store some data in an external, or off-chain, database. Don't worry; I describe off-chain data too.

TECHNICAL STUFF

I describe only the basic Ethereum block and chain details. The authoritative reference for Ethereum internals is the Ethereum yellow paper, at `https://ethereum.github.io/yellowpaper/paper.pdf`. You can also find a good third-party detailed discussion of Ethereum block structure internals at `https://ethereum.stackexchange.com/questions/268/ethereum-block-architecture`.

A *block* is a data structure that contains two main sections: a header and a body. Transactions are added to the body and then submitted to the blockchain network. *Miners* take the blocks and try to solve a mathematical puzzle to win a prize. Miners are just nodes, or pools of nodes, with enough computational power to calculate block hashes many times to solve the puzzle.

In Ethereum, the mining process uses the submitted block header and an arbitrary number called a *nonce* (number used once). The miner chooses a value for the nonce, which is part of the block header, and calculates a hash value using a hash function on the block header. The result has to match an agreed-upon pattern, which gets more difficult over time as miners get faster at mining blocks. If the first mining result doesn't match the pattern, the miner chooses another nonce and calculates a hash on the new block header. This process continues until a miner finds a nonce that results in a hash that matches the pattern.

The miner that finds the solution broadcasts that solution to the rest of the network. That miner collects a reward, in ETH (ether), for doing the hard work to validate the block. Because many miners work on blocks at the same time, it's common for several miners to solve the hash puzzle at almost the same time. In other blockchains, these blocks are discarded as *orphans*. In Ethereum, these blocks are called *uncles*. An uncle block is any successfully mined block that arrives after that block has already been accepted. Ethereum accepts uncle blocks and even provides a reward to the miner, but one that's smaller than the accepted block.

TECHNICAL STUFF

Ethereum rewards miners that solve uncle blocks to reduce mining centralization and to increase the security of the blockchain. Uncle rewards provide an incentive for smaller miners to participate. Otherwise, mining would be profitable only for large pools that could eventually take over all mining. Encouraging more miners to participate also increases security by increasing the overall work carried out on the entire blockchain.

The *header* of a block contains data that describes the block, and the *body* contains all transactions stored in a block. Figure 3-5 shows the contents of an Ethereum block header.

TECHNICAL STUFF

Ethereum uses the Keccak-256 algorithm to produce all hash values. The National Institute of Standards and Technology (NIST) Secure Hashing Algorithm 3 (SHA-3) is a subset of the Keccak algorithm. Ethereum was introduced before the SHA-3 standard was finalized, and Keccak-256 does not follow the SHA-3 official standard.

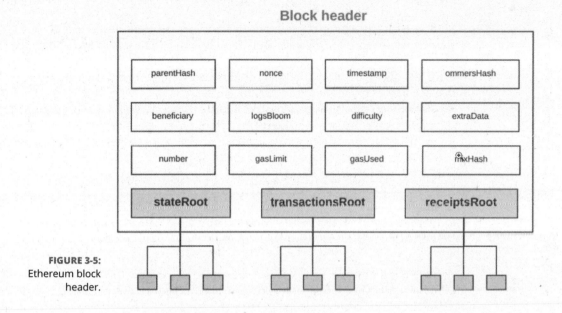

Block header

FIGURE 3-5: Ethereum block header.

Each Ethereum block header contains information that defines and describes the block, and records its place in the blockchain. The block header contains the following fields:

>> **Previous hash:** The hash value of the previous block's header, where the *previous block* is the last block on the blockchain when the current block gets added.

>> **Nonce:** A number that causes the hash value of the current block's header to adhere to a specific pattern. If you change this value (or any header value), the hash of the header changes.

>> **Timestamp:** The date and time the current block was created.

>> **Uncles hash:** The hash value of the current block's list of uncle blocks, which are stale blocks that were successfully mined but arrived just after the accepted block was added to the blockchain.

>> **Beneficiary:** The miner's account that receives the reward for mining this block.

>> **Logs bloom:** Logging information, stored in a Bloom filter (a data structure useful for quickly finding out if some element is a member of a set).

>> **Difficulty:** The difficulty level for mining this block.

>> **Extra data:** Any extra data used to describe this block. Miners can put any data here they want, or they can leave it blank. For example, some miners write data that they can use to identify blocks they mined.

>> **Block number:** The unique number for this block (assigned sequentially).

>> **Gas limit:** The limit of gas for this block. (You learn about gas later in this chapter.)

- **Gas used:** The amount of gas used by transactions in this block.

- **Mix hash:** A hash value combined with the nonce value to show that the mined nonce meets the difficulty requirements. This hash makes it more difficult for attackers to modify the block.

- **State root:** The hash value of the root node of the block's state trie. A *trie* is a data structure that efficiently stores data for quick retrieval. The *state trie* expresses information about the state of transactions in the block without having to look at the transactions.

- **Transaction root:** The hash value of the root node of the trie, which stores all transactions for this block.

- **Receipt root:** The hash value of the root node of the trie, which stores all transaction receipts for this block.

The body of an Ethereum block is just a list of transactions. Unlike other blockchain implementations, the number of transactions, and as a result the size of the blocks, isn't fixed. Every transaction has a processing cost associated with it, and each block has a limited budget. Ethereum blocks can contain lots of transactions that don't cost much or just a few expensive ones or anything in between. Ethereum designed a lot of flexibility into what blocks can contain. Figure 3-6 shows the contents of an Ethereum transaction.

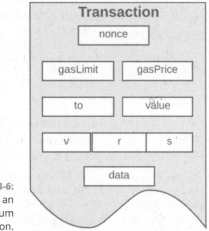

FIGURE 3-6: Contents of an Ethereum transaction.

Ethereum transactions contain the following fields:

- **Nonce:** Each Ethereum account keeps track of the number of transactions it executes. This field is the latest transaction, based on the account's counter.

The transaction nonce is used by the network to ensure that transactions are executed in the proper order.

>> **Signature:** The digital signature of the account owner, proving the identity of the account requesting this transaction.

>> **Gas price:** The unit price you're willing to pay to execute this transaction.

>> **Gas limit:** The maximum total amount you're willing to pay to execute this transaction.

>> **To:** The address of the recipient of this transaction. For transfers, the To address is the account that will receive the transfer. For calling functions, the To address is the address of the smart contract.

>> **Value:** The total amount of ether you want to send to the recipient.

>> **Data:** The actual data submitted as the transaction body. Each type of transaction may have different data, based on its functionality. For calling functions, the data might contain parameters.

As users submit transaction requests to nodes, the nodes create transactions and submit them to the transaction pool. Miners then pick transactions from the pool and build new blocks. After an Ethereum mining node constructs a block, it starts the mining process. The first miner to complete the mining process adds the block to the blockchain and broadcasts the new block to the rest of the network.

REMEMBER

You can look at the public Ethereum blockchain at any time by going to Etherscan at https://etherscan.io/. Etherscan lets you see blockchain statistics as well as block and transaction details.

Decoding block data

Etherscan presents blockchain data in a readable format. But in doing so, it hides some important details. Blockchain data isn't always stored in a format that is easily readable, at least to most people. For many reasons beyond the scope of this book, blockchain implementations store some data as a hash, not in a raw format. Storing data as hash values makes common querying and analytics operations more difficult than interacting with databases.

Each type of blockchain data has nuances in the way its data is formatted and stored. For example, a transaction's input data value in its raw format, shown in Figure 3-7, isn't very helpful. You can see this by clicking or tapping View Input As ⇨ Original.

FIGURE 3-7:
Original format of input data.

Etherscan can decode the input data for you. Click or tap the Decode Input Data button and Etherscan will try to translate the input data into easy-to-read input parameters for the called function. Figure 3-8 shows successfully decoded data for the cancelOrder() function. (In Figure 3-4, you saw that this transaction calls the cancelOrder() smart contract function.)

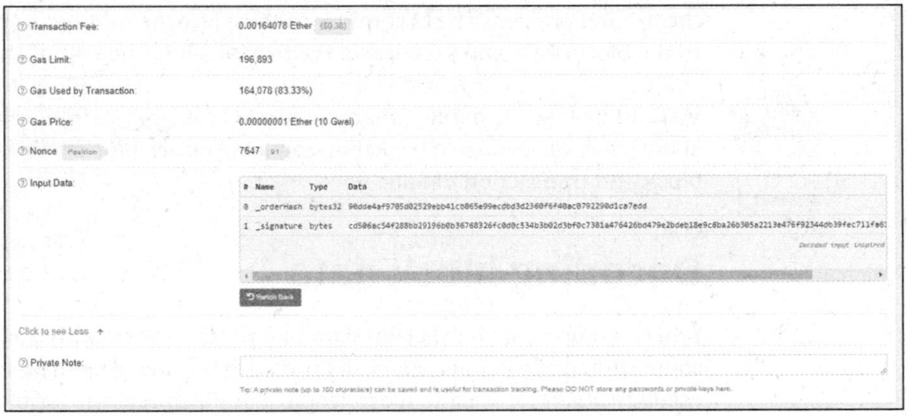

FIGURE 3-8:
Decoded data for the cancelOrder() function.

You don't get this level of detail in every transaction. This transaction called a function in a registered smart contract. *Registering* a smart contract means that the developer submitted the application binary interface (ABI) for the contract, along with the compiled bytecode. An *ABI* is a definition of a smart contract's state data, events, and functions, including each function's input and return parameters. Etherscan uses the ABI, if it is available, to provide more descriptive information. If the ABI is not available, Etherscan can display only the raw input data.

If you explore the Etherscan page, you'll notice the Event Logs, State Changes, and Comments tabs. I don't cover those here, but I do revisit them in Chapter 6. Transaction data isn't the only data you'll encounter in a blockchain application. Smart contract developers commonly use events to log notable actions in a smart contract. Data from these events are often of interest in the data analysis process. You'll see this type of data again.

Categorizing Common Data in a Blockchain

You've already seen most of the types of data you'll use when carrying out blockchain analytics. You've seen block header data, basic transaction data, and details contained in some transactions. You may have investigated the Etherscan user interface to view some event data, and even the effect a transaction has on the blockchain state. In this section, you learn more about the main categories of blockchain app data: transaction, events, and state.

Serializing transaction data

The core of blockchain data is contained in the transaction. A blockchain transaction records the transfer of some value from one account to another account. Additional information may be in the transaction, such as input data that records smart contract parameters, but not every transaction includes additional data.

Each transaction does include a timestamp showing the date and time the transaction was mined, so you can create a chronological list of transactions and see how value changed ownership at specific points in time and how value moved among accounts. This movement is serial. The serial nature of data storage can yield interesting information but can also be an obstacle to analyzing the data.

Unlike traditional data storage systems such as relational databases, final tallies or balances often have to be calculated over time. A traditional database can store the current balance of an account, while you may have to trace all blockchain transactions for an account to arrive at its final balance. The data is available, but it may take more work to get to it.

Blockchain gives you the flexibility of tracing transactions by account but doesn't always make it easy to query a single value. For example, suppose you want to know the balance of a specific account on a specific date. Finding the current account balance is easy, but finding the balance as of a specific date (and time), requires serializing the transactions for that account and calculating account increases and decreases up to the date and time in question.

If you're comfortable with databases and applications that access database data, searching transactions doesn't sound like such a bad thing to do. However, remember that a blockchain is not a database. The data in a blockchain is not stored in a manner that makes general purpose queries easy and fast. You can get the information you want, but you have to think about the effort to get that data in a different way.

The serialized transaction storage of blockchain data does provide the flexibility to trace and retrieve activity data in several ways. Here are a few types of queries you can satisfy by tracing blockchain transactions:

>> Find all transactions in which a specific account sent funds.

>> Find all transactions that resulted in a specific account receiving funds.

>> Find all transactions that occurred between two specific accounts.

>> Find all transactions that invoked a specific smart contract function.

After you fetch the data you want, you can trace the transactions, calculating the value change (that is, keeping track of the Value and Transaction Fee fields) to find the information you're looking for, such as a balance at a specific point.

Logging events on the blockchain

One of the more interesting aspects of blockchain data extends the information you can get from transactions. As mentioned, a transaction is the transfer of some value as a result of a smart contract function. Because the only way to create a transaction is to invoke a smart contract function, you can be sure that a transaction is the result of a function.

The previous statement may sound redundant, but it's extremely important. Smart contract functions can be simple or complex. As smart contracts become more complex, just knowing the function a transaction invoked, along with its input parameter values, isn't always enough information to describe what's going on. You need a way to record what happens inside transactions.

REMEMBER

Ethereum, and most popular blockchains second generation and beyond, support sophisticated smart contract languages. Ethereum's EVM (Ethereum virtual machine) is a Turing complete machine, so with enough resources, an Ethereum smart contract can calculate anything. Of course, in the real world, transactions eventually run out of gas, but the point is that your smart contract functions can be as complex as you want.

Go back to Etherscan and dig a little deeper into block 8976776's transactions. Examine the same transaction in Figure 3-4 (block 8976776 -> Transaction list -> Fourth transaction in the list's details). Click or tap the Event Logs tab at the top of the page. The Event Logs page shows a list of events that occurred during a smart contract function. Figure 3-9 shows the last two events for the current transaction.

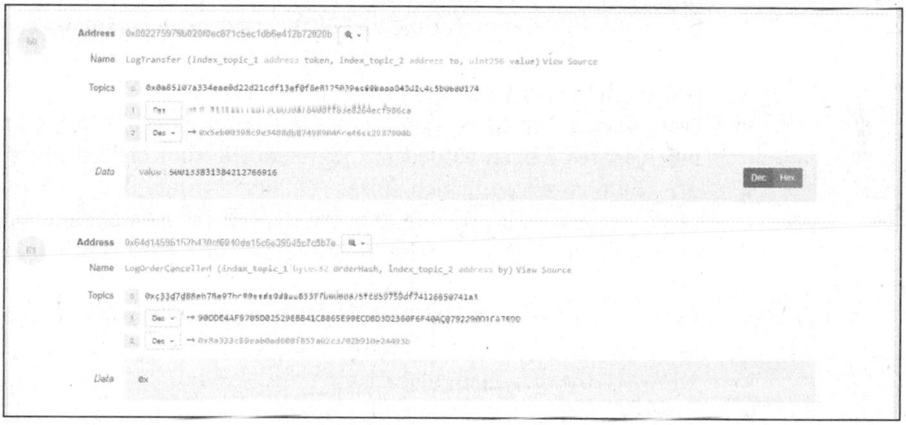

FIGURE 3-9:
Ethereum events
in Etherscan.

Note that these events have names — LogTransfer() and LogOrderCancelled() — and parameters. Smart contract programmers use events to create messages that Ethereum logs and saves. Events make it easy to notify client applications that certain actions have taken place in a smart contract and also to store important information related to a transaction.

TECHNICAL STUFF

Smart contract programmers use events to record internal details of how smart contracts operate. The programmer defines events and the parameters passed when the events are called. Then, during runtime, the smart contract invokes the event when something notable happens in the code. For example, when using the popular language Solidity for writing smart contract code, the emit command invokes an event. Any time a programmer wants to send a message to the client or record an action, the emit statement invokes an event to do just that.

Most smart contract programmers use event names that describe the action. So we would expect that the LogOrderCancelled() event is present because an order was cancelled in the transaction. Smart contract programmers can create events anywhere in their code. The most common purpose of an event is to record the occurrence of an action, such as cancelling an order. The event parameters, order-Hash and by, provide identifying information for the order that was cancelled and who cancelled it. Events take some effort to analyze but can yield interesting analysis data.

Storing value with smart contracts

The last main category of data associated with a blockchain is the state data. *State data* is the data that is most like traditional database data. Each smart contract can define one or more variables or structures to store data values. These values can include things such as highest order number (for an order entry contract) or a list of products (for a supply chain contract). State data make it possible to store data that contracts use each time one of their functions is invoked.

Although transaction data is stored in blocks on the blockchain, Ethereum stores state data not in blockchain blocks but in an external (off-chain) database. Each block stores a hash value that points to the root of that block's state trie in the off-chain database, which stores the block's state data. Storing data using a trie structure makes it possible to query the trie for a value, and validate the integrity of that value, without having to read the entire trie.

REMEMBER

Refer to Figure 3-5, which shows the contents of a block header, including the state root hash that points to the root of the state values for that block (which is stored in the off-chain database).

Unlike blockchain data, state data can change. Each time a function in a smart contract runs, it may change the value of one or more state data items. The transaction that caused the change is stored in a block on the blockchain, and log entries may be created by events, but state data changes are stored in the off-chain database.

TECHNICAL
STUFF

Each Ethereum client can select its own database for storing state data. For example, the Geth client uses LevelDB, and the Parity client uses RocksDB. Each database uses different methods for access, so the blockchain client you use for analysis should support a database that is familiar.

Examining Types of Blockchain Data for Value

Now that you know about the basic categories of data a blockchain stores, you can start to dig into what each type of data you'll find might mean. Few hard-and-fast rules for storing data exist. Each smart contract sets its own rules for defining and maintaining the data it needs to do its work.

Exploring basic transaction data

Every transaction contains basic information about crypto-asset ownership and transaction cost. The From, To, and Value fields record, respectively, the account that owns the value at the start of the transaction, the account to which the value is transferred, and the amount or cost of the asset that is transferred by the transaction.

The Input Data field may contain additional information about the transaction. This data field is often very different from one transaction to another. When the To field of a transaction refers to a regular Ethereum account, the Input Data field may contain supporting or additional transaction details. In these cases, the transaction serves primarily to record a transfer of cryptocurrency from one account to another. If the To field contains the address of a smart contract, the Input Data field will contain information about the function that the transaction invokes and the data sent to the function.

Part of the challenge in extracting blockchain data for analysis is classifying and making sense of the input data. The blockchain analytics process is more than just reading data and building models.

Associating real-world meaning to events

Although transaction data can reveal what a client requested and what value was transferred, it doesn't always provide many details of how the transaction played out. In other words, transaction data doesn't provide more than summary information. If you want to explore details of what happened during a transaction, you'll have to look elsewhere.

Because smart contract code can include complex calculations and data, it's often beneficial, and sometimes necessary, to store messages and data at points within the transaction. Most complex business transactions involve multiple steps, and mirroring real-world processes in code makes sense. For example, if you want to import wood from a foreign country to manufacture furniture, you'd follow a general sequence of steps:

1. The importer requests the product from the exporter.

2. The importer applies for a letter of credit from a local bank on behalf of the exporter.

3. The importer's bank issues a letter of credit and sends it to the exporter's bank.

4. The exporter ships the product.

5. Based on the terms of the letter of credit, the exporter may receive partial payment while the product is in transit. If partial payment is executed, the exporter's bank claims the payment due and the importer's bank transfers the specified payment.

6. When the importer receives the product, the importer notifies the bank and the importer's bank transfers the remaining funds to the exporter's bank.

Believe it or not, this process is simplified! I didn't even touch on export licenses or bills of lading. Even with this simple scenario, you can see that the process has many steps. In a real application, some of these steps might occur at different times and some might occur at the same time (such as in Step 5). It would be helpful if the blockchain stored status information about how the transaction was carried out, as opposed to storing just the amount transferred from one account to another.

Event logs provide that functionality. No events occur by default; smart contract programmers must request each one. Most smart contract code includes at least minimal event invocations. A best practice when developing a smart contract is to invoke an event any time a package of work of interest to the application's user is completed. That description of when to use events is a loose one and open to interpretation.

Knowing how the smart contract code that will supply data for your analytics projects works is important. In Chapters 5 and 6, you learn how to get smart contract source code and how to use it to build your data acquisition plan. But until then, remember that analyzing data in a blockchain environment requires familiarity with far more than just blockchain data.

Aligning Blockchain Data with Real-World Processes

Although understanding the data available through transactions, events, and contract state is important, you must understand what that data represents before you can make much sense out of it. An important part of any data analytics project (blockchain or traditional data) is to align data with the real world. In a blockchain environment, that understanding starts with smart contracts.

Understanding smart contract functions

You can think of smart contracts as programs that contain data and the functions to manipulate that data. One way to help understand smart contracts is to think of state data as nouns and functions as verbs. Associating smart contract elements with parts of speech helps to understand each element's purpose. You store data that represents something in the real world, such as an order, a product, or a letter of credit.

Functions provide the actions that applications take on data, such as creating an order, createOrder(), shipping a product, shipProduct(), or requesting a letter of credit, requestLoC(). Data analytics is focused on extracting meaningful and actionable information from data. It is important to understand the data available to you, along with how that data was created and what real-world things and processes it represents. Smart contract functions provide the roadmap to how data gets added to the blockchain and what that data means.

Assessing smart contract event logs

One process early in any data analytics project is assessing your available data. In a blockchain environment, that step should include assessing any events related to the smarts contracts you'll examine. One way to view events is as documentation of internal operations. These microtransaction artifacts often provide a level of granular data that you can't get anywhere else. Don't ignore the event logs – they may provide your best description of blockchain data and what it really represents.

Ranking transaction and event data by its effect

After you have a catalog of the data available to you, rank each data item's importance by its effect. A data item has greater effect when it corresponds to some entity attribute or action in the real world. Data that represents a letter of credit's approval status change is likely more important than the field that records the page count of the letter of credit document. All data is not equal. It is always up to you, the analyst, to focus on the important data and not spend too much time on data with little value. Properly ranking data value by its effect is a learned skill, and one that takes practice.

Chapter **4**

Implementing Blockchain Analytics in Business

U nderstanding how blockchain data gets stored and how to get to it is only the beginning of the analytics process. In fact, a good analytics process starts before that point. To find value in data of any type, you first must determine what you're after. Setting analytics goals helps you to avoid wasting time and effort (and most importantly, money) in the analytics process.

Always remember that technology exists to solve problems. A cool new gizmo isn't worth much unless it addresses a need. Data analytics is the same. If your analytics results do not meet a business need, your effort will be wasted. To avoid that situation, the first step towards launching any analytics project should be articulating a clear statement of the business justification and goals. Ask what information you're looking for and how it will benefit the business.

After you have a clear direction, you need to set up an analytics lab to gather, transform, and analyze your data. Depending on where the data resides, you may need to set up your own blockchain node as well. In this chapter, you learn how to align analytics with business goals and how to set up your own blockchain analytics lab.

Aligning Analytics with Business Goals

Blockchain technology alone cannot provide rich analytics results. For all that blockchain is, it can't magically provide more data than other technologies. Before selecting blockchain technology for any new development or analytics project, clearly justify why such a decision makes sense.

If you already depend on blockchain technology to store data, the decision to use that data for analysis is a lot easier to justify. In this section, you examine some reasons why blockchain-supported analytics may allow you to leverage your data in interesting ways.

Leveraging newly accessible decentralized tools

Most of this book focuses on manually accessing and analyzing blockchain data. Although it's important to understand how to exercise granular control over your data throughout the analytics process, higher-level tools make the task easier. The growing number of decentralized data analytics solutions means more opportunities to build analytics models with less effort. Third-party tools may reduce the amount of control you have over the models you deploy, but they can dramatically increase analytics productivity.

The following list of blockchain analytics solutions is not exhaustive and is likely to change rapidly. Take a few minutes to conduct your own Internet search for blockchain analytics tools. You'll likely find even more software and services:

>> **Endor:** A blockchain-based AI prediction platform that has the goal of making the technology accessible to organizations of all sizes. Endor is both a blockchain analytics protocol and a prediction engine that integrates on-chain and off-chain data for analysis.

>> **Crystal:** A blockchain analytics platform that integrates with the Bitcoin and Ethereum blockchains and focuses on cryptocurrency transaction analytics. Different Crystal products cater to small organizations, enterprises, and law enforcement agencies.

>> **OXT:** The most focused of the three products listed, OXT is an analytics and visualization explorer tool for the Bitcoin blockchain. Although OXT doesn't provide analytics support for a variety of blockchains, it attempts to provide a wide range of analytics options for Bitcoin.

Monetizing data

Today's economy is driven by data, and the amount of data being collected about individuals and their behavior is staggering. Think of the last time you accessed your favorite shopping site. Chances are, you saw an ad that you found relevant. Those targeted ads seem to be getting better and better at figuring out what would interest you. The capability to align ads with user preferences depends on an analytics engine acquiring enough data about the user to reliably predict products or services of interest.

Blockchain data can represent the next logical phase of data's value to the enterprise. As more and more consumers realize the value of their personal data, interest is growing in the capability to control that data. Consumers now want to control how their data is being used and demand incentives or compensation for the use of their data.

Blockchain technology can provide a central point of presence for personal data and the ability for the data's owner to authorize access to that data. Removing personal data from common central data stores, such as Google and Facebook, has the potential to revolutionize marketing and advertising. Smaller organizations could access valuable marketing information by asking permission from the data owner as opposed to the large data aggregators. Circumventing big players such as Google and Facebook could reduce marketing costs and allow incentives to flow directly to individuals.

There is a long way to go to move away from current personal data usage practices, but blockchain technology makes it possible. This process may be accelerated by emerging regulations that protect individual rights to control private data. For example, the European Union's General Data Protection Regulation (GDPR) and the California Consumer Privacy Act (CCPA) both strengthen an individual's ability to control access to, and use of, his or her personal data.

Exchanging and integrating data effectively

Up to this point, you've mainly learned about data stored on the blockchain environment. Although blockchain data is the focus of this book, much of the value of blockchain data is in its capability to relate to off-chain data. Most blockchain apps refer to some data stored in off-chain repositories. It doesn't make sense to store every type of data in a blockchain. Reference data, which is commonly data that gets updated to reflect changing conditions, may not be good candidates for storing in a blockchain.

Remember that blockchain technology excels at recording value transfers between owners. All applications define and maintain additional information that supports and provides details for transactions but doesn't directly participate in transactions. Such information, such as product description or customer notes, may make more sense to store in an off-chain repository.

Any time blockchain apps rely on on-chain and off-chain data, integration methods become a concern. Even if your app uses only on-chain data, it is likely that analytics models will integrate with off-chain data. For example, owners in blockchain environments are identified by addresses. These addresses have no context external to the blockchain. Any association between an address and a real-world identity is likely stored in an off-chain repository. Another example of the need for off-chain data is when analyzing aircraft safety trends. Perhaps your analysis correlates blockchain-based incident and accident data with weather conditions. Although each blockchain transaction contains a timestamp, you'd have to consult an external weather database to determine prevailing weather conditions at the time of the transaction.

Many examples of the need to integrate off-chain data with on-chain transactions exist. Part of the data acquisition phase of any analytics project is to identify data sources and access methods. In a blockchain analytics project, that process means identifying off-chain data you need to satisfy the goals of your project and how to get that data.

Surveying Options for Your Analytics Lab

Before you can start fetching data from a blockchain to analyze, you have to set up an access path to the data. You could use third-party analytics tools, but you would lose some control of the analytics process. In this book, you learn how to build simple models from scratch, so you'll be able to access blockchain data directly by interacting with smart contract functions.

In this section, you build a lab that allows you to write software to build models that access data stored in an Ethereum blockchain.

The first thing you might notice when building an Ethereum development environment is that you have a lot of choices. Overall, many choices are a good thing, but they make getting started a little more confusing. Remember that Ethereum is a complete blockchain environment. Running the blockchain is one thing — developing code for the blockchain is a bigger endeavor and requires more tools.

EVM (Ethereum virtual machine), the runtime environment for Ethereum smart contracts, is implemented in many languages. Each implementation allows Ethereum to run on a different platform, giving anyone setting up a new node choices in how to run the EVM. For example, if performance is the highest priority, a C++ implementation might be the best choice. But if the capability to integrate additional functionality with the EVM is a goal, a JavaScript or Python implementation might be a better choice.

The open-source community is a worldwide group of users and developers who contribute to projects in which they have a stake. Ethereum users and developers often engage in rigorous debates about how to best advance the product. These debates commonly result in different opinions about the best way to meet goals. One of the more common debates is over which user interface is better. One school of thought is that a *command-line interface (CLI)* is the most flexible and the easiest to script. This type of user interface tends to work best for lower-level utility-type tools. On the other hand, an integrated *graphical user interface (GUI)* is more user friendly and makes tasks such as software development easier. That's just one example of why you may see both CLI and GUI versions of tools.

As a result of diverse people contributing to the community, you'll find multiple software products that address the needs of each step in the development process. Several test network implementations exist because a group in the Ethereum community felt that making it easier to set up a test network would draw more developers to the Ethereum platform. Others focus on integrated testing tools or decided to extend their favorite editors and Integrated Development Environments (IDE) with extensions that support Solidity.

As you look at the available options in the tool categories, remember that each one exists because a group of Ethereum enthusiasts saw an opportunity to fill a feature gap. You might want to read through the features and benefits of some competing products to see how they differ.

TIP

If you want to get involved in the Ethereum community, check out the Ethereum website at https://ethereum.org/. At the bottom of the home page, you'll see a Community section with links to various ways to participate.

The tools you'll install and configure in this chapter are the ones you'll frequently see used by other Ethereum developers. You can find lots of online tips, tricks, and tutorials on using these tools for Ethereum development. The environment you build in this chapter will allow you to work through the examples in this book and learn from other online resources — without having to start over installing new tools.

Installing the Blockchain Client

Now that you're ready to build your Ethereum analytics lab, let's dive right in. You'll learn how to set up a PC running Microsoft Windows to be an Ethereum development platform. Even though you won't be developing smart contracts and blockchain apps, you do need a development environment to develop the analytics models that access your blockchain.

Windows isn't the only operating system that supports Ethereum. You can just as easily set up a macOS or Linux computer to support Ethereum. If you're running macOS or Linux, each tool in this chapter will work on your computer, too, although the installation steps might be a little different. Each tool's website will provide detailed instructions for each operating system.

Start by installing an Ethereum client. I chose Go Ethereum (Geth) as the Ethereum client you use in this book. Geth is written in the Go language and allows you to run a full Ethereum node, which means you'll have access to the complete Ethereum blockchain and also run a local EVM. Geth gives you the capability to mine ETH, create transactions and smart contracts, and examine any blocks on the blockchain. All remaining tools you'll install in this chapter will depend on Geth to provide the local EVM and allow access to the blocks on the blockchain.

TECHNICAL STUFF

The Geth website provides prepackaged installers for Microsoft Windows, macOS, and Linux operating systems. You can also download the Geth source code and build it for your own custom environment. If you're interested in playing around with devices other than just computers, you can conduct an Internet search and easily find instructions on setting up Geth on smartphones or a Raspberry Pi. That's the beauty of using open-source tools.

Start by downloading and installing Geth, as follows:

1. **Launch your browser and navigate to** `https://ethereum.github.io/go-ethereum`, **and then click or tap the Downloads link at the top of the page.**

    Your web browser will look like Figure 4-1.

2. **Click or tap the Geth button for your operating system.**

    Because I'm setting up a Microsoft Windows computer in this tutorial, I selected Geth 1.9.7 for Windows. (When you set up your computer, a newer version of Geth might be available. You should download and install the latest stable version of each tool.)

3. **Launch the executable file you just downloaded.**

4. **Click or tap I Agree to the GNU General Public License.**

    Always read any license agreement before agreeing to its contents.

REMEMBER

5. **Select the Development Tools check box, shown in Figure 4-2, and then click or tap the Next button.**

    Make sure that you choose to install the development tools in this window before continuing.

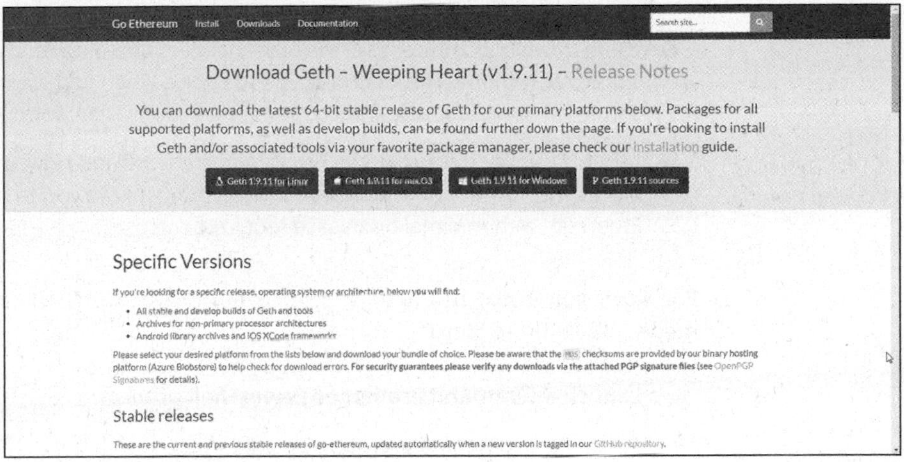

FIGURE 4-1:
The Go Ethereum
(Geth) Download
web page.

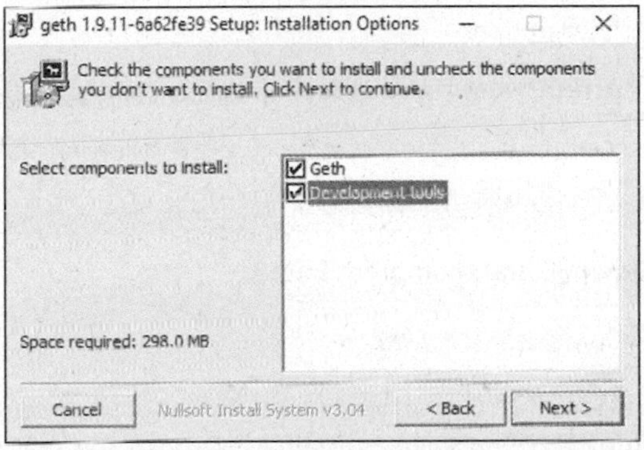

FIGURE 4-2:
Installation
Options window.

6. **If you want to install Geth to a different folder than the one that's displayed, change it to your desired destination folder.**

7. **To start the installation process, click or tap the Install button.**

8. **When the installation finishes, click or tap the Close button.**

After you've installed Geth, you can launch it to start the EVM and synchronize with the public Ethereum blockchain.

Many Geth startup options are available, but the only option you need for now is syncmode, which tells Geth how much of the blockchain to download. The sync-mode option has the following three values:

>> **full:** Download and validate the entire blockchain. This option requires the most time and disk space but can provide the fastest response because a full node doesn't ever have to request missing blocks from other nodes.

» **fast:** Download and validate the block headers and data for the most recent 1,000 transactions. This option is a good choice when you want to conserve some disk space but also want to store the most recent blocks locally.

» **light:** Download only the blockchain current state and request any missing blocks from other nodes as needed. This option allows you to operate Ethereum with minimal disk space requirements.

For now, you'll use the light syncmode option for Geth. To start Geth in light mode, follow these steps:

1. **Launch a command prompt or PowerShell prompt.**

    To launch a command prompt, type **cmd** in the search bar at the lower-left corner of your desktop and then click or tap the Command Prompt option. To launch a PowerShell prompt, type **PowerShell** in the search bar and select or tap the PowerShell option.

2. **Change the current working directory to the Geth install directory.**

    If you installed Geth to the default location, type the following and then press Enter:

    ```
    cd 'C:\Program Files\Geth\'
    ```

3. **Type the following, and then press Enter:**

    ```
    .\geth --syncmode "light"
    ```

    This command launches Geth in light mode. Make sure that you type two hyphens before syncmode. Figure 4-3 shows the Geth command to start a light Ethereum node.

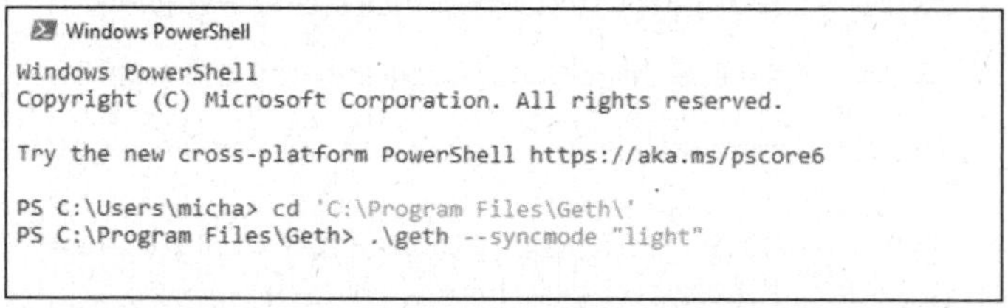

FIGURE 4-3: Geth light node startup command.

A Geth starts, it establishes a connection with the Ethereum network and begins synchronizing the current blockchain. Geth provides messages at each stage of its startup process to let you see what is happening. Figure 4-4 shows what the Geth messages looks like.

After Geth synchronizes the blockchain, you're ready to use the Geth blockchain client to fetch and analyze live blockchain data.

FIGURE 4-4:
Geth runtime
messages.

Installing the Test Blockchain

As you build and assess analytics models, you don't want to deploy any code to the live blockchain or launch long-running routines until you're sure that everything works correctly. You have to test your code in some non-live environment first. You'll need a blockchain to use during the development and testing process. Ethereum clients, Geth included, connect to the main public Ethereum blockchain by default, but you can connect to other blockchains as well. You can change the connection settings easily for development and testing.

Several tools make it easy to create and manage test blockchains. I chose Ganache for our test blockchain environment. According to the Ganache website (`https://truffleframework.com/ganache`), "Ganache is a personal blockchain for Ethereum development you can use to deploy contracts, develop your applications, and run tests." Ganache includes a handy set of tools to explore blockchain contents.

TECHNICAL STUFF

You aren't limited to prebuilt Ganache executables. Because Ganache is an open-source product, you can also download the Ganache source code and build it for your own custom environment.

To download and install Ganache, follow these steps:

1. **Launch your browser and navigate to** `https://truffleframework.com/ganache`.

   Your web browser will look like Figure 4-5.

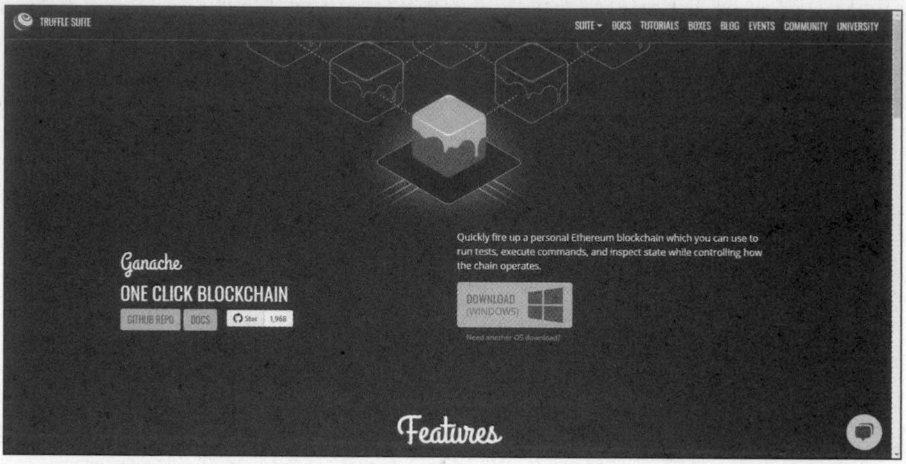
TRUFFLE SUITE
SUITE DOCS TUTORIALS BOXES BLOG EVENTS COMMUNITY UNIVERSITY
Ganache
ONE CLICK BLOCKCHAIN
GITHUB REPO
DOCS
Star 1,968
Quickly fire up a personal Ethereum blockchain which you can use to run tests, execute commands, and inspect state while controlling how the chain operates.
DOWNLOAD (WINDOWS)
Need another OS download?
Features

FIGURE 4-5: The Ganache Download web page.

2. **Click or tap the Download (Windows) button to download the Windows installer.**
3. **Launch the executable file you just downloaded.**
4. **To start the installation process, click or tap the Install button.**

   Ganache launches when the installation finishes.

5. **Decide whether or not to enable analytics, and then click or tap the Continue button.**

   Because this is the first time you're launching Ganache, you're asked to allow Google Analytics tracking, as shown in Figure 4-6. You don't have to do this, but allowing analytics helps the Ganache development team learn how different people use Ganache.

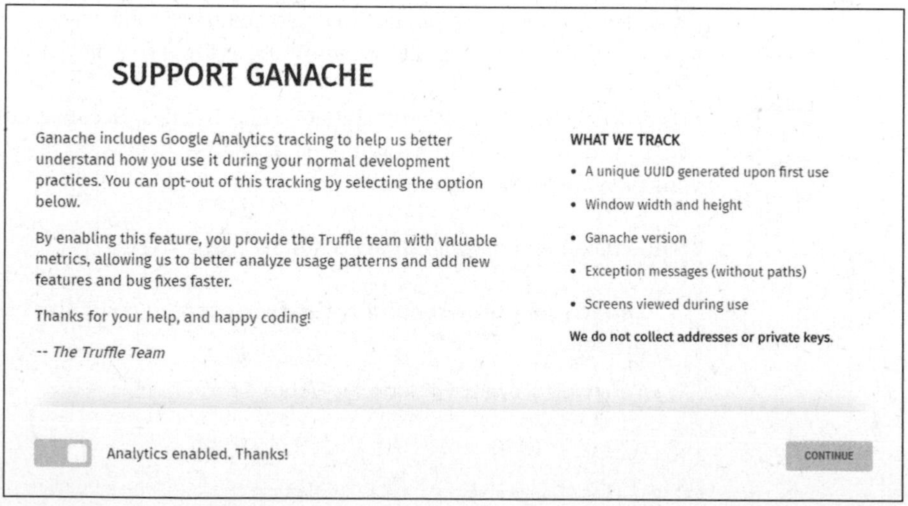
SUPPORT GANACHE
Ganache includes Google Analytics tracking to help us better understand how you use it during your normal development practices. You can opt-out of this tracking by selecting the option below.
By enabling this feature, you provide the Truffle team with valuable metrics, allowing us to better analyze usage patterns and add new features and bug fixes faster.
Thanks for your help, and happy coding!
-- The Truffle Team
WHAT WE TRACK
• A unique UUID generated upon first use
• Window width and height
• Ganache version
• Exception messages (without paths)
• Screens viewed during use
We do not collect addresses or private keys.
Analytics enabled. Thanks!
CONTINUE

FIGURE 4-6: Support Ganache Analytics window.

6. When Ganache launches, click or tap Quickstart.

You see the main Accounts window with basic server information and a list of accounts, as shown in Figure 4-7. Because the reason to install Ganache is to create your own blockchain, you'll need at least one account to access the blockchain. Ganache creates ten accounts for you, each with a balance of 100.0 ETH. You can create more accounts and give them all the ETH they need to test any smart contracts you write.

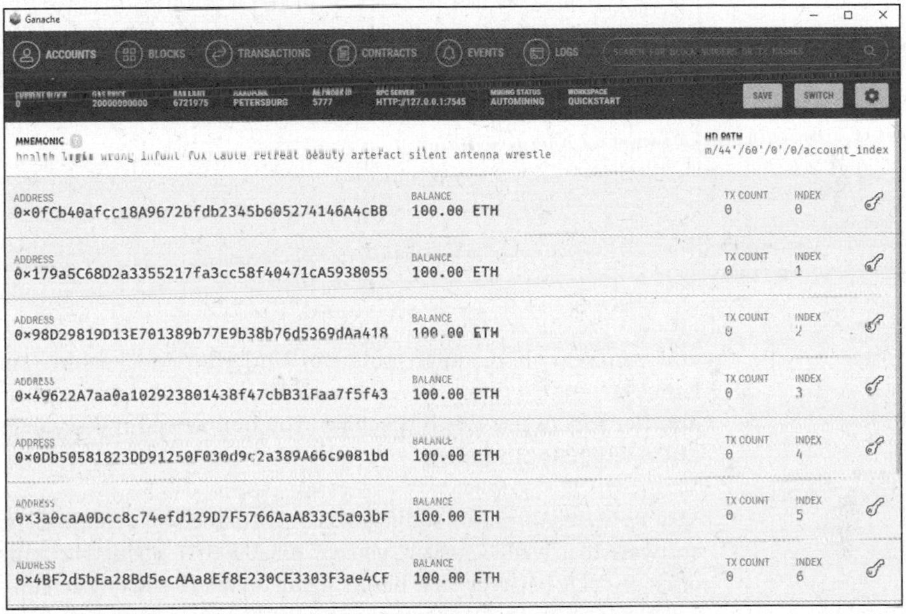

FIGURE 4-7: Ganache Accounts window.

That's all it takes to create your own Ethereum blockchain in Ganache. Of course, this blockchain is local to your own computer and isn't distributed to any other nodes. And because there aren't any other nodes on this network, there aren't any miners. This blockchain is set to *automining*, which means any new transactions are processed immediately. That setting makes it easy to test your smart contracts and models that access other smart contracts without having to pay miners to process your transactions.

When you're ready to start developing software for Ethereum, you'll need to tell your client and other tools which blockchain to use. Let's see where your new Ganache blockchain is located. In Ganache, click or tap the settings (gear) icon in the upper-right corner to launch the Ganache Settings window. Figure 4-8 displays the Server tab of the Ganache Settings window.

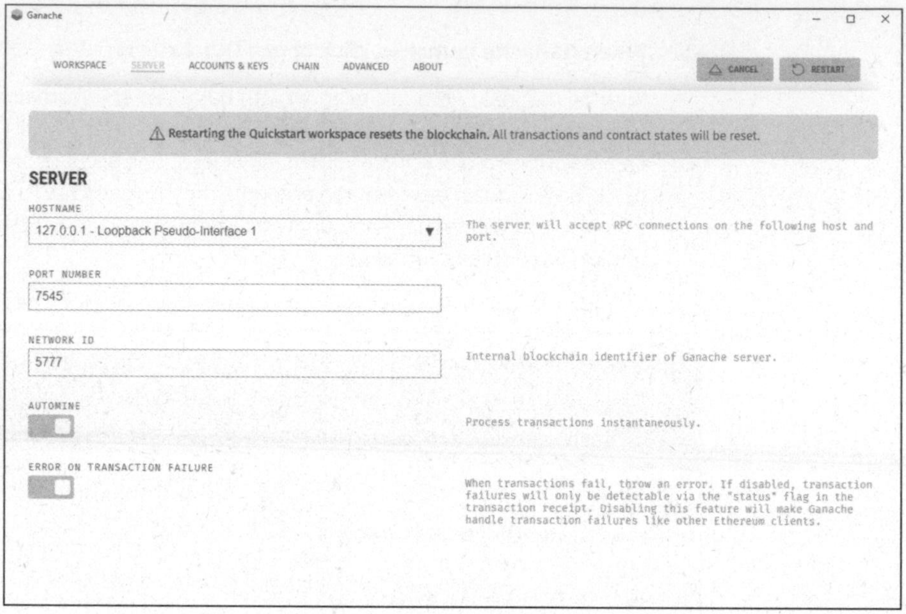
Ganache
WORKSPACE
SERVER
ACCOUNTS & KEYS
CHAIN
ADVANCED
ABOUT
CANCEL
RESTART
Restarting the Quickstart workspace resets the blockchain. All transactions and contract states will be reset.
SERVER
HOSTNAME
127.0.0.1 - Loopback Pseudo-Interface 1
The server will accept RPC connections on the following host and port.
PORT NUMBER
7545
NETWORK ID
5777
Internal blockchain identifier of Ganache server.
AUTOMINE
Process transactions instantaneously.
ERROR ON TRANSACTION FAILURE
When transactions fail, throw an error. If disabled, transaction failures will only be detectable via the "status" flag in the transaction receipt. Disabling this feature will make Ganache handle transaction failures like other Ethereum clients.

FIGURE 4-8: Ganache Settings window's Server tab.

You can see where other tools can find your blockchain. The Hostname, Port Number, and Network ID values show you what you need any time you want another tool to use this blockchain. You don't need these values yet, but now you know where to find them.

Also note the Automine setting, which is enabled by default. Before you deploy your software to a live blockchain, you can disable this setting and enter a number of seconds to delay between new blocks being added to the blockchain. Manually specifying a delay between block creations helps to simulate the effect of miners that you'll encounter in a live blockchain. Testing will be more complex but also more realistic.

TIP

Before you leave the Settings window, look at the settings on the other tabs (Workspace, Accounts & Keys, Chain, Advanced, and About). The Ganache Quickstart guide has details about these settings at `https://truffleframework.com/docs/ganache/quickstart`.

Installing the Testing Environment

The software development process is made up of multiple steps. In addition to just writing source code, you have to compile your code, deploy it to a test environment, test the code, and measure how well the code performs against your specifications. Then you need to fix any flaws and repeat the testing process until you're satisfied with the code's operation.

After you complete testing, you need to transition your software from a test environment to a live environment. For this transition, you need to submit your smart contracts to a live blockchain and place any other code where your clients can access it. All tasks related to testing and deployment should be repeatable and as automated as possible. A comprehensive testing framework helps to standardize these tasks and make the entire development process more manageable.

I chose Truffle as the testing environment you'll use for the examples in this book. You may have noticed that the test Ethereum network, Ganache, is part of the Truffle Suite. One of the reasons I chose both Truffle and Ganache is due to the easy integration of these tools. In the rest of this section, you learn how to install Truffle.

Getting ready to install Truffle

Before you can install Truffle, you have to ensure that your computer meets the prerequisites. Open your browser and navigate to `https://truffleframework.com/docs/truffle/getting-started/installation` to see the Truffle installation requirements, which are shown in Figure 4-9.

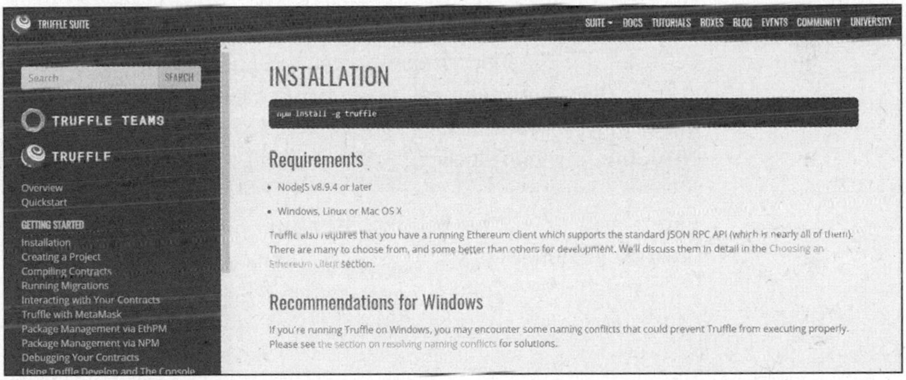

FIGURE 4-9:
Truffle
installation
requirements.

The main requirement for Truffle is to have NodeJS version 8.9.4 or higher installed. NodeJS is an open-source project that provides a runtime environment for code written in JavaScript. JavaScript was originally designed to run in web browsers, but NodeJS makes it easy to run JavaScript code outside a browser.

It's easy to find out whether NodeJS is installed. Open a command shell or Power-Shell window, type the node command, and press Enter. You'll get a simple ›prompt or an error message telling you that NodeJS is not installed. Figure 4-10 shows the error message you'll see in Windows PowerShell if you don't have NodeJS installed.

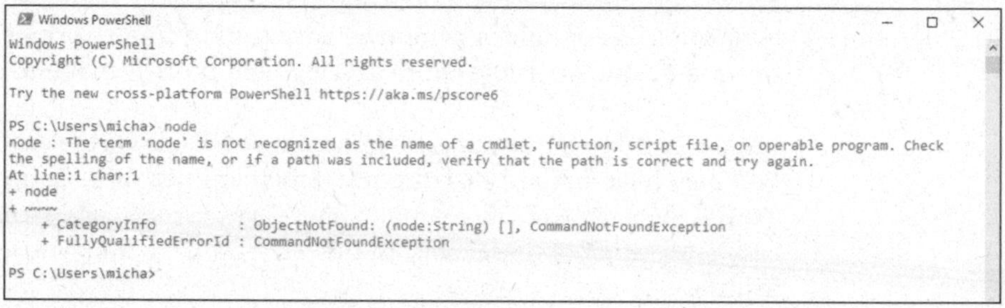

FIGURE 4-10: Error message in PowerShell when NodeJS isn't installed.

If you do have NodeJS installed, skip to the next section, "Downloading and installing Truffle." If you don't have NodeJS installed, follow these steps to download and install it:

1. **Launch your browser and navigate to** `https://nodejs.org/en/`.

   Your web browser will look like Figure 4-11. The NodeJS website detects your operating system and suggests the versions for that operating system. Because I'm using Microsoft Windows, I saw download links for Windows.

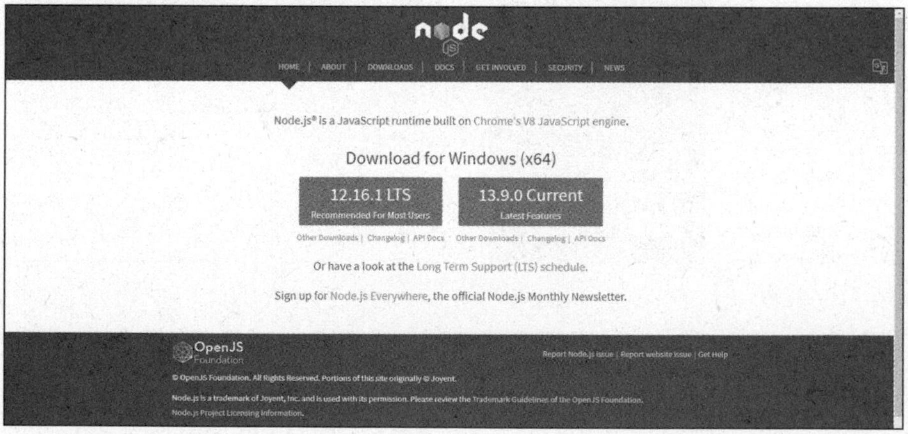

FIGURE 4-11: The NodeJS Download page.

2. **Click or tap the button for the version you want to install to download the Windows installer.**

   You can download the latest version or the latest stable (long-term support, or LTS) version. I chose the LTS version for the examples in this book. (When you set up your computer, a newer version of NodeJS might be available. You should download and install the latest LTS version.)

REMEMBER

   If you want to install NodeJS on a computer that isn't running Microsoft Windows or want to build your own version of NodeJS, click or tap the Other Downloads link. This link takes you to a page with options to download source code or installer packages for multiple operating systems.

3. **Launch the executable file you just downloaded.**

   Click or tap the Next button to start the installation process.

4. **Read the end-user license agreement, accept it, and then click or tap Next.**

5. **Select NodeJS installation options in the next three windows:**

   a. *Enter the install destination (or accept the default), and then click or tap Next.*

   b. *In the Custom Setup window that appears, click or tap Next to accept the defaults.*

   c. *In the next window, select or tap the Automatically Install the Necessary Tools option and then click or tap Next.*

6. **To install NodeJS, click or tap Install.**

7. **To complete the NodeJS part of the installation process, click or tap Finish.**

8. **Install the NodeJS tools.**

   Press or tap any key in the next two windows to run the scripts to install the supplemental NodeJS tools.

You can verify that NodeJS is installed with a simple command. Open a command shell or PowerShell window, type the following command, and press Enter:

```
node --version
```

This time when you enter the node command, you should see a message showing you the installed NodeJS version. Figure 4-12 shows the version message in Windows PowerShell.

After you have NodeJS installed, you're ready to install Truffle.

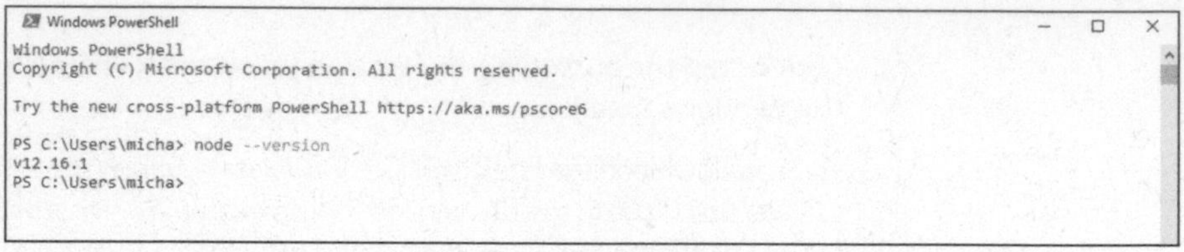

FIGURE 4-12:
The NodeJS
version message.

Downloading and installing Truffle

The NodeJS environment makes it easy to find and download new packages, including Truffle. The Truffle installation process requires you to enter just a single command.

To install Truffle, open a command shell or PowerShell window, type the following command, and press Enter:

```
npm install -g truffle
```

Figure 4-13 shows this command and the results. Truffle is installed and almost ready to be used.

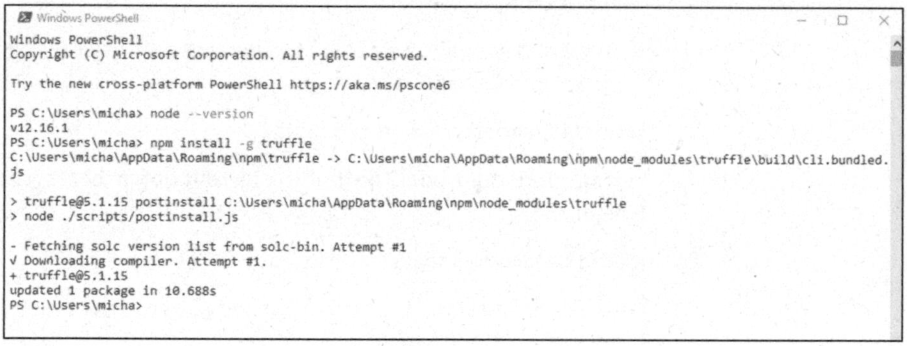

FIGURE 4-13:
Installing Truffle.

Truffle organizes development activities into projects. That way you can work on multiple projects with different configuration requirements. For example, you could set up a different testing blockchain for each of several projects. Let's look at the basics of setting up a project in Truffle.

Each Truffle project must have its own folder. The first thing to do to set up a Truffle project is to create a project folder. If you'd rather download the project files instead of creating a new empty project, go to www.dummies.com/go/blockchaindafd and extract the project archive file to a directory of your choice.

To create a new empty project named bcAnalytics, for example, open a command shell or PowerShell window, type the following command, and press Enter:

```
mkdir bcAnalytics
```

Make the new project folder your current directory by typing the following command and pressing Enter:

```
cd bcAnalytics
```

Then, to initialize your new Truffle project, enter this command and press Enter:

```
truffle init
```

Figure 4-14 shows these commands for initializing a new Truffle project.

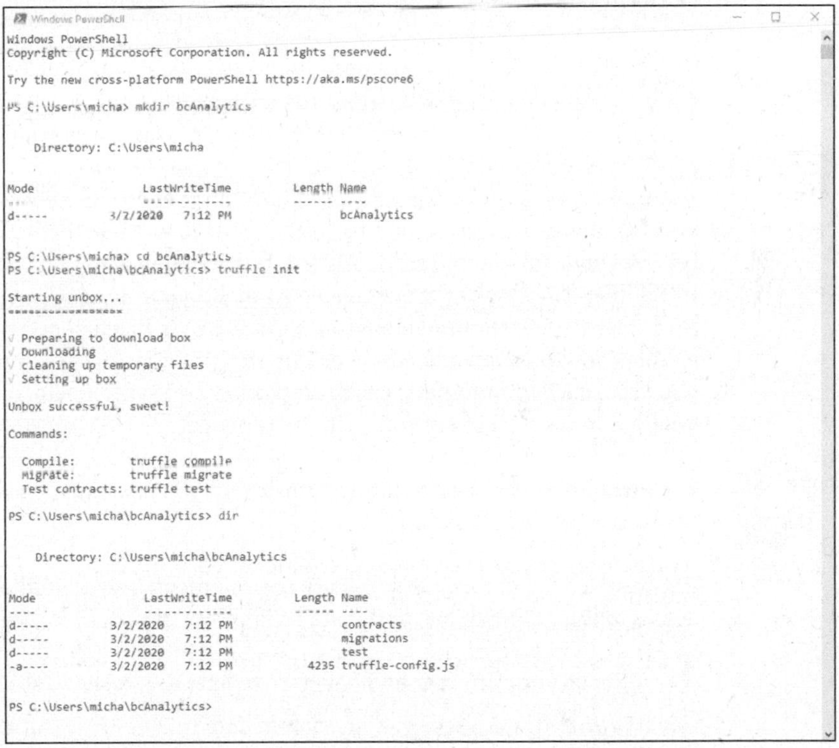

FIGURE 4-14:
Initializing a new Truffle project.

That's it! You now have a new Truffle project named bcAnalytics. That's all you'll do at this point. You can use File Explorer or the `dir` command to look at the bcAnalytics folder to see the files and new folders that Truffle created. You learn more about how Truffle uses these to define projects when you start writing your own smart contracts. But for now, you're ready to install the last tool to complete your Ethereum development environment.

Installing the IDE

Now that all foundational pieces are in place, you're just about ready to start writing code. The most visible part of software development is writing the source code. Many developers consider writing code to be the first productive step in the software development process, but that is far from the truth. Before you start writing any code, you should carefully and completely plan and design your application.

You'll save yourself far more time in the development process by taking time up front to plan. Planning will reduce the number of times you'll have to rework your code when what you write the first time doesn't do everything you need it to.

After you have a thorough plan and know what code you need to write to meet all your application's goals, you're ready to start writing the source code that will become your final application. Although you can use any text editor to write code in Solidity, many tools are available to make your development activities easier. An integrated development environment (IDE) is like a super editor that not only enables you to create and edit code but also provides many supporting features as you type, such as automatic code completion and syntax help. A good IDE can save you lots of time and help you write better code.

TIP

Use an editor or IDE that you find comfortable. Try several options before you settle on the tool you'll use.

For the exercise in this book, you use the Microsoft Visual Studio Code IDE to write source code. To download and install Visual Studio Code, follow these steps:

1. **Launch your browser and navigate to** `https://code.visualstudio.com/`.

Your web browser will look like Figure 4-15.

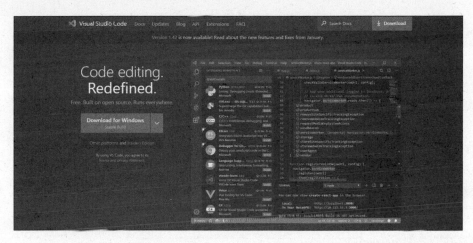

FIGURE 4-15:
The Microsoft
Visual Studio
Code download
web page.

2. **Click or tap the Download for Windows button.**

   If you want to install Visual Studio Code on a computer that isn't running Microsoft Windows, click or tap the down arrow next to the Download for Windows button. You'll see a list of links to download a Visual Studio Code installable file for macOS, Windows, and Linux.

3. **Launch the executable file you just downloaded by clicking the Next button on the Setup — Visual Studio Code window.**

4. **Read and accept the license agreement, and then click or tap Next.**

5. **Select Visual Studio Code installation options in the next three windows.**

   a. *Enter the install destination (or accept the default), and then click or tap Next.*

   b. *In the Select Start Menu Folder window, click or tap Next to accept the defaults.*

   c. *In the next window, if you want to place a shortcut to Visual Studio Code on your desktop, select or tap the Create a Desktop Icon option. Then click or tap Next.*

6. **To install Visual Studio Code, review your install options (see Figure 4-16) and then click or tap Install.**

   Your settings should look similar to the ones in Figure 4-16, with the exception of the destination location.

7. **When Visual Studio Code finishes installing, click or tap Finish to complete the installation process and launch the Visual Studio Code IDE.**

The Visual Studio (VS) Code IDE is now installed. Figure 4-17 shows the default Visual Studio Code tabletop and Welcome window. The welcome window contains lots of helpful information for getting started using the VS Code IDE.

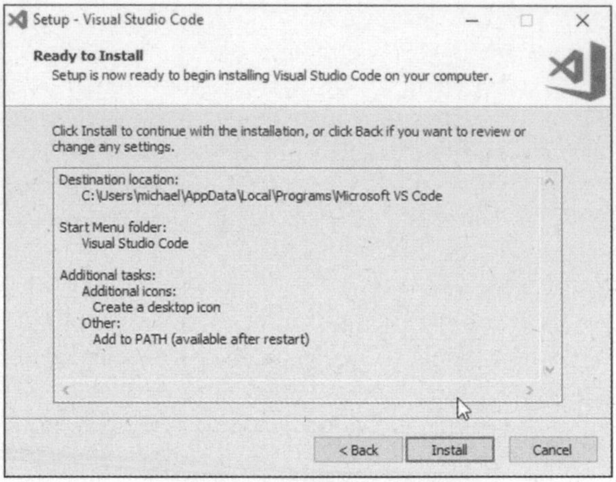

FIGURE 4-16:
Visual Studio
Code install
options window.

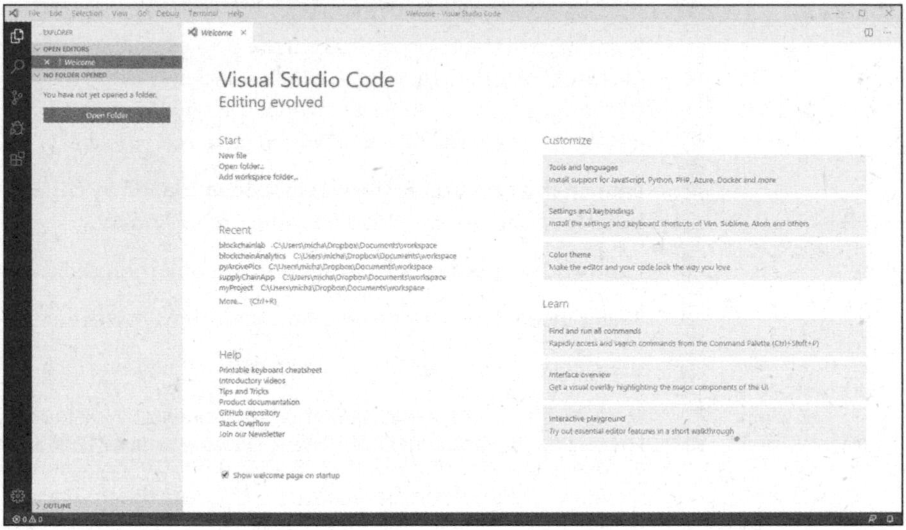

FIGURE 4-17:
The Visual Studio
Code IDE
desktop.

If you close the Welcome window, you can always open it again from the Help menu. It's the top option in the Help menu.

TIP

You have one more step to complete the installation of your Ethereum development environment. To get the benefit of VS Code's syntax highlighting, code completion, and other features, you need to add an extension so that VS Code understands Solidity. The easiest way to add an extension to VS Code is right from the IDE.

On the left border of the VS Code tabletop, click or tap the Extensions icon (the square within a square) icon. In the Search Extensions in Marketplace text box, type **Solidity**. A list of extensions that match your search term appears. Find the extension with the title "Ethereum Solidity Language for Visual Studio Code by Juan Blanco" and click or tap the green Install button for that extension. When you successfully install the Solidity extension, your VS Code window will look like Figure 4-18.

Congratulations! You've successfully built an Ethereum Solidity application development environment. Now you're ready to start developing blockchain analytics models.

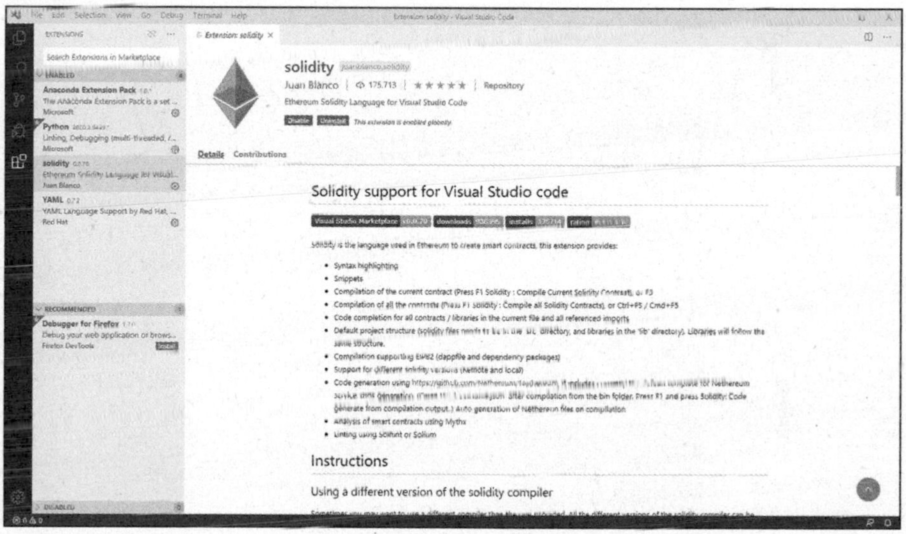

FIGURE 4-18:
The Visual Studio Code IDE with the Solidity extension.

Chapter **5**

Interacting with Blockchain Data

n Chapter 4, you build a lab environment to support Ethereum blockchain development. With a fully functioning lab you can develop, test, and even deploy your own smart contracts. You can either build your own local blockchain or connect to one of several public blockchains. You need a stable blockchain platform to carry out any type of blockchain analytics. The analytics process is simple at its core: Fetch interesting data from a blockchain, build a model to analyze that data, and execute your model to look for information your data may reveal.

Although the process sounds simple, each step has its own obstacles. That's why we're taking things slowly. You've spent a lot of time exploring what kinds of data a blockchain stores, and I hope you've been thinking about how that data could reveal interesting information. Regardless of whether you want to carry out analysis on public or private blockchain data, the process is foundationally the same. First, you explore the data to identify interesting data. Second, you build a model to make sense of your data and fetch the data you need for your model. Third, you use the model to carry out the analysis process and then present the results. You learn a lot more about each step in the rest of this book, but before you can move on to build models, you need some way to fetch blockchain data and carry out the analysis process.

Your blockchain lab provides the server side of the data repository, but you don't have a component in your ecosystem yet to efficiently interact with the blockchain data. Although your test environment does allow you to test smart contract code, it doesn't provide a way to easily access and evaluate your blockchain data. In this chapter, you learn how to identify, install, and set up an analytics client that you'll use to build models to analyze your blockchain data.

Exploring the Blockchain Analytics Ecosystem

In Chapter 4 you set up a blockchain lab. That lab included an Ethereum client (Geth), a test blockchain (Ganache), a testing framework (Truffle), and an IDE (VS Code). These components give you the ability to develop, test, and deploy Ethereum smart contracts and provide the core of a decentralized app (dApp).

The one piece of the puzzle that is missing is the end-user client component. Although Truffle gives you the ability to interact with Ethereum blockchain, the process isn't easy or elegant. To develop a viable dApp or any application that interacts with a blockchain, you must add another component to your lab: an effective way to write code that writes to and, more importantly, reads from the blockchain. You're about to learn about a few great options that allow you to easily interact with blockchain data.

Reviewing your blockchain lab

Your existing blockchain lab consists of several important pieces:

>> **Geth:** The Geth (Go Ethereum) client implements the EVM on a local device. The EVM is the software that runs smart contract code and makes a computer or device a blockchain node. You can use Geth to connect to the live mainnet Ethereum network, any of the public test networks, or any other Ethereum network (public or private).

>> **Ganache:** Ganache is one of the two products we've chosen from the Truffle Suite. Ganache provides a local, private blockchain that is handy for developing and testing smart contacts. Ganache also includes handy tools, such as a block explorer you'll use to examine block contents that help build effective analytics models.

>> **Truffle:** Truffle is a smart contract development framework. You won't use all of the rich Truffle features in this book, but you'll get a good taste (pardon the pun!) of how Truffle can help the overall smart contract development process.

>> **Visual Studio Code:** VS Code is one of many IDEs you can use to write code various many languages. I chose VS Code because it makes writing programs and scripts easier in Solidity (for smart contracts) and analytics models (we'll use Python). It also handles with ease many other languages and file formats, such as delimited text files.

You might wonder what you can do with your blockchain lab right now and why you need to add more tools to get ready to build analytics models. Everything you have in place gives you the tools and ecosystem to develop, test, and deploy smart contracts to a local or remote blockchain. That means you can either create your own blockchain or connect to someone else's network and create transactions through your own smart contracts.

You don't have a convenient way to interact with smart contracts yet. Although Truffle allows you to invoke smart contract functions from the Truffle console, it isn't pretty. The command-line interface is provided for its simplicity and utility value, not for its user interface elegance. To interact with blockchain data you need a more convenient way to fetch data and create new transactions that end up in new blocks.

The one additional component to add to your blockchain lab is an analytics client. I call it an analytics client to separate it from the Ethereum client. Your Ethereum client, Geth, implements the EVM that makes your computer or device an Ethereum network node and runs smart contract code. Ethereum clients are clients from the perspective of the blockchain but can also be viewed as a server component from the end user's perspective.

Identifying analytics client options

Lots of options for analytics clients are available. The main requirement is that the client provide access to the blockchain data. That's a loose requirement and one that you can meet in many ways. In general, when choosing a client option, there's a trade-off between user-friendliness and flexibility. Options that are the friendliest for users often provide the fewest options and least flexibility. That makes sense because providing more options almost always makes things more complex. But if you want maximum flexibility that allows you to build detailed models, you generally have to give up some ease of use.

When carrying out analytics in any environment, you generally have three options, each with its own strengths, weaknesses, and cost:

>> **Hire someone to do the work.** This option is by far the most expensive but the easiest. By outsourcing your analytics, you avoid much of the ecosystem and time investment. If you work well with the person or firm who carries out the analytics and can create detailed specifications (and have the budget), this option might be a good one for you.

>> **Use an existing blockchain analytics tool.** A growing list of tools and other software products supports blockchain analytics. Many tools are specific to blockchain implementations (Bitcoin or Ethereum specific) and generally focus on one type of data. It might be worth examining some of these tools to see if any meet your needs. Table 5-1 provides a partial list of available blockchain analytics tools.

>> **Develop your own models from scratch.** This last option is the one I focus on in this book. Writing code to develop your own models is almost always the slowest option (with respect to time invested from design to deployment) but offers unrivaled flexibility. When you write your own code, you can build models tailored to your needs. Even with this last approach, several options are available. The right decision depends on your language of choice and comfort level with the provided features. Table 5-2 lists several popular libraries you can use to write your own code to interact with a blockchain.

TABLE 5-1   **Blockchain Analytics Tools**

Product	Description	Where to Find It
Chainalysis	Company offering multiple products focused on associating real world identities with blockchain activity	www.chainalysis.com
CipherTrace	Solutions that support blockchain forensic investigations	https://ciphertrace.com/
Crystal	Analytics solutions to support due diligence and compliance needs	https://crystalblockchain.com/
Neutrino	Bitcoin-centric analytics service provider (acquired by Coinbase in 2019)	https://neutrino.global/
OXT	Bitcoin-centric analysis tool to support financial compliance requirements	https://oxt.me/
SAS Visual Investigator	General purpose analysis tool supporting forensics investigations and compliance requirements	www.sas.com/en_us/software/intelligence-analytics-visual-investigator.html

TABLE 5-2   **Ethereum Blockchain Access Libraries**

Library	Description	Where to Find It
web3.js	The most popular JavaScript library used to interact with Ethereum smart contracts	`https://github.com/ethereum/web3.js/`
ethers.js	A JavaScript alternative to web3.js, based on lessons learned from initial Ethereum deployments and implementations	`https://github.com/ethers-io/ethers.js/`
ethjs	A lightweight JavaScript library that provides a subset of web3.js functionality with a much smaller footprint	`https://github.com/ethjs/ethjs`
web3.py	A Python implementation of the popular web3.js library; I chose to use this library since Python is a popular analytics language	`https://github.com/ethereum/web3.py`

Choosing the best blockchain analytics client

Don't get confused by all the options available. The best blockchain analytics client depends on your needs. Before looking at the range of possible solutions, take some time to clearly document your analytics goals. Write down a short list of goals that describe your reasons for pursuing analytics answers in the first place. If you can't clearly explain your reasons for analyzing your data, chances are you haven't thought things through enough. You can save yourself lots of time and money by taking more time to come up with a clear statement of purpose. After you have that, you can make a better decision on the best analytics client for your circumstances and goals.

Because the purpose of this book is to explore blockchain analytics basics, you'll use the functions from analytics libraries to build analytics models. Later, you may decide to use a purpose-built product or even write your own from scratch, but in going through the exercises in this book, you'll gain a broader understanding of what those tools are doing for you.

If you have a background in analytics, chances are you have experience in the R statistical package or the Python language or both. Because Python is such a popular language for data analytics and one of the more popular Ethereum blockchain libraries is written in Python, I chose to use the Python library, web3.py, as the Ethereum client you'll use in the examples for this book. You'll also use several Python analytics libraries to avoid having to write every model from scratch. I show you how to install an analytics platform named Anaconda, which comes with most of the Python libraries you'll need to build a variety of models.

If you already know Python, you'll be able to jump right into the code I present. If you don't know Python, many resources are available to help you get up to speed in this powerful language. Following are five free and for-fee resources to help you get started:

>> **A Byte of Python:** A free online book on programming in Python, at https://python.swaroopch.com/.

>> **Codecademy:** A well-designed, structured 25-hour Python course. Requires a Codecademy subscription. Go to www.codecademy.com/learn/learn-python-3.

>> **Google's Python Class:** A Google education course, including videos, on learning Python. Go to https://developers.google.com/edu/python/.

>> **Learn Python the Hard Way:** A classic book on Python programming. This resource isn't free, but it's well worth the price. Visit https://learnpython thehardway.org/book/.

>> **Envato Tuts+:** A Python tutorial with many links to additional resources, at https://code.tutsplus.com/articles/the-best-way-to-learn-python--net-26288.

Adding Anaconda and Web3.js to Your Lab

In this section, you add the Anaconda platform and the web3.py library to your blockchain analytics lab. The Anaconda platform gives you easy access to a collection of software tools and Python libraries you'll need for the examples. The web3.py library allows you to write Python scripts that invoke smart contract functions and interact with blockchain data.

If you haven't built your lab, go back to Chapter 4 and follow the instructions to build the basic lab first. This section assumes that you at least have VS Code and Ganache installed.

Verifying platform prerequisites

Installing the few additional components your blockchain analytics lab needs is easy. However, you must have Python already installed on your computer. In this section, you first check to see if Python is installed and then install if necessary.

REMEMBER

You may see references to Python 2 and Python 3. These are major versions of the Python language. Keep in mind that Python 2.7 was *deprecated* (reclassified as no longer used) as of January 1, 2020. That means you should not install any Python version lower than 3.0 unless you have specific legacy software that requires it. For all new projects, you should only install Python version 3.0 and higher.

Checking the installed Python version

To see if your computer already has Python installed, follow these steps:

1. Launch a command prompt or PowerShell prompt.

To launch a command prompt, type **cmd** in the search bar at the lower-left corner of your desktop and then click or tap the Command Prompt option. To launch a PowerShell prompt, type **PowerShell** in the search bar and select or tap the PowerShell option.

2. Type the following and then press Enter:

```
python --version
```

This command will display the version of Python installed or an error message indicating that Python can't be found. Figure 5-1 shows that Python version 3.8.0 is installed on my computer.

```
Windows PowerShell
Windows PowerShell
Copyright (C) Microsoft Corporation. All rights reserved.

Try the new cross-platform PowerShell https://aka.ms/pscore6

PS C:\Users\micha> python --version
Python 3.8.0
PS C:\Users\micha>
```

FIGURE 5-1:
Python version
command.

If Python is not installed, you must follow the instructions in the next section to install it before proceeding. If a version of Python lower than version 3.0 is installed, you should install a higher version.

TECHNICAL STUFF

You can install multiple versions of Python on one computer. In many cases, you can install Python 2.7 and Python 3.x (where x is some minor version number greater than 0) on a single computer. You can either change your system PATH based on which version you want to run or use the python command to run Python 2.7 and the python3 command to run Python 3.x.

Installing Python (if needed)

Follow these steps to download and install the Python language on your computer:

1. **Launch your browser, navigate to** `https://www.python.org`, **and then click or tap the Downloads link at the top of the page.**

   Your web browser will look like Figure 5-2.

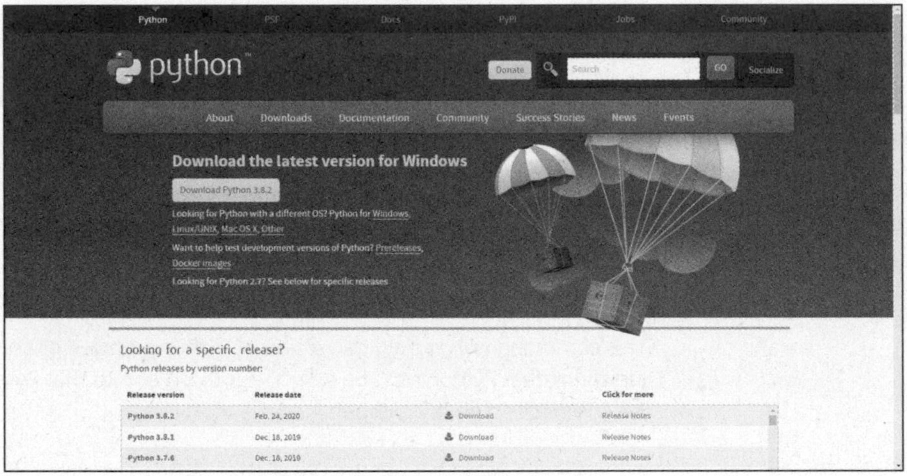

FIGURE 5-2:
The Python
Download web
page.

2. **Click or tap the Download Python button.**

   I selected Python 3.8.0. (When you set up your computer, a newer version of Python might be available. Download and install the latest version available.)

3. **Launch the executable file you just downloaded.**

   The Python Setup window appears.

4. **Select or tap Add Python to PATH check box (see Figure 5-3), and then click or tap Install Now.**

5. **When the installation finishes, click or tap the Close button.**

Installing the Anaconda platform

The *Anaconda platform* is a popular environment for building and managing data science projects using the Python and R languages. When you install Anaconda, also installed automatically are over 250 packages, including nearly all the Python libraries you need to build the models in this book. You could install each library yourself, but installing Anaconda is easier.

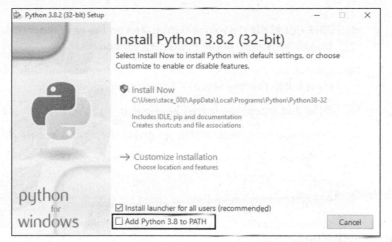

FIGURE 5-3:
Python Setup
window.

In addition to getting lots of packages, Anaconda provides GUI and command-line interfaces, easy integration with many analytics tools, and the powerful Conda package manager for installing anything else you might need.

Installing Anaconda is easy. You'll use the open-source and freely available version of Anaconda called Anaconda Distribution. To download and install Anaconda Distribution, follow these steps:

1. **Launch your browser and navigate to** www.anaconda.com/distribution/.

Your web browser will look like Figure 5-4.

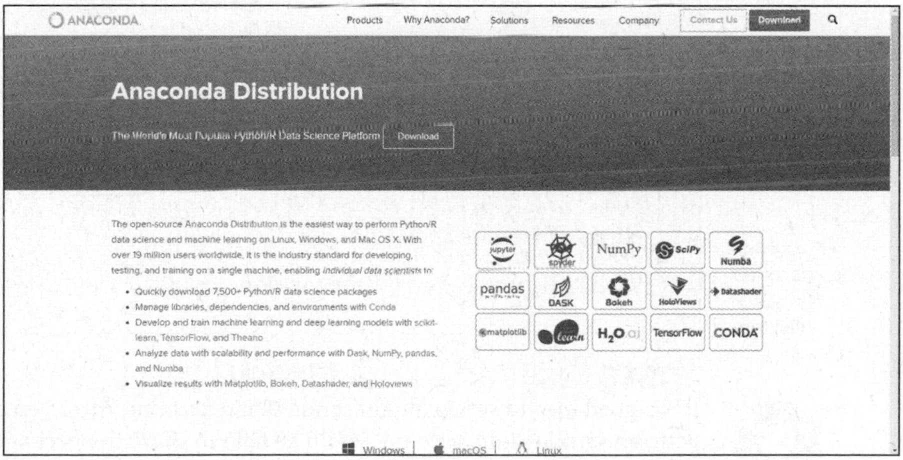

FIGURE 5-4:
The Anaconda
Distribution
download web
page.

2. **Click or tap the Download button, and on the next page click or tap the Download button under Python 3.x version.**

3. **Launch the executable file you just downloaded, and then click or tap the Next button on the Setup — Anaconda window.**

4. **Read and accept the license agreement, and then click or tap I Agree.**

5. **Select Anaconda installation options in the next three windows.**

   a. *Select or tap the option to indicate whether Anaconda should be installed for your user only (Just Me) or for All Users, and then click or tap Next.*

   b. *Enter the install destination (or accept the default), and then click or tap Next.*

   c. *Select or tap the Register Anaconda as My Default Python 3.x option. Then click or tap Install.*

6. **When Anaconda finishes installing, click or tap Next in the next two windows, and then click or tap Finish to complete the installation process and launch Anaconda.**

The Anaconda Platform is now installed. Figure 5-5 shows the default Anaconda Navigator desktop. The desktop window contains links to popular tools and lots of helpful information for getting started using Anaconda.

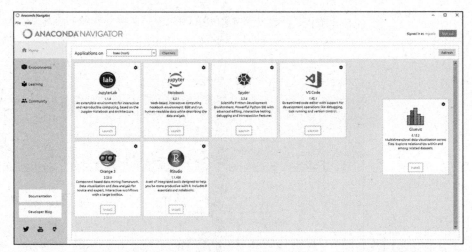

FIGURE 5-5:
The Anaconda Navigator desktop.

It's a good idea to set up an Anaconda Cloud account. After you create and log into your Anaconda Cloud account, you'll be able to share the packages, notebooks, and complete environment with other users (or even with yourself on other computers). Go to https://anaconda.org/ to create your Anaconda Cloud account and learn more about its advantages.

Installing the Web3.py library

One of the libraries Anaconda doesn't include is the one you'll use as your block-chain client, web3.js. Installing the web3.py library is easy, requiring a single command pip (PIP Installs Packages). Unfortunately, the pip utility isn't installed in Anaconda by default either, so you have to install it first.

The next task in making your Python Ethereum blockchain library available is to install the package installer for Python, pip, and then use pip to install the web3.py package. Follow these steps to install pip and web3.py:

1. **Launch the Anaconda Navigator. From Anaconda, click or tap the Launch button under VS Code to launch VS Code.**

   To launch a command prompt, type **cmd** in the search bar at the lower-left corner of your desktop and then select or tap the Command Prompt option. To launch a PowerShell prompt, type **PowerShell** in the search bar and select or tap the PowerShell option.

2. **Click or tap Terminal in the VS Code menu bar, and then click or tap New Terminal to open a new terminal window.**

3. **Type the following at the prompt in the terminal window, and then press Enter:**

   ```
   conda install pip
   ```

   Figure 5-6 shows the results of the conda install pip command. Now that you have the pip command installed, you can use it to install the web3.py library.

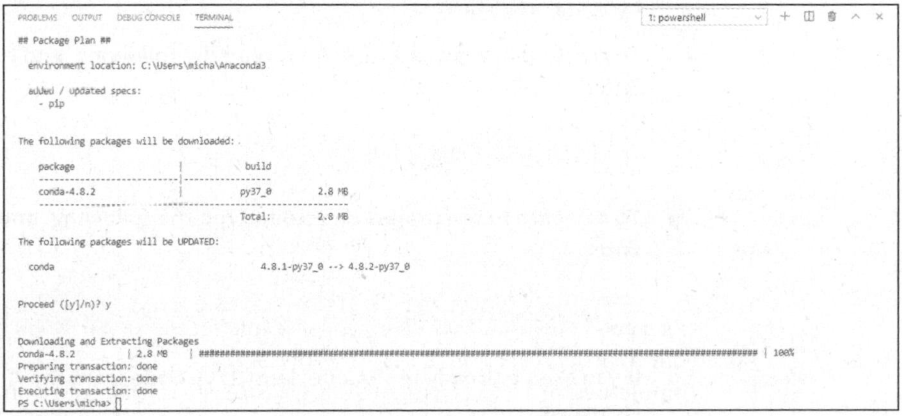

FIGURE 5-6:
The conda install pip command.

4. **Type the following at the prompt in the terminal window, and then press Enter:**

```
pip install web3
```

Figure 5-7 shows the `pip` command to install `web3.py`.

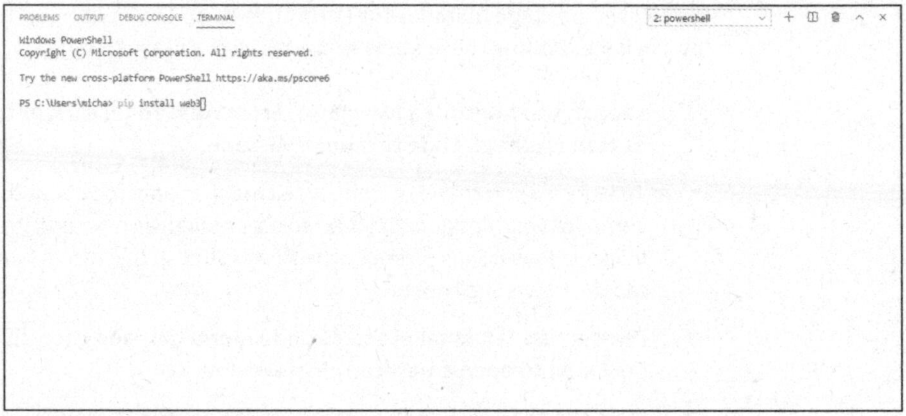

FIGURE 5-7:
The `pip install web3` command.

Setting up your blockchain analytics project

The last steps before you will be ready to start writing Python code to access a blockchain is to set up a project in VS Code. Follow these steps to create a new project and configure VS Code for your analytics code:

1. **Launch a command prompt or PowerShell prompt (or open a new terminal in VS Code).**

2. **To create a new project directory, type the following, and then press Enter:**

```
mkdir blockchainlab
```

3. **To navigate to the project directory, type the following, and then press Enter:**

```
cd blockchainlab
```

4. **If you aren't already in VS Code, launch VS Code from the Anaconda Navigator.**

5. **Open the blockchainlab folder:**

    a. Click or tap the Open Folder button or choose File ⇨ Open Folder from the menu bar.

    b. Navigate to the blockchainlab folder you just created and click or tap Select Folder to open it in VS Code.

Figure 5-8 shows the commands for Steps 1-3.

```
PROBLEMS   OUTPUT   DEBUG CONSOLE   TERMINAL                                    1: powershell

Windows PowerShell
Copyright (C) Microsoft Corporation. All rights reserved.

Try the new cross-platform PowerShell https://aka.ms/pscore6

PS C:\Users\micha> mkdir blockchainlab


    Directory: C:\Users\micha


Mode                LastWriteTime         Length Name
----                -------------         ------ ----
d-----        3/3/2020   1:20 PM                blockchainlab


PS C:\Users\micha> cd blockchainlab
PS C:\Users\micha\blockchainlab> []
```

FIGURE 5-8:
Commands to
create a new
project directory.

After you're in VS Code, you should carry out one more step to complete your analytics lab setup. This last step isn't strictly necessary, but it extends VS Code to support any Python code you write.

TIP

Many VS Code extensions provide integrated Python language support, but you'll install the default extension for now. You can always replace it with an alternative extension if you find another one that provides functionality you prefer.

Click or tap the extensions icon (shown in the margin) on the left border of the VS Code tabletop. In the Search Extensions in Marketplace text box, type **Python**. You'll see a list of extensions that match your search term. Find the extension with the title Python from Microsoft and click or tap its green Install button. When you successfully install the Python extension and click or tap the Python extension in the extension list, your VS Code window should look like Figure 5-9.

Congratulations! You've extended your Ethereum blockchain analytics lab to allow you to interact with the blockchain data.

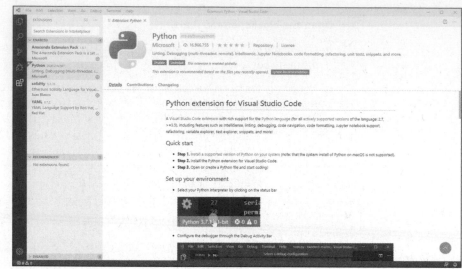

FIGURE 5-9:
Visual Studio
Code IDE with
Python extension.

Writing a Python Script to Access a Blockchain

Before you can access a blockchain using Python (or any other language), you must establish a few things. First, you must set up a connection to your block-chain. Your analytics client (your Python code) will need to establish a connection with an EVM to interact with the blockchain. This simple process requires only two steps.

Before starting, you must ensure that you have an available connection to a running blockchain node. For our purposes, we'll use Ganache. Launch Ganache, then click or tap Quickstart to create an EVM running on port 7545, which is the default. (You can change the port in Ganache settings.)

After you have Ganache running, create a new file in VS Code with the name showSupplyChain.py and type the following Python code, which will carry out the steps to connect to your Ganache blockchain (and define a couple variables you'll soon need):

```python
import json
from web3 import Web3


ganache_url = "http://127.0.0.1:7545"
web3 = Web3(Web3.HTTPProvider(ganache_url))
```

```
with open('SupplyChain.abi') as f:
  abi = json.load(f)


address = web3.toChecksumAddress('ADDRESS')
```

The first two lines import the `json` `web3.py` libraries and makes their functionality available to your Python script. The next two lines define the host and port number for your Ganache instance (you can find those values on the main Ganache window) and then create a connection to Ganache. The two lines that follow load the smart contract's ABI from a file (more on that in a minute). And finally, the last line assigns the address on the blockchain where the smart contract you'll use resides, which provides the rest of the information `web3.py` needs to interact with your blockchain.

You can find the ABI (more on that in a minute) and contract address in multiple ways. To keep things simple, we'll use the Remix IDE to find the values. You could use Truffle or other methods, including `web3.py`, but those methods are more complex. The Remix IDE is a convenient way to write and deploy smart contracts without having to configure more software components.

Interfacing with smart contracts

Most of the interesting data stored in Ethereum is a result of smart contract functions. Unlike Bitcoin, which focuses on account value transfers, Ethereum supports far more data than just transferring an amount from one account to another. Smart contracts allow users to invoke functions that store state data and generate events stored in logs. Having access to smart contract information is fundamental to accessing the data stored in an Ethereum blockchain.

Essentially two types of blockchains exist: unspent transaction blockchains and smart contract blockchains. A complete description of each type is beyond the scope of this book, but *unspent transaction blockchains,* such as Bitcoin, simply add up transactions over time to calculate any account's current balance. Alternatively, *smart contract blockchains,* such as Ethereum, store state values and other complex data in addition to recording individual transactions. The difference may seem subtle, but it changes the way you look at blockchain data and how you access it. You focus on the Ethereum model in this book.

Because much of your blockchain interaction will depend on smart contract data states and events, you need a way to define to Python what data you can access on the blockchain. The Ethereum compiler creates an *application binary interface (ABI)* when it compiles smart contract source code into bytecode. The ABI is a JSON data structure that defines a smart contract's function signatures, its state variables, and any events it supports. In short, the ABI describes all the data and functionality of a smart contract. With a smart contract's ABI, you can write code to interact with any data created and managed by a smart contract. You also need to know the address on the blockchain where your smart contract code is stored. After you provide the ABI and contract address to web3.py, it has all the information needed to locate and interact with the smart contract's data.

This smart contract context approach to data might be different from what you're used to. In most traditional database applications, the schema defines data layouts. With the schema, you can write queries to fetch and update any data in the database. Blockchain state storage is very different. Each smart contract likely stores and manages data differently from other smart contracts. That means you need the ABI for every smart contract whose data you want to analyze.

If ABIs are readily available, needing an ABI for analytics work isn't a big problem. Analytics carried out on your own smart contract data shouldn't pose any ABI availability issues. However, if you want to access data via someone else's smart contracts, you'll need to either request the ABIs from the smart contract author or use the published ABI for registered smart contracts. Otherwise, you'll have a tough time decoding the block data. You focus on accessing data through ABIs in this book.

The next step in any Python script to access blockchain data is to define the smart contract's ABI and its address. You'll use the smart contract's address to invoke its functions (to get to its data) and to parse through its logs.

Finding a smart contract's ABI

If you have access to a smart contract's source code, finding the ABI isn't difficult. Although you can use Truffle to compile a smart contract and provide the ABI, I show you an easier way to get the info you need.

TIP

This discussion focuses on homegrown smart contracts — that is, you or your organization developed the smart contract and the source code is available to you. If the smart contract you want to use isn't yours and the source code isn't available, the next step is to determine if it's published in a shared repository. In later chapters, you discover how to use published smart contract ABIs instead of compiling them yourself.

Remix is a web-based Ethereum smart contract IDE that provides some of the same functionality of Truffle and VS Code. It doesn't do everything the Truffle and VS Code do, but it does make deploying smart contract code easy. And because Remix makes it easy also to get a smart contract's ABI and deployed address, you use it here to deploy the SupplyChain.sol smart contract.

TIP

If you read *Ethereum For Dummies* (Wiley), you'll recognize the `SupplyChain.sol` smart contract. The version you use in this book is an enhanced version of the smart contract presented in *Ethereum For Dummies*.

The `SupplyChain.sol` smart contract implements a simple supply chain application. You'll use that smart contract to interact with and analyze blockchain data. Follow these steps to use Remix to deploy the `SupplyChain.sol` smart contract to your Ganache blockchain and then use Python to invoke the smart contract's functions:

1. **Launch your browser and navigate to** `https://remix.ethereum.org/`, **and then click or tap the Solidity button to select the Solidity programming environment.**

   Your web browser will look like Figure 5-10.

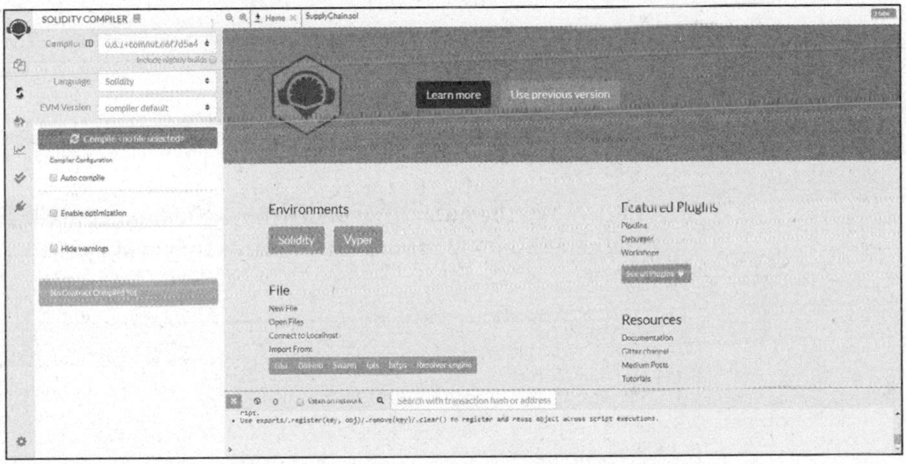

FIGURE 5-10:
The Remix web
page.

2. **Click or tap the create new file icon, type** SupplyChain.sol, **and then click or tap OK.**

   If you don't see the File Explorers pane, click or tab the File Explorers icon in the left menu.

3. **Open the** `SupplyChain.sol` **file in VS Code, copy all the text in the file, and then paste the contents of** `SupplyChain.sol` **in the Remix blank editor window.**

TIP

   You can download all code for this book from www.dummies.com/go/blockchaindafd.

   Now that you have the code for `SupplyChain.sol` in the IDE, Remix can compile it and then deploy it to your Ganache blockchain in the next steps.

4. If the Solidity Compiler pane is not visible, click or tap the Solidity compiler icon in the left menu bar (labeled in Figure 5-11).

FIGURE 5-11:
The Remix Solidity compiler page.

5. Click or tap the Compile SupplyChain.sol button to compile your smart contract.

6. Click or tap the ABI button under the Compilation Details button to copy the generated ABI to your clipboard, as shown in Figure 5-12.

FIGURE 5-12:
Copying the SupplyChain. sol smart contract ABI in Remix.

7. **Open or launch VS Code, and then create a new file with the name** SupplyChain.abi.

If the SupplyChain.abi file already exists, open the file and press Ctrl+A to select all text. (You're about to overwrite any existing text.)

8. **Paste the contents of your clipboard (the ABI you copied from Remix) into the VS Code editor for** SupplyChain.abi **and save the file, as shown in Figure 5-13.**

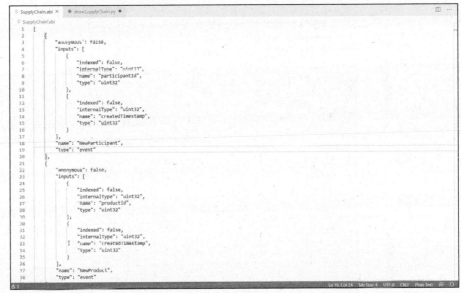

FIGURE 5-13: Copied ABI value in the Supply Chain.abi file.

9. **Open** showSupplyChain.py **in VS Code. Or, if you still have the file open, just switch to the showSupplyChain.py tab.**

TIP

Note that in showSupplyChain.py, lines 9 and 10 open the SupplyChain.abi file you just created and read its contents into the abi variable. Your Python file should look like Figure 5-14.

10. **Make sure that your Ganache blockchain is running.**

11. **In Remix, click or tap the deploy & run transaction icon (shown in the margin), and then click or tap the Environment drop-down and select Web3 Provider.**

FIGURE 5-14:
VS Code
showSupply
Chain.py.

```
 showSupplyChain.py > ...
  1  import json
  2  from web3 import Web3
  3
  4  ganache_url = "http://127.0.0.1:7545"
  5  web3 = Web3(Web3.HTTPProvider(ganache_url))
  6
  7  web3.eth.defaultAccount = web3.eth.accounts[0]
  8
  9  with open('SupplyChain.abi') as f:
 10      abi = json.load(f)
 11
 12  address = web3.toChecksumAddress('0xE9D226EC6190087Ac76E76Fc89094ac8a8e34a5d')
 13  # Initialize supplyChain contract
 14  contract = web3.eth.contract(address=address, abi=abi)
```

12. In the External Node Request window, change the Web3 Provider
Endpoint value to http://localhost:7545.

Steps 11 and 12 configure Remix to connect to your Ganache blockchain. Your
web browser will look like Figure 5-15.

FIGURE 5-15:
Connecting Remix
to your Ganache
blockchain.

13. Click or tap OK to close the External Node Request window.

14. Deploy the SupplyChain.sol smart contract to your Ganache blockchain
by clicking or tapping the Deploy button.

15. Copy the contract's deployed address to the clipboard by clicking or
tapping the Copy Value to Clipboard button next to the Deployed
Contracts entry for supplyChain.

Your web browser will look like Figure 5-16.

TIP

If you deploy a contract multiple times, use the last deployed contract address
(the one at the bottom of the list).

FIGURE 5-16:
Copying a
deployed
contract's
address.

16. **Return to VS Code, then replace the** `ADDRESS` **string in line 12 with the contract's deployed address you just copied from Remix.**

After you replace the `ADDRESS` string (in line 12) with the contract's deployed address value from Remix, your Python file should look like Figure 5-17.

Now that you have all the basic pieces in place in your Python script, you can run it! It doesn't really do anything yet, but it shouldn't give you any errors.

```python
showSupplyChain.py ●
showSupplyChain.py > ...
1    import json
2    from web3 import Web3
3
4    ganache_url = "http://127.0.0.1:7545"
5    web3 = Web3(Web3.HTTPProvider(ganache_url))
6
7    web3.eth.defaultAccount = web3.eth.accounts[0]
8
9    with open('SupplyChain.abi') as f:
10       abi = json.load(f)
11
12   address = web3.toChecksumAddress('0xE9D226EC619D087Ac76E76Fc89094ac8aBe34a5d')
13   # Initialize supplyChain contract
14   contract = web3.eth.contract(address=address, abi=abi)
15
16   productCount = contract.functions.product_id().call()
17   participantCount = contract.functions.participant_id().call()
18   transferCount = contract.functions.owner_id().call()
19
20   print()
21   print('Products: ',productCount)
22   print('Participants: ',participantCount)
23   print('Ownership transfers: ',transferCount)
24
25   # Display the participants
26   for i in range (0, participantCount):
27       print(contract.functions.participants(i).call())
28
29   print('Participants: ',contract.functions.participant_id().call())
```

FIGURE 5-17:
VS Code
showSupply
Chain.py (with
contract address).

17. **To run the Python file, click or tap the right-pointing arrow in the upper-right corner of your VS Code window.**

Running your code from VS Code launches the Python interpreter and executes the current script. At this point, your script doesn't do anything exciting — that will come soon. Your VS Code window should look like Figure 5-18.

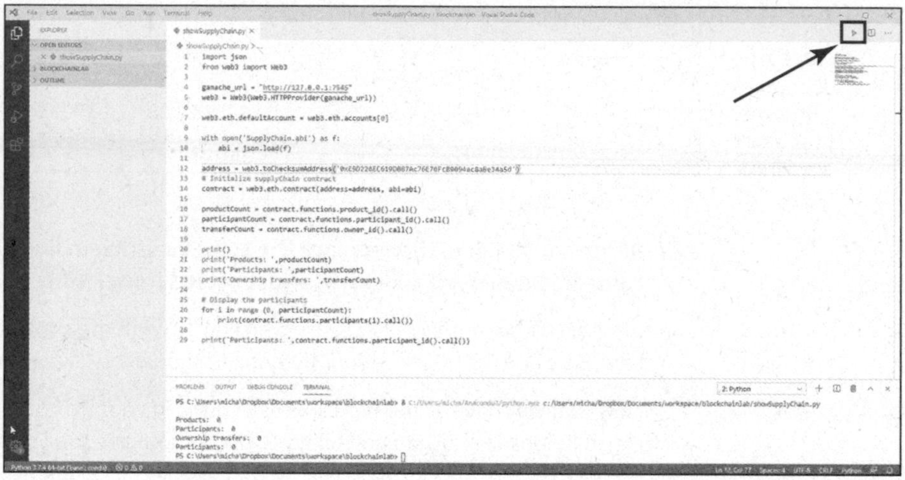

FIGURE 5-18:
VS Code after running showSupply Chain.py for the first time.

TIP

If you get any errors, carefully review your Python code for any misspellings. VS Code will try to help you by underlining any errors with a red squiggle line. If you see that, hover your cursor over the error to get more information about the error.

WARNING

Your code will work only after you've copied the ABI and current contract address from Remix. If you download the code from the book's site and try to run it without providing your ABI and address, it won't run.

Building a Local Blockchain to Analyze

You just have a few more steps to have a fully functioning and populated blockchain analytics lab! Because you're starting with a blank Ganache blockchain, one easy way to populate it with data is to let your smart contract's functions do the work for you. You'll need to use smart contract functionality to interact with any blockchain, so now is a good time to learn how to do it!

Connecting to your blockchain

Before you can interact with data stored in any blockchain, you have to connect your analytics client (your code written using web3.py) to the blockchain. The good news is that you already did that in the preceding section. You used a running Ganache instance and Remix to deploy your smart contract to your Ganache blockchain. You can deploy smart contracts and find their addresses in other ways, but regardless of what method you use, the takeaway is that you need the ABI and the deployed address for any smart contract data you want to access.

The first 14 lines of showSupplyChain.py (refer to Figure 5-17) set up the connection to your blockchain. If you want to use a different blockchain, you can easily connect to it by changing the value of ganache_url to reflect your desired blockchain's host and port number. (Of course, if you aren't using Ganache, you should change the variable name to be consistent with its use.)

After you're connected to the blockchain, you can start interacting with its smart contracts and data.

Invoking smart contract functions

The main type of data you'll use for analytics is smart contract data. Transaction and event data may be of interest as well, but we'll focus on smart contract state data for now. The most direct way to access smart contract state data is to invoke smart contract functions to do the work for you.

The first step in invoking smart contract functions is to choose the functions that will do what you want. For now, we want to add data to the blockchain. If you look at the source code for the SupplyChain.sol smart contract, you'll see that three functions look like they add data:

```
function addParticipant(string memory _name, string memory _pass, address _pAdd,
    string memory _pType) public returns (uint32)

function addProduct(uint32 _ownerId, string memory _modelNumber, string memory _
    partNumber, string memory _serialNumber, uint32 _productCost) public returns
    (uint32)

function newOwner(uint32 _user1Id ,uint32 _user2Id, uint32 _prodId) onlyOwner(_
    prodId) public returns(bool)
```

TIP

Reading smart contract source code is one way to find useful functions. An easier way to identify functions is to check smart contract documentation.

The addParticipant() and addProduct() functions add new state data, and the newOwner() function moves a product to a new owner, creating the product's track as it moves along the supply chain.

Invoking a smart contract function involves two steps: Invoke the function and then wait for the results. Because invoking a function to add data to the blockchain creates a transaction, that transaction won't complete until the block that contains your transaction is mined. In Ganache with the automining feature enabled, completing transactions and adding a block to the blockchain are instantaneous. In a real blockchain, there will be some delay.

Here are the two steps to app a new product to the supply chain blockchain (replacing the strings NAME, PASSWORD, ADDRESS, and TYPE with data):

```
tx_hash = contract.functions.addParticipant('NAME','PASSWORD',
    web3.eth.accounts[int('ACCOUNT')],'TYPE').transact()
web3.eth.waitForTransactionReceipt(tx_hash)
```

The first line of Python code invokes the addParticipant() function for the attached contract, passing the desired input parameters and creating a transaction. The second line of Python code waits for the block that contains the new transaction to be mined and stores the transaction receipt in tx_hash.

To quickly build a blockchain you can use for analytics. I've supplied a Python script, buildSupplyChain.py, and three input files to define the participants, products, and supply chain movements, respectively. I used Python to open the input files and read their contents to provide input parameters to the three functions mentioned previously. You can download these files from www.dummies. com/go/blockchaindafd. After you download the file, extract its contents to your blockchainlab folder. Then just open the buildSupplyChain.py script in VS Code, change the smart contract address value in line 15 to your smart contract's deployed address, and run it.

Fetching blockchain data

Now that you have a Ganache blockchain with some data in it, you can read that data and then display or analyze it. This next step is a small step forward from the preceding section. You already know how to invoke smart contract functions, so you can just invoke functions that fetch data to get all the data you need from smart contract state values.

TIP

Using the smart contract function method to fetch data relies on the functions each smart contract contains. If the get() function doesn't provide all the smart contract data, you can fetch it in other ways, but using provided functions is generally the easiest way to get the data you need.

The complete showSupplyChain.py Python script (provided on the download site) shows how to use smart contract functions to fetch blockchain data. I used a simple Python loop for each type of data and iteratively invoked the get() functions that return the desired data. The main difference between adding data and fetching data is that you aren't creating transactions when just fetching data. That's why the code uses the call() method instead of the transact() method at the end of each function invocation.

Note that I used simple loops for the participants and products, and then used a nested loop structure to iterate over all ownership transfers for each product. Figure 5-19 shows the completed showSupplyChain.py Python script. If you've run the buildSupplyChain.py script, you can run the showSupplyChain.py script now to see data from your blockchain.

For the rest of the book, you learn how to extend this basic functionality to build and execute your own blockchain analytics models.

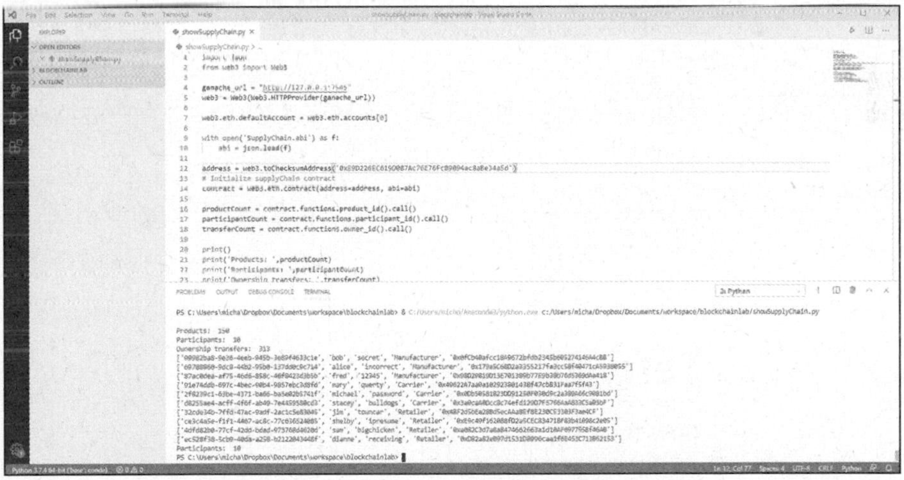

FIGURE 5-19:
Completed show
SupplyChain.
py Python script.

2
Fetching Blockchain Chain

Chapter **6**

Parsing Blockchain Data and Building the Analysis Dataset

In Chapter 5, you learn how to connect to an Ethereum blockchain and read data that smart contracts manage. Blockchain data consists of more than just smart contract state data, and over the next few chapters you learn how to identify and access transaction details and logs as well. No hard rules exist for accessing blockchain data for analytics; each project may have different requirements and need different types of data.

One important aspect of blockchain analytics to understand is the nature of blockchain apps and data. Blockchain technology is not just a new type of database. In fact, storing data in a blockchain that doesn't need to be there is expensive. Because a fee is required to store data in a blockchain, the only data that should get stored is data that benefits from transparency, integrity, and immutability.

In this chapter, you learn how to fetch blockchain data and pair it with externally stored data (data that isn't stored in the blockchain) to provide complete input to your analytics models.

Comparing On-Chain and External Analysis Options

When you build analytics models, you have two basic options: real-time parsing or two-step analysis. With real-time parsing, you read data from the blockchain, fetch any related data that you need from other sources, and then provide the complete dataset to the code that analyzes the data. On the other hand, two-step analysis (which may contain more than just two steps) first fetches data from the blockchain and stores it in some off-chain repository. The second step then uses traditional methods to find related data to complete the input requirements for the analytics models.

For example, assume you're analyzing your supply chain data to identify inefficient carrier (shipping) participants. You could read all the ownership data to determine the timestamp when a carrier picked up products and delivered those products. You could compare the performance of different carriers for similar pickup and drop-off locations to see if one carrier is better than another.

One problem with such a simple comparison is that is doesn't take anomalies into account. If adverse weather delayed delivery, that shouldn't negatively affect a carrier's performance result. In that case, you could query a weather database for the dates and times along the delivery route to identify any major weather events. Consuming weather data would require querying an external data repository. Most analytics models that provide actionable results (results that you can use to make decisions) will probably need more data than just what you can find in the blockchain. Integrating external data is a major part of building an effective model.

Considering access speed

Determining access methods and data needs are processes. You should consider whether you'll need to carry out this analysis multiple times or just once, and whether you'll need external data. You also should consider the volatility of your blockchain and external data. If any data changes frequently, you might need to revisit it often.

After you have a good understanding of your data needs, you'll need to assess your analysis platform capabilities. If you have the network bandwidth to transfer all the data you need on demand and the processing capability to execute your models, you have the option to collect data and analyze it in place. If you're limited in any way, you may need to examine alternative methods to economize either data transfer or processing.

TIP

You don't have to follow the process in any specific order, but it's helpful to determine your own approach sequence and try to stick with it. Although data analytics projects are all unique, standardizing as much of the process as you can will help you avoid reinventing the wheel.

Regardless of how fast your analytics lab computer may be, fetching data from a blockchain will not be as fast or efficient as getting similar data from a database. Today's database management systems are the results of several decades of optimization and generally do a good job of delivering requested data rapidly. In many cases, your blockchain analytics models are based on blockchain data, so you'll find yourself reading blockchain data and then querying off-chain repositories (such as databases) for additional data to complete the dataset entry.

TECHNICAL STUFF

I'm using a few terms rather loosely here. *Data repository* means any data storage method, such as a database or just a text file. *Dataset* means any collection of data, similar to a database table or collection of tables. And *dataset entry* means a collection of data items or fields that refer to one data item. You can think of a dataset entry as a row in a traditional database.

The takeaway for this section is that blockchain access is slower than databases, and you're likely going to need to access both to feed your analytics models. In fact, it's common to need extra data from multiple external sources to complete the data picture. If all your external resources are databases, the process of fetching data is relatively simple. Unfortunately, real-life analytics often requires data from other sources, including online services, external files, and even other blockchain entries. Managing the data input complexities is one of the first challenges in any analytics project.

Comparing one-off versus repeated analysis

One important driver for your decision about when to process data is whether the model is for a one-off analysis or will be run multiple times. Simply put, if you need to run a model only once (perhaps for a quick look at your data to answer a single question), you probably don't need to put much effort into storing data in an off-chain repository.

WARNING

Never believe that "this is just a one-time query." After you deliver the results of that "one-time query," you'll often get a follow-up request to run it again with fresh data. Even though the specs for your analytics model may state that a particular model will be run only once, it's good practice to treat it as though you'll run it again.

Because any blockchain data collection process requires a minimum of one pass through the blockchain (you have to touch your data at least once), you can consider that first pass as a *sunk cost* of the model. That means you must invest the time and effort to pass through your blockchain data at least once regardless what you do with the data. When you make that first pass, you may just process (analyze) it then, and you may decide to store it somewhere else for later analysis. Either way, your approach will depend on the first pass.

The variable performance cost starts after the first pass. It's important to consider the "what's next?" question when you start thinking about collecting data for an analysis model. Try to avoid "going to the well" more than once. You may think I'm recommending that you always save data in an external repository, but that isn't the case. If you need to visit data only once, you don't need to store it for later.

At this point, you may be thinking that I'm recommending that you always assume that you'll run models more than once but I just said that sometimes you visit data only once. If you're wondering how both can be good advice, think about the volatility of your data. If your data changes frequently and each model run's results depend on current data, even if you run a model multiple times you want to use fresh data each time. That means you'll be visiting your blockchain frequently.

One of the many compromises you'll learn to make when analyzing data is in deciding between performance, reusability, and time-to-results (deadlines). In general, you should strive to meet project deadlines. If you can build a model that is easily reusable and executes efficiently and still meets project deadlines, you're on track to building effective models!

Assessing data completeness

In the early stages of any data analytics project, one of the hardest parts is evaluating your data inventory. The first step is to simply list the blockchain data available to you. Initially, a list of data you can directly acquire comes from the state variables exposed by smart contracts. You can find that information from smart contract documentation or looking at the source code. Additional exploration will likely result in additional nuggets of data you can use. The key is to look beyond what is obvious in the first pass.

TECHNICAL STUFF

If you're comfortable with reading JSON (a common data format when you call many blockchain functions), you can use the smart contract's ABI to provide information about available data. I prefer looking at the smart contract source code because it shows me not only what data is there but also how the smart contract uses the data.

Although I haven't explicitly covered techniques for fetching all forms of data available from a blockchain, Table 6-1 lists the forms of data available from a blockchain. You'll soon learn how to write Python code to fetch each type of data you see in the table.

TABLE 6-1 **Forms of Data Stored in a Blockchain**

Data	Description	Example
Transaction	Information stored in the transaction, including from account, to account, amount, and function (with parameters) — if the transaction calls a smart contract function.	In Chapter 3, Figure 3-4 shows a transaction that calls the cancelOrder() smart contract function and shows the parameters passed to the function.
State	Variables defined in smart contracts. You can fetch the current value or the value from any block on the blockchain.	The SupplyChain.sol smart contract (provided at www.dummies.com/go/block chaindafd) includes state variables that store a list of participants, products, and ownership records.
Event log	Event names and any provided parameters when the event occurs during the execution of a smart contract.	In the SupplyChain.sol smart contract (provided at www.dummies.com/go/block chaindafd), the newOwner() function fires the TransferOwnership event, providing the productId, fromOwner address, and toOwner address.

After you understand the data available from blockchain queries, you'll determine what additional data you'll need. For example, if you want to analyze shipping efficiency based on pickup and drop-off locations and shipping duration, you need address information for participants. The SupplyChain.sol smart contract doesn't store any physical address information, so you need to get that information elsewhere. In the next section, you learn some techniques for identifying and fetching external data.

Integrating External Data

Good blockchain app design should limit the data stored in blocks. Blockchain technology focuses on data transparency and integrity, not bulk data storage or performance. If all you want to do is store lots of data, blockchain may not be the best technology to use. Lots of existing database management products will do that. Blockchain technology shines when an app needs to store information directly related to the transfer of value from one owner to another.

The transfer of ownership transaction generally needs only a small set of data to record the transaction. There may be lots of supporting data, such as demographic other descriptive data, but only the data necessary to define a transaction needs to be stored on the blockchain. In fact, storing too much data in blockchain blocks can increase the overall cost of using blockchain technology.

TIP

Some requirements, such as the European Union General Data Protection Regulation (GDPR), dictate that organizations honor any consumers' requests to remove their private data. To support the "right to be forgotten," organizations must make it possible to remove any private information from their data systems, including blockchains. The current approach is to limit the data stored in blockchain blocks to hashes of identifiers to records (pointers to off-chain data) in external databases, as opposed to storing any *personally identifiable information (PII)* directly on the blockchain. Although you can't remove the hash from the blockchain, you can remove the data to which it refers. Removing the off-chain PII satisfies the "right to be forgotten" even though the blockchain data (pointer) still exists. In such a case, the blockchain data wouldn't point to any valid off-chain data. Removing the off-chain data that a blockchain data item points to effectively creates an orphan condition. A compromise of orphaned blockchain pointers is just one more case in which blockchain data may be incomplete for data analysis.

Because blockchain data is likely to have a narrow scope due to design goals or mandate, it's common to start with data you fetch from the blockchain and then find related data to complete the story. For example, the `SupplyChain.sol` smart contract defines the participant UUID (universally unique identifier). A UUID is an identifier that should be unique across all applications and uses. This UUID could be used as a key to a record in a traditional database application. After you retrieve a participant *struct* (a structured collection of data items or fields) from the blockchain via the smart contract `getParticipant()` function, you could easily fetch the corresponding details from a database using a simple SQL (Structured Query Language) statement.

Determining what data you need

The key (pardon the database pun) to figuring out what data you need lies in understanding what data you have and what is missing. If you want to determine whether a carrier is efficient or not, you need pickup location, drop-off location, and performance metrics. The `SupplyChain.sol` smart contract doesn't store any of that data. An ownership struct record that records the transfer of ownership from one participant to another includes only a reference to each participant and the timestamp the transfer occurred. You can find the UUID of each participant, but that's about all you can get.

TECHNICAL STUFF

A common strategy to storing real-world data on a blockchain is to store a unique identifier for that data, often called a *key,* in a block on the blockchain. This key value is the same as the primary key of a data record stored in an off-chain database. This practice allows apps to relate on-chain and off-chain data transparently. As long as the off-chain data can change without affecting the integrity of the on-chain data, this approach is a great way to combine blockchain and non-blockchain data. If off-chain data integrity is important, the off-chain data repository (often a database management system) must ensure that its data maintains integrity. That's one of the clear advantages of blockchain data — integrity is blockchain's middle name. (Well, not really its middle name, but one of its best features.)

Assuming the UUID refers to a participant defined more fully in an off-chain database, you can use the UUID to look up additional data to complete the data picture. Always assume that the data you can find in a blockchain satisfies your analytics requirements. Although that is often not the case, assuming that it is means you'll occasionally find simple cases in which you don't need external data. Most of the time, however, you'll need to consult some external data source to get the data you really need.

A tried-and-true method for determining what data you'll need is to create a mock-up. After you understand the analytics requirements, build a model that will satisfy those requirements and define the inputs your model will need. Then map those inputs to data you can find from your blockchain. The unmapped inputs represent data that you may need to find somewhere else. Those unmapped inputs form the starting point of your data scavenger hunt.

Extending identities to off-chain data

One way to think about relating on-chain and off-chain data is to look at data from the perspective of identity and ownership. Suppose a blockchain stores some data about you. It could be data supporting a decentralized shopping app, a medical management app, or even a home energy conservation app. Regardless of the type of data, you want your personal data to be kept private and associated only with you. You don't want your data to be confused with anyone else, and vice versa.

You'll get the best results when relating off-chain data to on-chain data by first determining the on-chain data's identity. If the blockchain's smart contracts were designed to support off-chain integration, each data item should have an eternally recognized identifier. In simple terms, there should be some smart contract state data that makes it easy to relate on-chain data with off-chain data. If you're familiar with traditional relational database systems, you'll know that extending identities beyond the blockchain is similar to relating data across tables.

For example, in a database system, it is common to store product orders in at least two tables, orderHeader and orderDetails. The orderHeader table contains information that describes the entire order, such as the customer who placed the order and the shipping address. The orderDetails table contains multiple records for each order, and each record describes one line on the order. Both tables contain an orderNumber field that the database management system uses to figure out which orderDetails records belong to which orderHeader record.

TECHNICAL STUFF

In this example, the orderNumber field is the primary key of the orderHeader table and a foreign key in the orderDetails table. That's how database management systems relate, or join, table contents.

In a blockchain context, you need something like the orderNumber field to identify data, regardless of where it lives. For personal data, a customerNumber (as long as that number is recognized in both systems), passport number, driver's license number, or some other unique identifier is necessary to easily relate on-chain and off-chain data.

If you just don't have a convenient identifier such as a UUID available, you may have to build your own cross-reference table. As long as you know how data is related, you can build your own table that defines the connection between on-chain and off-chain data. This approach takes extra effort but may be the only way to maintain the data identity you need to build your analytics dataset.

Finding external data

Before you can write any code to fetch data for your analytics models, you must identify the data you need and locate where it lives. Further, you'll need to assess the access methods available for the desired data and what you may need to do to get permission to fetch that data. Not all data you want is easily available, and some that is requires a fee to access.

When searching for data to build your model's input and training datasets, the best place to start is to describe all the data you need and then highlight what you currently don't have. The next step depends on what data you need. As much as is possible, start looking for external data that is close and easily accessible. If you can fetch off-chain data from your own organization's databases or other data repositories, you'll likely have a much easier time acquiring the data you need than relying on other sources.

The best place to find external data depends on the type of data you need. Start with an Internet search for the data missing from your model's input requirements. In today's data-driven global environment, you'll likely find multiple places to get the data you need. Table 6-2 lists just a few external data sources to get you started. (Don't stop here, though. You can quickly find lots more places to get good data.)

TABLE 6-2   **Sources of External Data**

Data Source	Description	Where to Get It
Data.gov	U.S. government's ongoing effort to make all government data public and freely available	`www.data.gov`
U.S. Census Bureau	All kinds of demographic information about U.S. citizens and residents	`www.census.gov/data.html`
CIA World Factbook	A wide range of historical and current information on 267 countries	`www.cia.gov/library/ publications/ the-world-factbook/`
HealthData.gov	U.S.-based health-related data covering 125 years	`https://healthdata.gov/`
Registry of Open Data on Amazon Web Services (AWS)	A repository of publicly available datasets covering a wide array of domains, from business to science to social impact	`https://registry. opendata.aws/`
Google Dataset Search	A Google search engine dedicated to helping users find sets of data	`https://toolbox.google. com/datasetsearch`

As you search for the best data repositories for your models, pay attention to access methods and restrictions on the data's use. A great repository isn't helpful if getting the data is slow or difficult, or if the use is restricted to a point that you can't legally use it. Finding out how to acquire the data and about restrictions and costs up front will save you frustrations later.

Identifying Features

In data analytics, *features* are the variables the algorithms analyze. For example, when analyzing the effect of income and education on the probability of defaulting on a loan, a person's income and education levels — but not his or her gender — are primary features. It may make sense to consider whether the gender feature should be included, but the original goal of analyzing income and education doesn't consider gender.

One of the most important decisions an analyst makes is determining which features to include in a model. You should include every feature that contributes to meaningful results and exclude all features that fail to contribute to a meaningful result. That sounds easy, but it can be difficult. Deeply assessing feature selection and assessment techniques is beyond the scope of this book, but you will learn about the most common ways to select the best features.

Describing how features affect outcomes

The main reason to care about feature selection is that choosing the wrong features will give you poor results. Remember that features are variables that you consider in your analysis. Each feature provides input that affects the output. If you're trying to determine how efficient competing carriers are when transporting goods between locations, the color feature of each truck likely doesn't contribute any value to your analysis.

WARNING

Just because truck color may not contribute to this analysis, it may be important to answering other questions. Many of today's delivery vans have white roofs because analysis revealed that it can drastically reduce the internal temperature in summer months. Lower internal temperatures means lower energy consumption and helps protect packages in the van. The importance of any feature depends on the questions you're asking.

Two main methods exist for determining the best features to select for your model. Try each of the approaches and use the one that gives you the best results. As you gain experience using each method, you'll be more comfortable and better prepared to reduce the number of features your models consider. And by reducing features, you'll increase accuracy, reduce training time, and provide clearer results.

Comparing filtering and wrapping methods

The two main approaches to selecting features are filter methods and wrapper methods. They each have the same goal: Identify the most meaningful features to produce the best analysis results. Let's briefly look at each method.

Filtering features

Filtering methods depend on scoring each feature and then using only the features with high scores. Various scoring methods exist, including Pearson's correlation, LDA, ANOVA, and chi-squared. The main assessment selection depends on whether the data that a feature contains and the expected result of the model is continuous or categorical. *Continuous data* refers to open-ended data that can vary along a range between minimum and maximum values. *Categorical data* can be only one of a previously defined list of values (such as true/false, yes/no, or a month of the year).

In the *feature filtering process*, you simply assign each feature a specific score, based on the selected scoring mechanism. You sort the features by score and use only the ones with high scores. No magic score threshold exists; you have to look at each scoring list to determine where to draw the line between high and low scores.

Filtering is always carried out as a preprocessing step. You select features before you use the model to analyze data.

Wrapping features

The other common way to select features is to use a wrapping method. Wrapping methods are more computation intensive but can provide better results when feature selection depends heavily on data. The process used in a *wrapping method* is to arbitrarily select a subset of features, run the model on your training data, and then assess the quality of the results. Then do the same thing with a different subset of features.

TIP

Selecting the training data to use is another discussion. To ensure the most accurate results, your training data must be representative of the real data. If the training dataset doesn't accurately represent the complete dataset, your feature selection and overall model results will not be optimal.

The wrapping method also depends on the ability to determine whether or not a selected set of features returns meaningful results. If you can't tell whether or not results are valid, a wrapper method may not help you select features.

Building an Analysis Dataset

Although it is possible, and sometime even advantageous, to carry out analytics as you pass through blockchain data, let's look at how to build an analysis dataset. In this section, you learn how to fetch data from an Ethereum blockchain, relate it to external data, and create a new repository of data to use for analysis.

You start simple. You read participant data from an Ethereum blockchain and a simple comma-separated value (CSV) text file, and create a new CSV file to store the new dataset. You can build on this basic process to fetch data from any number of sources to build a comprehensive dataset for your analytics models. In more realistic scenarios, you'll probably find data from databases or online services. (You discover how to get data from other sources in later chapters.)

Connecting to multiple data sources

Each data source requires a unique connection from your Python script. You've seen how to connect to text files and your blockchain. Setting up a database connection or a web service connection isn't all that different. For this example, you create three connections: the Ethereum blockchain, an input CSV file that contains participant details, and an output CSV file for you to store the dataset you'll build.

Here is the Python code to create the three connections (you can find the full code for `buildDataset.py` on the book's download site at www.dummies.com/go/blockchaindafd):

```
from web3 import Web3

# Set up a connection to the blockchain
ganache_url = "http://127.0.0.1:7545"
web3 = Web3(Web3.HTTPProvider(ganache_url))

# Open the participantDetails.csv file to read participant details
fileHandleIN = open('participantDetails.csv', 'r')

# Open the dataSet.csv file to store our constructed dataset
fileHandleOUT = open('dataSet.csv', 'w')
```

Now you can read data from the blockchain, relate it to data from the `participantDetails.csv` file, and store the complete list of data items in the `dataset.csv` file.

Building a cross-referenced dataset

The process of building the cross-referenced dataset involves the three steps mentioned in the preceding section:

1. Read a participant from the blockchain by using the `getParticipant()` smart contract function.

2. Find the participant's details from the `participantDetails.csv` file.

3. Write the complete participant data to the `dataset.csv` file.

Cleaning your data

The data you've used in the preceding example is based on clean data. A *clean input dataset* means that all the data you need exists and is already in the right format.

In real life, you may not find details for one or more participants. And some of the individual details may be missing or don't have data in the right format. For example, a postal code may contain letters instead of just numbers. (Having letters in a postal code value is fine in Canada but not in the United States.)

In other cases, you'll find that data you read from different sources uses different scales or base units. A common example is when querying weather data. Temperature may be expressed in Fahrenheit or Celsius. It doesn't matter which one you use, but you must be consistent. You can't easily compare and analyze numbers expressed using different scales.

Another example is grading information for classes. If different classes use different grading scales, you may find it difficult to compare and analyze grades across multiple classes. The common fix for scale mismatches is to select a common scale and transform all data to that scale, a process called *normalization*.

In addition to scaling issues, you must determine how to handle missing or malformed data. Each situation is unique, and you'll have to make decisions based on each data item's status and importance to the model. Your chosen model's sensitivity to missing or malformed data will go a long way toward helping you decide how to handle data that doesn't conform to the ideal standards. As you develop procedures to acquire and assimilate your analytics dataset, try to transform data, as appropriate, into a standard format for analysis.

TIP

Although it's a good idea to clean data as you acquire it, avoid losing the original data's granularity in the process. You don't want any cleaning process to degrade the level of detail your original data contained. Cleaning should make your models more accurate, not less accurate.

Now you know how to read smart contract state data, relate it to off-chain data, and then create a more complete dataset for analysis. In the next chapter, you start building analytics models on your blockchain data.

Chapter **7**

Building Basic Blockchain Analysis Models

I n previous chapters you learn about blockchain data, how it's stored, and how to get your hands on it. Of course, you need to understand your data before you can start to make sense of it. After you know how to identify and get access to the data you need, the next logical step is to figure out what secrets it may hold. That's the whole idea behind data analytics.

You can look at data in lots of ways. You just need to decide what method you want to employ and then build a model to carry out your selected method. Sounds simple, right? If you approach the problem deliberately, it can be pretty simple.

Knowing your objectives for data analytics drives your decisions when selecting the right models. Remember Alice's dilemma from Lewis Carroll's book, *Alice's Adventures in Wonderland,* as she talks to the Cat:

"Would you tell me, please, which way I ought to go from here?"

"That depends a good deal on where you want to get to," said the Cat.

"I don't much care where—" said Alice.

"Then it doesn't matter which way you go," said the Cat.

Just like Alice, if you don't have an idea what you want to find from your data, analytics becomes little more than hunting and guessing. You don't have to know exactly what you're looking for up front, but you do need to have some idea of where to start looking. You can let your data tell you its story, but you need to ask the right questions and understand the results.

You can use models to identify similarities that may not be obvious, unusual ways in which data items are related, and even new ways to group your data. In this chapter, you learn about the most common types of analytics models and how each one can yield results from your data. After you learn about the main types of analytics models, you'll be ready to pair that with your knowledge of blockchain data to unlock secrets your blockchain may be hiding.

TIP

Data analytics is kind of like hunting for buried treasure. One way to find buried treasure is to walk along a popular beach with a metal detector. You have to scan lots of sand, but every once in a while your metal detector alerts you to something under the surface. Then you start digging to see if there is something of value. Analyzing data is similar in that you may have to look at a lot of data before you find something interesting — and even then, it may just turn out to be an old tin can.

Identifying Related Data

One of the first types of analytics models is identifying related data and using discovered relationships to make predictions of behavior or classification. For example, if you find that all blue fish in a sample of tropical fish like to eat worms, it's likely that any new blue fish introduced into your environment will also eat worms. In this simple example we don't say anything about non-blue fish, so you can't always extrapolate your findings. Some findings are that obvious, but some aren't. Data analytics shines when it reveals findings that aren't obvious. The non-obvious findings are the ones you can use to make decisions to pursue the results you want (such as higher profits).

Note that in the following descriptions I use the term *dataset entry* to refer to all data that relates to a specific real-world item, or object. In database terms, a dataset entry would be a record or row. Think of all the data items that describe a fish, such as species, color, size, and fin placement. Taken together, these pieces of data make up a fish record, or a fish dataset entry. Each piece of data is called a *feature.* For example, a fish's species feature would correspond to a database's field or column.

Using different terms can get confusing. If you're used to databases, you're likely comfortable with record (or row) and field (or column). However, because most literature about analytics and data mining uses the term *feature*, I use it here.

Following are the main analysis models that assess how data is related:

>> **Clustering models** show how similar features imply that dataset entries are related. For example, clustering models can show if most customers in a specific age range prefer one type of cellphone over another.

>> **Association models** show the probability of multiple dataset items being present in a single transaction. A common association model can show whether a customer who purchases milk is likely to also purchase bread at the same time. (By the way, the answer is generally yes.)

>> **Classification models** can help identify broad groupings of data based on selected features. Marketers use classification models to help identify potential customers after analyzing features of existing customers. They figure that broad categories of customers, such as expectant mothers or college students, tend to purchase similar items. They use that information to make informed targeted recommendations for additional purchases.

In the rest of this chapter, you learn the most common analytics techniques for identifying related data.

For this book, I built a simple supply chain blockchain app that contains manufacturing and shipping information for TVs. Don't worry — you'll use your blockchain in upcoming chapters. This chapter provides a basic overview of common analytics models using text files as input data. Subsequent chapters have you look at the supply chain data for TVs and apply different analytics models to discover what the blockchain data says about how these TVs get from the manufacturer to the retailer.

Grouping data based on features (attributes)

In data analytics, data attributes are called *features* and I use that term from now on. One way to group data is by examining features and determining which objects (data items) are similar based on similar features. For example, do TVs that sell for a lower price tend to sell better at a specific retailer? Or do retailers in specific areas (postal code ranges) sell more larger or smaller TVs? These questions are the kind that a clustering model might answer.

WARNING

Don't expect every model you try to reveal meaningful data. Many models just don't result in actionable information. As you gain more experience with analytics, you'll get a better feel for when to use specific models for data you encounter. Even then, you'll probably have to look at your data multiple ways to find the right view that gives you interesting results. Don't get discouraged — keep looking.

Clustering techniques are generally called *unsupervised analysis* (or even *unsupervised learning*) techniques. These techniques are called *unsupervised* because they don't impose any preconceptions. In other words, you let the data tell you what clusters exist, instead of fitting data into predefined clusters. Unsupervised techniques look at your data and provide clues of hidden structures.

Some data lends itself well to clustering, while other data doesn't visually appear to organize into well-defined clusters. Figures 7-1 and 7-2 show data that represents customer ratings of a retailer. The x-axis shows the rating each customer gave, ranging from −3 (below average) to 3 (above average). The y-axis shows how long, in months, each customer has shopped with the retailer.

Figure 7-1 shows that the data appears to be organized into four clusters. New customers, perhaps happy with front-end incentives, rate the retailer above average. Customers who have shopped with the retailer for 2 to 3½ months or longer than 6 months provide below average ratings, while those who have shopped between 3½ months and 6 months provide above average ratings. If the retailer offered incentives for new customers and then again at 3 months, that could explain the various clusters.

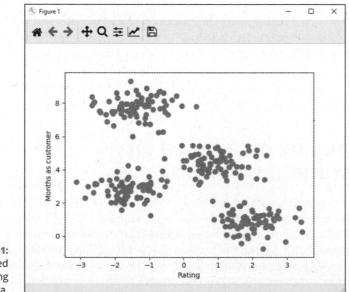

FIGURE 7-1:
Clustered customer rating data.

While obvious clusters are easy to see, it's important to represent clustering mathematically to use the model for prediction of future behavior. One technique, *k-means clustering,* calculates the most likely center point, called the *centroid,* of each cluster. Mathematical models gives analysts the ability to observe similar behavior that may not be obvious. In this case, the retailer can further explore why ratings change based on length of time as a customer and, more importantly, what they can do to increase overall ratings. Figure 7-2 shows the same data with centroids and different colors for each identified cluster.

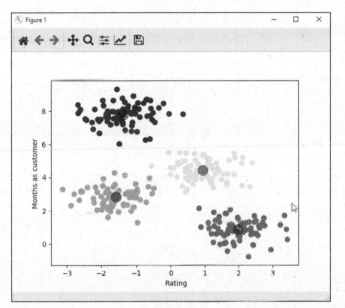

FIGURE 7-2:
Clustered
customer rating
data with
centroids and
colors.

At other times, the data doesn't appear to be clearly grouped. Figure 7-3 shows a scatter plot of customer ratings (x-axis) and the relative number of reviews a customer has posted (y-axis). It isn't easy to see clear clusters in this plot, indicating that a strong correlation may not exist between rating and number of reviews posted. Customers who post a below-average number of reviews generally post lower ratings, but it isn't easy to predict how customers who post with average or above-average frequency will rate the retailer.

Regardless, the k-means clustering algorithm can identify three distinct clusters, shown in Figure 7-4.

TECHNICAL
STUFF

Clustering techniques aren't generally used in isolation. They are used either during early phases of analysis or in with other techniques. Clustering is helpful in identifying groupings that may not be initially obvious. After such clusters are identified, they can be further studied for causation or prediction usefulness.

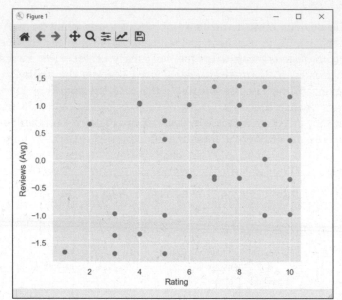

FIGURE 7-3:
Weak clustered
customer rating
data.

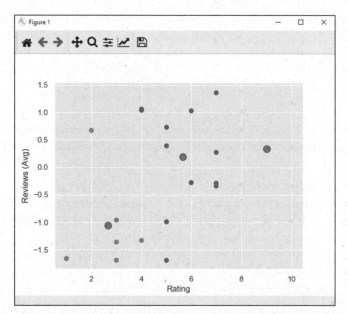

FIGURE 7-4:
Weak clustered
customer rating
data with
centroids and
colors.

Determining group membership

You just learned that clustering techniques reveal groupings of data, which can be invaluable when initially examining your data. However, many analysis projects require some capability to use past data to predict future behavior. *Classification analysis* techniques provide a mathematical approach to determining likely outcome based on known characteristics. For example, you can use classification to predict whether a person is likely to default on a loan based on that person's current income and past credit history. Classification is a supervised learning technique. With *supervised learning,* you define a set of labels, or groups, and the model decides which label to assign to new input data.

WARNING

Classification models that you build focus exclusively on data, not people. However, because humans build the models, it isn't difficult for human bias to influence how such models are created and used. The way you use analytics results can lead to decisions that affect people. There is a fine line between classification and profiling. Be very careful when making decisions based on classification results. Classification models built with substantial human bias, such as basing loan default results on race or religion, may yield discriminatory results and could even lead to illegal decisions.

Classification is one approach to analytical prediction. The general approach to building supervised learning models is to use a dataset with known labels to *train* the model, and then provide unlabeled data for the model to suggest a label. In simple terms, your model learns how to come up with a correct answer by studying known features and outcomes, and then lets you test it by providing a new object with different attributes.

You learn about several classification methods in Chapter 10, but for now, let's stick with one of the simplest approaches, a *decision tree.* Table 7-1 shows a short list of historical loan default data. For this simple example, you're looking at only a few features, namely, a person's gender, marital status, job status, home state, and loan default status. The finance company for which you work wants you to use this data to predict if loan applicants are likely to default on their loans.

TABLE 7-1

Loan Default Data

Gender	Marital Status	Has a Job?	Home State	Defaulted?
Male	Single	No	GA	Yes
Male	Married	Yes	NC	Yes
Female	Single	Yes	TN	No
Male	Married	No	VA	No
Female	Married	No	MS	Yes
Female	Married	Yes	TX	No
Female	Single	No	SC	Yes
Male	Single	Yes	MD	No

Using the data in Table 7-1, the only feature that does a good job of predicting if a person is likely to default is whether that person holds a job. Each person lives in a different state, so that feature doesn't help us predict anything, and the remaining features are evenly split with respect to outcomes. Even the combination of gender and marital status fails to help us make a prediction. Only the person's job status is a reliable indicator of whether that person will default on a loan — and that makes sense.

Real-world analytics is rarely this obvious. In most cases, you can't just look at a table of data and predict future outcomes. Instead, you go to the trouble of building models you can use to predict future results based on historical data. As mentioned, one of the simplest classification models is the decision tree. You learn how to build a blockchain-based *decision tree* in Chapter 10, but the model essentially builds a tree based on the data you provide that you can then use to make decisions. If you build a decision tree from the data in Table 7-1, it should like the tree in Figure 7-5.

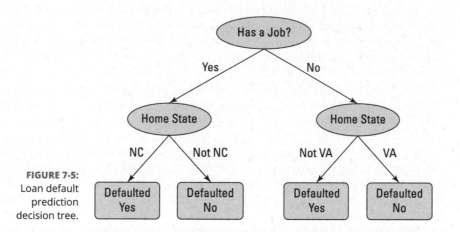

FIGURE 7-5: Loan default prediction decision tree.

Using Figure 7-5, it's easy to see that the only meaningful feature is job status. After you determine whether an applicant holds a job, all other information about that person carries the same weight in determining if the person is likely to default on a loan.

WARNING

Be careful when characterizing results. This simple loan default classifier can determine only that a loan application is likely to default (or not), based on very limited information. No analytics model is perfect. You should never base decisions on analytics models only; you should always corroborate model output with other available input. In other words, analytics results should align with other data.

One of the hardest parts of using any analytics model is identifying the best features that will produce the highest quality results. You discover more about basic feature selection in Chapters 9 through 12. For now, always ensure that the features you select make sense. For example, including the type of car a loan applicant drives could indicate that person's lifestyle, but considering the color of that car's interior likely isn't an important feature.

TIP

Avoid discarding any feature too quickly. Even though a car's interior color may seem inconsequential, if your initial data survey shows a strong correlation between car interior color and loan performance, take another look at it. Unexpected results can be due to bad data, inappropriate model selection, or just a dynamic that you previously hadn't understood. Data analytics can be hard because many correlations aren't initially obvious, but the work you invest in finding what isn't obvious can be productive.

Discovering relationships among items

The last main type of related data analytics looks at how different object relate to one another. Previous methods examined how features of a single object made that object similar to other objects. *Association analytics* techniques helps to identify when objects routinely exist together in specific contexts (often, in the same transaction). For example, suppose you work for a grocery store chain. One common type of association analytics technique is *market basket analysis,* which identifies items that a customer often purchases together.

TECHNICAL STUFF

One of the earliest surprising results of grocery store market basket analysis was the finding of a strong correlation of baby diapers and beer on Thursday and Sunday evenings. Further research found that young fathers often were tasked with buying baby diapers on Thursday to get ready for the weekend, and again on Sunday to prepare for the upcoming week. These young fathers also commonly picked up a six-pack of beer while in the store. Shrewd retailers started placing beer displays between the diaper aisle and the checkout (to remind the dads to not forget the beer). Ignoring the stereotyping evident in this example, retailers were able to increase their beer sales as a result.

The most common algorithms are simple but tedious. The *apriori technique* just counts items in transactions and reports the probabilities of any item appearing in a transaction. It starts with individual items, then recounts the entire dataset using pairs of items. It keeps adding items to the transaction set until it runs out of data. Additional rules help the process avoid recounting itemsets that aren't meaningful. The algorithm is tedious, but advanced techniques for implementing it make it a valuable technique. (There is a lot more to the apriori algorithm, but that's good enough for now.)

Regardless of the type of technique used, the goal of association is to help identify situations in which one choice has a high likelihood of being accompanied by another choice. The capability to associate choices is the basis of *recommender engines* (software that looks at past choices and make predictions of what you might choose next). Huge organizations such as Netflix, Amazon, Google, and pretty much any other enterprise trying to sell you something use recommender engines to prompt you to buy more.

Suggestive selling isn't new. Long ago, fast-food providers learned that fries were a common addition to sandwiches (and a high profit item). They had restaurant cashiers ask customers, "Do you want fries with that?" Subsequently, they began offering meal bundles to make it easier to implement what their market basket analysis told them.

Today, nearly every website you visit provides recommendations of further actions you should take. "Click here to find out more about the most amazing deal ever!" Recommender engines use association techniques to analyze your activities online (often in real time) to pick a common action for you to follow. The uncanny accuracy of recommender engines is why it feels like they're in your head. Because humans are basically creatures of habit, it isn't all that difficult to look at general norms and predict a likely next step. That's the power of association techniques.

Making Predictions of Future Outcomes

Organizations turn to data analytics for many reasons. Although gaining a better understanding of your data is a compelling reason to use analytics, it doesn't do much good unless you can make actionable decisions based on what you learn. Your goal may be to identify similar characteristics among features of your products or customers. Such finding could lead you to add, change, or remove services to cater to customer preferences. Additionally, you could identify previously unknown relationships between your products or services and use that to make suggestions to your customers.

Although discovery can be a valuable outcome of data analytics, one of its most common uses is in prediction. As you learned in the preceding section, humans tend to be creatures of habit. In fact, nature generally prefers repeatable and predictable outcomes. For instance, long ago weather used to be viewed as a constantly changing set of circumstances that could not be easily understood. Then, as budding meteorologists began studying past weather and what led up to specific weather events, reliable forecasting became possible. Today's weather forecasting is little more than building models from historical data, providing current conditions, and asking the model to predict what happens next.

If you're a weather enthusiast, you've probably heard meteorologists refer to different model predictions, such as the European model or the Weather Research and Forecast model. Each model refers to a data analytics model (some mathematical formula) that uses historical weather data to predict future events. Each model produces slightly different output because it looks at input data a little differently. Just like asking friends for advice, no model is always perfect and some work better than others in specific situations.

You've already seen one type of prediction model: the decision tree. A decision tree is a simple model and works well for categorical data. *Categorical data* has a limited range of data values, such as yes/no, true/false, or small lists, such as days of the week or months of the year. The other type of data you'll encounter is continuous data. *Continuous data* is almost always numerical and can be values in a wide range. Examples of continuous data include temperature readings, salaries, measurements, and any values with range limits.

TIP

Some values, such as product ratings, can be interpreted as either categorical or continuous. Because most ratings are limited to values of 1, 2, 3, 4, or 5, you could interpret such data as a range or as distinct values. Different models handle data types differently, so the ability to interpret data as different types gives you more flexibility when selecting models.

The goal of *prediction analytics* is to build and train a model that accurately predicts future outcome based on available information. You have to analyze existing historical data, make assumptions to create a formula on that data, and then apply your formula to new data to predict some outcome. The process starts with examining the data you have. That's why you started looking at clustering techniques. If you can identify any data clusters, you might be able to use that information to identify interesting features.

After you identify the features for your model, you move to a phase in which you find a formula that best represents the existing (historical) data. This process is called *training your model.* In this phase you keep tweaking your formula to best fit your training data. After the model it trained, you're ready to feed it new data to see how well it predicts future outcomes.

In the next sections, you learn how to avoid common pitfalls and build more accurate models.

Selecting features that affect outcome

One of the primary factors in building a good analytics model is to select all the features that most directly affect outcome and exclude any features that do not affect outcome. In practice, that's a tough balance to achieve. Data analytics focuses on studying how historical data can help predict future outcomes and the extent to which individual features play in outcomes is not always obvious. Simply using intuition when assessing a feature's importance is not enough. You need a more reliable method.

You can select features in two main ways: filter methods and wrapper methods. *Filter methods* are faster but may not be the most accurate, so they may be a good choice when building a model quickly is more important than the model's accuracy. *Wrapper methods* build models iteratively, incorporating machine learning techniques to determine which features affect the results to the greatest degree. Wrapper methods are slower and more computationally expensive but produce more accurate feature selection sets.

Filtering features quickly

Filtering feature selection methods, such as *chi-squared* test and *information gain,* evaluate the effect each feature has on the result. *Filtering feature selection methods* are generally quick and easy to calculate; all that is needed is access to the data stored in each feature and the recorded result. The idea is to compare each feature to the result to determine if a feature is statistically significant to the outcome (result.) For example, in the earlier loan default example from Table 7-1, the loan applicant's home state had no effect on whether that applicant would be likely to default on the loan.

Filtering methods are simple ways to determine if individual features contribute, in a material way, to the known result in a training set. If the feature doesn't contribute to a training set result, it is assumed that it shouldn't be a component of future predictions. The main drawback of filtering methods is that they generally do not evaluate the effect of composite features. For example, the home state feature by itself may not be significant, but it might be when considered along with marital status. Determining the effect of composite and dependent features takes more work.

Wrapping feature selection for high accuracy

Wrapping feature selection approaches, such as *forward feature selection* and *backward feature elimination,* employ machine learning to determine sets of features that most affect outcome values. The main approaches to *wrapping feature selection* is to either start with an empty feature set and build a set of the most influential features or start with all features and iteratively eliminate those that do not materially affect outcome. Either way, the goal is to end up with a set of features that affect the model's predictions the most.

Wrapping methods require more time and effort, but generally provide a more accurate feature selection than filtering methods. Filtering methods are more common in the early analysis phase when most activity focuses on surveying data. Later phases focused on building accurate models are more likely to benefit from wrapping methods.

Beating the best guess

Most questions have best guess answers, and predictions in business environments are no different. Data analytics is successful when its models predict outcomes with a higher probability than the best guess. Assume that for any average day, 25 percent of the people who visit an online shopping website will purchase at least one product. (By the way, that's a great average!) That means you'll assign every customer a purchase probability of 0.25.

However, using data analytics, you find that customers who log into your site and have purchased more than three times in the last month have an 80 percent chance of making a purchase in this visit. Now that's a customer you should focus on. The goal is to develop models that allow you to identify customers who are most likely to purchase from you. They are the customers who keep you in business. Data analytics makes it possible to look at a customer's demographic and activity data (features) and draw conclusions about how likely it is that they will put money in your pocket.

TECHNICAL STUFF

You've learned about analytics and its capability to make predictions, a feature often called *predictive analytics*. Another fascinating aspect of analytics that I don't describe in this discussion is *prescriptive analytics*, where you analyze data and figure out strategies to affect outcomes. For example, you can identify ways to potentially turn website visitors into paying customers, instead of just predicting which ones will buy from you.

The idea behind beating the best guess is demonstrating that your model is better. A common way to do this is to establish a *null hypothesis* and an *alternative hypothesis*. Suppose your model examines the effect of holding a job on whether a loan applicant is likely to default on a loan. The null hypothesis states that job status has no effect on loan defaults. The alternative hypothesis states that job status is a good predictor of whether a person will default. To determine if the job status is a good discriminator or not, simple evaluate each hypothesis and see if the results are different. Clearly, job function does affect loan default (from Table 7-1), so you must reject the null hypothesis. Therefore, the alternative hypothesis is accepted and job function is a good potential feature for your model.

The best analytics models not only beat the best guess but do so with the highest accuracy possible. Often multiple models beat the best guess. It is important to examine as many models and options as feasible to find the best solution.

TIP

The best solution is almost always the best solution for now. Supervised learning models depend on training data. As your data changes over time, the model's accuracy may change, for better or worse. It is important to retrain models with current data to ensure the highest ongoing accuracy.

Building confidence

Data analytics models provide results but always with a caveat. Predictions are never guaranteed. Some level of uncertainty always exists when predicting any outcome. The degree to which you can trust a prediction is that prediction's *confidence.*

When you assess any data, you'll likely see some data that just doesn't seem to fit. Data points that don't fit with most of the rest of a set of points are called *outliers.* Outliers can exist for many reasons. Perhaps the measurement was faulty, the object's behavior was unusual, or something else weird just happened. Regardless of the reason for outliers, their existence can have a negative effect on model building and use. Confidence can help you deal with outliers and model accuracy deviations. Because real-world data isn't perfect and symmetric, deviations from any model's projections of outcomes will always exist. Stating a confidence value makes it possible for a model to still be accurate even if it provides a prediction that doesn't turn out to be true.

Confidence levels, or *intervals,* are often expressed as percentages. A confidence level of 95 percent means that the model is expected to provide correct results 95 percent of the time. That's not bad, but a 99 percent (or even higher, such as 99.99 percent) confidence level is preferred. Building and training a model that makes predictions with a confidence level higher than 99 percent requires a lot of work, but such a model can be a valuable business tool.

For normally distributed data, most data centers around a *mean,* also called *average,* value, with decreasing data points as you move away from the mean value. Figure 7-6 shows a set of normally distributed data with the mean value in red (the center line) and the confidence interval boundaries in blue (the two outer lines). The values outside the confidence interval (on both the positive and negative ends) are the *tails* of the distribution. Because some data under the distribution curve's tails falls outside the confidence interval, confidence analysis is sometimes called *two-tail analysis.*

Now look at Figure 7-7, which shows the same data and mean value as in Figure 7-6, but with a 99 percent confidence interval. Note that the confidence interval barriers are farther apart and fewer data points fall outside the confidence interval. A higher confidence interval tells you that in this case, 99 percent of all predictions should lie between the confidence interval bounds. As the confidence value increases, the number of outliers should decrease.

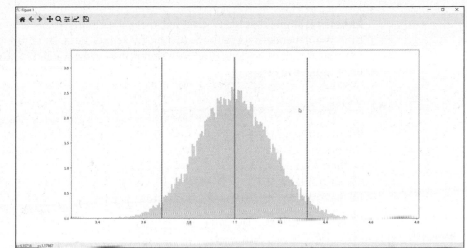

FIGURE 7-6:
Normally
distributed data
with mean and
95 percent
confidence
interval.

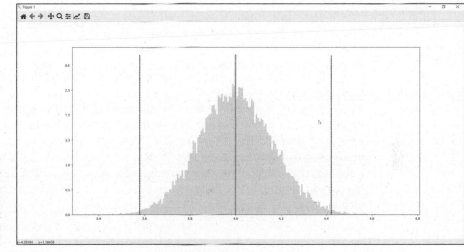

FIGURE 7-7:
Normally
distributed data
with mean and
99 percent
confidence
interval.

Analyzing Time-Series Data

Sometimes data exhibits characteristics that don't fit nicely into regular models. For example, suppose that you were asked to analyze stock prices for a specific security and predict future price levels. You'd quickly find that models you've seen up to now may not work well because they ignore variations due to time. Stock prices fluctuate throughout the year. Some stocks perform better at different times of the year than others. These fluctuations can be due to production capabilities, demand, or just consumer trends.

Another example that lends itself to time-series analysis (looking at data in which time is a dependent variable) is airline passenger data. In Figure 7-8, it's easy to see that the number of airline passengers has grown steadily since 1949, but in what appear to be spurts.

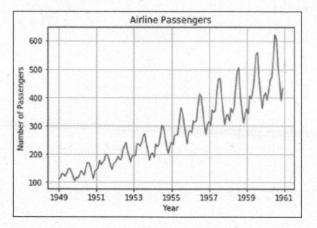

FIGURE 7-8:
Airline passenger data.

The relative highs and lows within each year represents seasonal variations throughout the year. Airline travel peaks during summer months. One of the first steps when applying time-series analysis techniques is to map time-based variations of data to a metric, such as an average or a weighted trend, that is easy to view and interpret. To remove, or compress, seasonal variations, you can apply a *moving average* (an average value based on previous values that dampens fluctuations) to create a trend line. The moving average imposes a dampened view of data movement that tends to minimize seasonal variations. Figure 7-9 shows the same airline passenger data with a calculated trend line.

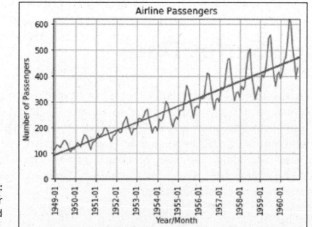

FIGURE 7-9:
Airline passenger data with a trend line.

A trend line makes it easier to compare time-based data that includes seasonal variations because it helps flatten, or dampen, cyclical variations. However, a trend line also squashes much of the data's details, so it's important to consider all the components that make up time-based data. When analyzing time-based data, there are at least four types of visualization you should consider to fully understand your data:

>> **Raw:** This visualization is the original, or raw, view of your data. Figure 7-8 shows a raw time-based data visualization.

>> **Trend:** A trend line may be used by itself or superimposed on another view. Trends help you visualize how data changes over a longer period of time without showing other variations. Figure 7-9 shows a trend line superimposed over the raw data visualization.

>> **Seasonality:** Another type of visualization extracts changes over time and visually depicts seasonal variations, without overall basic value changes. It looks somewhat like the raw data if the trend line were flat.

>> **Residuals:** This last type of time series visualization shows any other variations observed in data that can't be explained through seasonality or time based variation.

The overall goal of time-series analysis is to provide time- and date-sensitive information and predictions for data that depends on the time of its occurrence. Many real-life business applications depend on current predictions, and time-series analysis casts predictions to specific time periods.

Exploring growth and maturity

One of the applications of time-series analysis is for situations in which products, services, or entities change over time. Many factors, both internal and external, may affect the accuracy of analysis model results. The most accurate models consider temporal influences, as necessary, to calculate predictions.

Although not all data is temporal sensitive, many financial models must take timing into account. A model to predict stock prices for 2001 won't be accurate for predicting tomorrow's prices. Likewise, predicting the passenger load for a flight in March will be far less accurate without taking seasonality into account. Time-series analysis allows analysts to include seasonality, environmental factors related to time, and additional known influences to build the most accurate model possible.

Identifying seasonal trends

Toy manufacturers have known about seasonal influences for many decades. The demand for toys tends to increase, sometimes at a dizzying pace, as Christmas approaches. Awareness of such trends drives business decisions necessary to meet anticipated demands. Planning across all aspects of supply chain, manufacturing, and distribution would be insufficient without sophisticated models based on seasonal variations.

Toy manufacturing procurement planning is quite different for February and September. As you would expect, February planning focuses on acquiring raw materials for aggressive manufacturing, while September's focus is on distribution. Time-series analysis techniques help analysts build models that meet the needs of the sponsoring organization, regardless of the time period being considered.

Describing cycles of results

You learned earlier that you can use trend lines to smooth variations observed in raw data. Trend lines make it easier to see long-term trends (growth trends, I hope) but hide any cyclic variations between periodic norms. In many cases, including the airline passenger data graphs in Figure 7-8 and 7-9, data tends to cycle each year. If the intra-year cycles are of interest, the seasonality and residual views may help. These last two views of the four standard time-series analysis views help amplify variations observed in cycles. When selecting features, a high observed variation in residuals may imply that something unexplained is going on and you should consider additional features.

Although time-series analysis is more complex than some other types of analysis, it can provide valuable insights into how your data changes over time and how you can uncover timely nuggets of value from it.

Now that you know about the main types of analytics, you're ready to learn how to use Python to implement analytics models and then apply those models to blockchain data.

Chapter **8**

Leveraging Advanced Blockchain Analysis Models

A successful and productive data analytics project is more than just an understanding of statistics. You learned about some basic models in the previous chapter, but just covering models isn't enough. Lots of resources can help you learn how to build basic and sophisticated data analytics models. This book is unique in that I cover how to use those models in a blockchain environment. But even aligning blockchain data with analytics models isn't enough to justify the effort.

The true value of data analytics in any environment lies in the proper alignment of the chosen models and the data to satisfy business goals. Without high-quality current data, even a great model won't deliver the best results. Even if you build the perfect model that delivers the highest accuracy, it will almost certainly degrade over time. You must perpetually retrain models with fresh data to maintain valuable results. If you don't, you'll be making decisions based on increasingly older data.

This need for pertinent and fresh data means you'll have to provide the partici-pants who feed your models with reasons to stay around. Providing incentives for participants to keep providing data, reducing the cost of participation, and foster-ing a collaborative environment should be the goals of a healthy consortium.

Your blockchain environment (or the community within a public blockchain envi-ronment) likely won't thrive without care and feeding. The best way to encourage a healthy blockchain data environment that grows and matures is to provide incentives to continually contribute, make it as easy as possible to do so, and encourage collaboration among all participants. In this chapter, you learn about blockchain- and analytics-specific approaches to pursue these goals.

Identifying Participation Incentive Mechanisms

Many data analytics projects take place in completely public or isolated environ-ments. It's common to carry out analytics on publicly available data for macro results and then use silos of internal data for micro results. This approach often ends up providing valuable insight but sometimes doesn't illuminate middle ground activities. Macro results can help explain industry-wide trends and even direct strategic decisions at scale. On the other hand, micro results can help enter-prises see what's going on in their own environments.

What is often missing is a view of activity that occurs in a specific enterprise's market segment. For example, a large amount of data is available for the automo-bile manufacturing domain. If an organization participates in the automobile manufacturing supply chain, it would likely be able to access and analyze general supply chain information, as well as its own internal data. It may not, however, be able to acquire rich data that focuses on its specific product line in the context of its part of the supply chain.

Medium and large organizations generally participate in information-sharing consortiums but limit the data they share to avoid leaking unnecessary intellec-tual property. These data-sharing limits result in unnecessarily generic data. The trick to building effective analytics models is to ensure that you have the data your models need to provide the results to meet their goals. You can do that by provid-ing incentives for data providers to contribute richer data. You can accomplish the goal of getting the data your models need in several ways.

Complying with mandates

The most obvious method to use when incentivizing participants to contribute data is to mandate contributions. This approach may seem to be the most straight-forward but doesn't always result in the highest quality data. *Mandates* can exist in many forms, including legislation, regulation, industry standards, professional organization standards, or even consortium participation agreement requirements. Regardless of the type of mandate, organizations will eventually classify mandates as liabilities they must satisfy and do so by meeting only the absolute minimums. Unless another incentive exists, most organizations will not expend effort and cost to exceed the minimum mandated effort.

Mandates scoped to the individual user are likely to result in the lowest level of observed compliance. Users tend to agree to terms without completely reading user agreements and will perform mandated minimum activities only if those activities are required to complete the desired functionality. In other words, many users will jump through hoops only if they must do it to get to the information they want. Forcing users to perform for functionality or data is a dangerous game. They will likely grow tired of the extra effort and simply choose to not participate.

Mandating proper behavior and participation will commonly result in lower overall participation. Even if your terms of use clearly state that participation is dependent on contribution, users will likely grow frustrated and leave. And when users withdraw, they take with them potentially valuable data that your organization needs to thrive.

Due to the many drawbacks of relying solely on mandates, it is recommended that organizations not use such a monolithic approach to compelling participation in a blockchain network. A better solution is to inform participants of the benefits to them of participation, and then offer interesting incentives for being good contributors.

One of the benefits of working in a blockchain environment is that blockchain tends to attract participants who value decentralization and a lack of central control. This attitude commonly exists with a higher sense of community involvement and a willingness to contribute for the greater good. Although you can't assume that all blockchain participants will be altruistic, some organizations have found that participants in a blockchain environment tend to be easier to motivate than users in traditional environments. In the next sections, you learn about a few alternatives to the heavy-handed approach of mandating good behavior.

Playing games with partners

One of the most successful methods to incentivizing behavior is turning the activity to be incentivized into a game. Educators have long known that an effective way to reduce the tedious nature of learning and increase overall retention is to use games in the educational process. Treating the learning process as a game, along with the ability to earn points or status, increases student interest and participation.

Gamification describes applying game design to real-world environments. Most people like playing some types of games. Games involve challenges, a safe environment for solving those challenges without long-term real negative effects, and the potential of a reward for success. Many gaming systems engage players with interesting characters and storylines, and provide a path to earning rewards and character growth. Applying gaming elements to real-world environments has shown positive results in encouraging participation in group projects.

WARNING

Don't confuse gamification and game theory. *Game theory* is a mathematical approach to studying complex system agent interactions. In other words, game theory seeks to formalize the process of explaining social situations among competing participants, or players. *Gamification* is the application of game design elements to a non-game context, such as a project or blockchain application, for the purpose of enhancing participation.

Airlines, hotels, and grocery stores are just three examples of businesses that have capitalized on this concept. Many organizations across many industries have loyalty programs, which reward participants with points, badges, or even discounted prices. Participants provide their identifying information along with activity data. In exchange for the rich data participants provide, they earn increasing levels of status and perks.

TIP

It isn't hard to see the power of loyalty programs and status. Fly with a commercial airline, and you can see the airline treat its status customers differently than regular customers. It's humorous at times to watch flyers with status flaunt that status, which just demonstrates the power of gamification.

Gamification may be one way to motivate participants in your blockchain environment to perpetually contribute quality data. If you can develop a program that offers real (or perceived) value in exchange for providing data, you could materially improve the longevity of your analytics models.

Rewarding and punishing participants

Another approach to incentivizing participants is more straightforward. Instead of subtly offering increased status through gamification, you respond in kind. Your application can monitor data submission behavior and provide rewards or punishment based on the quality of participation. Although this may sound a bit like gamification, it differs in that rewards and punishment are driven by some central entity, while gamification is generally driven by the individual participant.

TIP

With gamification, each participant gets as involved as he or she desires. Those who want to reach a higher status level must roll up their sleeves and get busy earning it. A reward/punishment system is more like a school semester. Each participant earns or loses something of value based on periodic reviews of behavior.

Because data quality matters more than quantity, there should be agreement on the definition of good and bad data. In a blockchain environment, you could bake the definition into the smart contracts that collect the data. As long as the smart contract designers define specific metrics that collect and store the desired quality of data, blockchain consensus would provide the authority for determining how well participants contribute to the blockchain dataset's quality.

Similar to successful miners, participants who contribute high-quality data, and do so on a perpetual basis, could earn cryptocurrency or some other measure of value. Participants who provide low-quality data could lose value in penalties. Such mechanisms, as long as they're deemed fair to all participants, could help maintain an overall high quality of available data.

Managing Deployment and Maintenance Costs

The preceding section focuses on ensuring participants continue to provide current, high-quality data. However, before participants settle into the ongoing interaction phase, they must join the network and provide the resources necessary to participate initially. This step can involve provisioning infrastructure, building a blockchain image, and providing connectivity for app users.

Sometimes the cost and effort required to initially participate in a blockchain environment are more than a new organization can justify. Let's look at some of the issues and how you can lower the cost of admission and increase the overall value for your blockchain environment.

Lowering the cost of admission

Blockchain application development isn't cheap. It requires all the effort, personnel, and project structure consistent with traditional application development, in addition to the unique skills required for the new technology. Some early blockchain adopters mistakenly operated under the impression that a decentralized environment meant lower overall costs. Although it may be possible to argue that decentralization reduces the total of infrastructure investment for any participating entity, those traditional costs are often redistributed to other areas.

Traditional software development activities rely on either an on-premises or cloud-based application footprint. Application developers design and write their software to run from a specific set of servers or devices. Although an application may be made up of many components across various device types (services, middleware, interfaces, clients, and so on), the application's functionality is generally centralized to a core functionality platform.

TECHNICAL
STUFF

This traditional application architecture description is generic and leaves the door open to lots of interpretation. The idea is that traditional applications, even distributed applications, run within some centralized footprint. You can generally draw a picture of a traditional application that depicts all components and who owns (and maintains) which components.

Data-repository architecture is similar to application architecture in that it traditionally exists as a centralized component. The most popular data repository in use by enterprise applications is the centralized database. A database may be a relational database or supported by any number of newer technologies. More and more larger data repositories in the last few years have begun to deviate from the traditional relational model toward a key-value pair architecture. Regardless of the storage architecture, most current data repositories are largely centralized.

TIP

A centralized data-repository or application architecture doesn't strictly mean a single copy exists in a single location. Application distribution is common, where an application owner may run copies of the application software on many servers across geographically diverse datacenters. Likewise, most enterprise data repositories are replicated across multiple servers for fault tolerance and load balancing. *Decentralization,* as I discuss it, refers to a low-level property of transparently distributing data and functionality across every node in a peer-to-peer network.

Becoming a participant in a blockchain network requires more than simply connecting to the network. The size of the Ethereum mainnet blockchain is currently in the neighborhood of 2 TB. Therefore, if you want to run an archive Ethereum node, you'll have to allocate at least 2 TB disk space just to store the existing blockchain. And because a blockchain only grows, the storage requirement won't ever decrease. You can set up a full node, or if you want to use substantially less local disk space, you can set up a light node. Light nodes download only the essential block headers at first and will download block contents when you need them.

WARNING

Don't assume all blockchain sizes are equal. The 2 TB size estimate is for the Ethereum mainnet blockchain only. Private (or consortium) Ethereum blockchains, as well as any non-Ethereum blockchains, will be different sizes and require different amounts of disk space to store.

To make matters worse, carrying out data analytics using blockchain data will almost always require substantial additional off-chain storage. Due to the processing overhead for blockchain technology, it is recommended that you pass through the blockchain data to create an off-chain repository, and then use the off-chain repository for analysis. Extracting and analyzing data directly from the blockchain is possible, and you'll see both techniques in Chapters 9 through 12. Regardless which approach you use, you'll likely need to store some data off-chain.

For these and many other reasons, joining a blockchain network comes with a non-trivial cost of admission. If your goal is to encourage participants to join and perpetually contribute to your network and available data, removing as many barriers to participation as possible is important.

Virtualization is a promising approach to lowering the cost of admission. You don't have to provide physical infrastructure to create a blockchain network node. Commercial cloud services such as Amazon Web Services (AWS) may be a good choice for spinning up a blockchain node. Costs are associated with processing and network traffic, but those costs are generally lower than the investment of setting up a physical node. Exploring virtualized options may allow more organizations to consider participation in your blockchain environment.

Leveraging participation value

The performance of any investment, whether personal or business, comes down to the value you receive in exchange for the assets you contribute. If the perceived payback value is greater than the amount invested, the investment is generally viewed as profitable. Even though you may have lowered the cost of participating in your blockchain network, an entry cost and additional ongoing costs will still exist.

One of the key factors in determining whether a blockchain investment is sound is the payback you get for participating. The point of this chapter is to discuss how to leverage advanced blockchain analytics models, which you accomplish by getting value from accurate models. You get accurate models by carefully building models to give you the information you need and supplying those models with the best data. That's how we got to this point in the discussion.

TIP

I use the term *you* a lot. That term could refer to you as an individual or to your overall organization. Data analytics is rarely a solo endeavor. In almost all cases, you (individual) will be working on some analytics project within an organization. Because blockchain technology is built on a network of peers, it stands to reason that you'll be working with other nodes and will need their participation to keep your model's data current and relevant.

Leveraging participation value and analytics models boils down to giving your data providers a reason to continue playing the game. Of course, the game is more than something you do in your leisure time. The game I'm talking about is the pursuit of your organization's business. Data analytics can provide the advanced information for you to make strategic decisions to stay ahead of your competition. Possessing that edge is the primary reason for investing so much effort and resources in incentivizing your business partners and customers to keep providing you with quality data. Your models, and perhaps the viability of your business, depend on it.

Because you already know how the value of good data, the key to acquiring that data is to maintain relationships with your business partners and customers. As long as you keep them happy and keep providing them with good enough incentives, most of them will likely continue to contribute the quality data you need. By offering those incentives, you're leveraging the value of their participation by collecting data that has more value than the incentives you offer to get it.

Aligning ROI with analytics currency

Up to now, I've discussed data value in only generic terms. At some point, you have to put real numbers on the data's value. The best strategy for determining whether your investment in blockchain data analytics is worthwhile is to measure your model's performance. That task sounds simple, but in a dynamic and often hectic business environment, it's often easier said than done.

The key to determining your analytics return on investment (ROI) is simple. The first step is to create a baseline. For example, if the goal of your analytics project is to find ways to increase sales, record your sales before taking any action indicated by your analytics results. If the organization wants to reduce the number of loans that end up in default, record loan origin and terminations data. All too often, organizations fail to start with a baseline. If you don't know what normal is, it's difficult to determine whether the changes you make are better or worse.

TIP

Another important piece of information to collect with baseline data is the opportunity cost associated with any change in behavior. For example, your organization should know how much an increase in sales affects bottom-line profit. Likewise, in the loan default scenario, the organization should know the cost of each loan default.

Next, keep track of how much you've invested in defining your problem, collecting data, and building models. This step is basic project management. Most investment in any analytics project is personnel investment, although there may be some non-trivial infrastructure and other technical costs.

After your models provide actionable results, the next logical step is to implement changes based on those results. For example, if your analytics models show that loan applicants with graduate degrees show a much lower default rate than those with less education, your organization would likely want to take action on that finding. Perhaps they would change the underwriting process to prefer higher educational levels. Although a cost would be associated with changing existing procedures, it should be minimal.

After some period of time, current data should be compared with pre-action data (data collected before any action based on analytics results was taken). Because you should already know the cost or benefit of any behavior change, calculating the effect of the analytics model's output should be straightforward. The value of the model's output is the model's *currency,* and capitalizing on that benefit is the goal of data analytics.

Collaborating to Create Better Models

By now, you've seen the importance of data quality to building a successful model. Your best (and perhaps only) hope to meet your blockchain data analytics goals lies in your ability to create and maintain a spirit of collaboration between your organization and its partners and customers. Although that sounds altruistic and somewhat obvious, remember that blockchain technology is built on the premise of exchanging value between untrusting participants.

So, from a philosophical perspective, your goal is to collaborate with entities whom you do not trust. Wait, that can't be right. From a purist's view, every node in a blockchain network lacks trust with other nodes. However, that doesn't mean you have to distrust everyone in a blockchain network. The untrusted environment really means no trust relationship exists with other blockchain nodes. You trust your bank (I hope), but you don't trust anonymous blockchain nodes with your bank balance. However, you do trust the blockchain technology with your crypto-bank balance.

TECHNICAL STUFF

Technically, you don't trust blockchain technology with your crypto-bank balance. You trust that the technology properly validates all transactions that effect your cryptocurrency balance. If every transaction is valid, the resulting account balance is valid. This difference in defining trust in a blockchain environment is subtle but important.

The whole idea of realizing value from data analytics over time depends on identifying your data value centers and keeping them happy enough to keep the data flowing. The easiest way to do that is to establish a mutually beneficial relationship with your data providers and nurture that relationship.

Collecting data from a cohort

Historically, commercial organizations have pursued making profits as a singular entity. The model of partnering with customers, or even competitors, to increase profits is fairly new. Under the right circumstances, partnering with customers or competitors or both may be beneficial to all parties. A robust data analytics partnership may be one of those circumstances.

Assume that your organization has decided to develop ongoing data analytics to increase profitability. Such a project will succeed only with clear goals, sophisticated models, and high-quality data that doesn't become stale. The last requirement, current, high-quality data, is the greatest ongoing concern. The best way to ensure that your data stays relevant and fresh is to enlist the data providers in your endeavor.

Team members generally contribute to any endeavor more freely. One way to enlist the help of your customers or partners is to build a team, or cohort, environment. This step takes time and effort but can result in your organization gaining access to rich data that you can turn into accelerating profits. The process may start with a few customers or partners but can grow as results turn into profits (or clearer information on how to best pursue profits). Either way, analytics can help provide a clearer picture of the current landscape, and that clarity is worth investing in.

Building models collaboratively

Collaboration isn't only a goal for collecting data. Because the process of selecting, building, and training models is iterative and requires substantial resources, partners may help spread the investment as well. If you include partners (both business partners and customers) in the model-building process, you may be able to reduce your own organization's resource commitments while increasing the quality of design input.

Because the general goal of analytics collaboration is to create a cohort environment, including potential cohort members in the design phase may be a good start. As with any software development process, involving stakeholders early in the design phase often increases the sense of ownership and decreases post-design objections. If your business partners and customers understand the overall goals of your analytics project from the beginning, they're more likely to support it, from a perspective of both interacting with the resulting product and more willingly providing the data you'll need for your models.

One of the first tasks in building collaboration among multiple partners is to educate the partners of the benefits of participation. This is where the techniques from the previous sections come into play. Providing incentives for partner participation isn't effective unless you have an ongoing education campaign to advertise the benefits. Such efforts can go a long way toward making partners feel as though they're part of a team, as opposed to simply providing data for someone else to make money with.

Another way organizations that sponsor data analytics activities can build consensus and team spirit is to reinforce the attitude that everyone is on the same team. When partners believe that their contributions benefit the larger community, they have a greater motivation to contribute. In some cases, contributions exceed requested minimums. When you build and maintain a team environment, the benefits can often be far more than those initially perceived. Teams that work well together are greater than the sum of the individual participants.

Assessing model quality as a team

Encouraging team participation is a great start, but it isn't the end game. After any model has been operationalized (put into production), it will invariably degrade over time without ongoing maintenance. Even a great model depends on relevant data. If you don't update a model with newer data, its accuracy will suffer. Quality assurance is critical to any analytics model's longevity. Remember that the purpose of any model is to provide information that is actionable and leads to an improvement in one or more metrics. You must be able to use a model's results for some good purpose.

A model may help explain previously misunderstood phenomena, predict future behavior, or even suggest actions to encourage desired behavior. Regardless of a model's specific purpose, its designers go through the effort to create a model only if there is an expectation for profit.

TIP

Profit doesn't always refer directly to money. Analytics results may be used to increase participation in a certain context, which may not lead directly, or at all, to increased money. For example, suppose a non-profit-industry marketing organization is made up of members who are all in the same business, in this case, dairy farmers. They've decided to form a marketing organization to help inform the public of the health benefits of dairy products. Success is measured by awareness and sentiment, not direct revenue. Of course, the hope is that a better public perception of their products will lead to increased revenue, but that isn't the direct result desired.

Because the quality of any model's results is directly related to the quality of the data on which it is built, the primary focus of operational efforts should be on data quality. Some organizations engage in elaborate incentive programs to attract bulk data and then carefully assess and clean the data they acquire. This approach provides a wider range of data, but it has drawbacks. Using this approach, the responsibility to assess quality and clean data lies with a single authority. Ongoing data handling requires personnel and budget. Also, as much as that authority may attempt to be objective as it handles data, removing all bias from the data preparation process is nearly impossible.

An alternate approach to distributing the workload and minimizing central bias is to engage your participants to consider quality before they submit data to your model. This approach takes far more work up front but can minimize the post-deployment workload necessary to maintain models. When designing incentives for partners to contribute, consider offering increasing benefits for higher quality data.

TECHNICAL
STUFF

In this chapter I talk a lot about high-quality data. The quality of any data depends on how well it meets the design goals for its use. In data analytics, high-quality data generally means no feature values are missing, all values are in an understandable format and within defined ranges, and the data accurately represents what it's supposed to represent. Further, the data represents a sample that is of use to the model.

It may be worth the effort to develop an incentive model that can define data quality standards with enough granularity for all partners to understand and comply. If that incentive model links incentives with submitted data quality, you'll be able to leverage the resources of your partners to not only continue to provide you with the data your models need but also carry out much of the data cleansing efforts before the data is submitted.

Developing a strong team approach to data analytics can help any organization leverage the power of data. Turning customers and users into partners through collaboration and offering mutual benefits can be a win-win scenario and foster loyalty. The benefits you gain from approaching an analytics project from a partnership perspective can be far greater than just good data you can use to make money. In the next chapter, you look at some specific model types and how you can put the data you acquire to good use.

3

Analyzing and Visualizing Blockchain Analysis Data

IN THIS CHAPTER

» **Finding clusters of data**

» **Exposing relationships between dataset items**

» **Choosing the right algorithm for your data**

» **Assessing the value of your model with diagnostics**

» **Writing Python code to find clusters of data**

Chapter **9**

Identifying Clustered and Related Data

You find out about some of the most common analytics models in Chapter 7 and how to help ensure that you have the data your models need in Chapter 8. Now you're ready to dig into specific models to discover how to choose the best one for your goals, write the code in Python to implement the model, and assess its accuracy and relevance.

One of the first steps in analyzing any dataset is to determine the structure and relationships among data items. Allow your data to tell any stories that are right below the surface. Some of these stories will take work to uncover, but other findings will almost jump out at you.

Cluster analysis and association rules analysis are both straightforward methods of letting your data do the talking. You may find that your data shows internal relationships (between features) or external relationships (between different data items) you may not have previously recognized. For example, it may turn out that your megastores sell out of strawberry toaster pastries when a hurricane approaches (yes, that really happened). Cluster analysis and association rules analysis can reveal characteristics or conditions consistent with observed behavior.

Cluster analysis can help organizations of all types identify indicators for both positive and negative behavior. They can use that knowledge to predict behavior, or even incentivize (or discourage) behavior by altering related conditions. Retailers can offer incentives to increase sales or can detect fraud earlier than their competitors by utilizing the knowledge clustering analysis can provide. Association rules analysis can reveal correlations between different data items, such as items that are frequently purchased together. In this chapter, you learn how to choose the right clustering and association rules algorithms for your goals and use Python to implement your chosen models.

Analyzing Data Clustering Using Popular Models

One of the first techniques analysts use to find hidden structures in data is clustering. The idea is simple. You graph the relationship between two or more features and then identify *clusters*, or groups, of objects. Objects on the graph that are close together are generally related in some way. *Clustering* can help you visualize groupings in your data that may not be obvious and can lead to *segmenting*, or classifying your data for further analysis.

Clustering is generally an *unsupervised technique*, which means there are no predefined cluster labels. Unlike *supervised techniques*, in which the algorithm already knows the target classes, you don't know what clusters exist (or even how many clusters exist) until you carry out the analysis. Clustering is often a preliminary step in the analysis process that can help direct further analysis activities.

Delivering valuable knowledge with cluster analysis

The primary benefit of *cluster analysis* is that it helps identify items that are similar. Tight clusters (those in which objects are very close to the center of a cluster) can indicate strong similarities, while more sparse clusters indicate weaker similarities among objects. One common use of clustering techniques is in medical imaging and diagnosis. Clustering can compare images of cells or other tissue and identify areas in which features of one object (patient) appear similar to features of another object or group of objects. Cell or tissue image similarities help researchers and physicians identify trends of shared behavior among multiple patients.

Recognizing trends and similarities is a foundational goal of data analytics. In project management, we strive to repeat the successes but not the mistakes. A crucial factor in repeating success is being able to recognize why things worked and led to success. Data analytics, and clustering in particular, can provide the capability to study many features of project activities and recognize how different feature values affect outcomes. Identifying how successful activities are similar to one another but different from unsuccessful activities is a first step in repeating success. Clustering can reveal any such similarities.

Examining popular clustering techniques

Many clustering algorithms are in use, but one of the most popular ones is the k-*means* technique, which is based on calculating the distances between data points and works well for numeric data. The k-means method returns a set of clusters, along with the center points of each one. The centers of the discovered clusters are called *centroids* and may not correspond with observed data points. Centroids serve to approximate the relative centers of clusters of observed data. If you want to assess how well multiple features define similarity between objects, k-means is a great place to start.

TIP

Data analytics provides methods for examining data often organized as a table. Although not strictly required, most datasets have multiple rows (or lines) of data, each with a collection of features (or attributes). Most analytics techniques assume data is organized in a tabular format. I refer to different rows in a dataset as *unique objects* and different attributes of an object as *features*. Some analytics focus on features, and others focus on objects.

If your data includes categorical data, the k-*modes* technique works better by counting differences between feature sets. The k-modes technique can be helpful when examining the similarity of survey answers when the answers are yes/no or have a limited list of options. Another alternative to k-means is the *partitioning around medoids (PAM)* technique. The PAM method chooses a data point closest to the true center of a cluster and determines cluster members by calculating each point's distance from a medoid. A *medoid* is similar to a centroid from the k-means method, except medoids must be values from the observed data. If your model deals with categorical data, you want all clusters to be centered on actual categorical data values, unlike the approximations that are fine for continuous data. Lots of resources for learning about clustering techniques are available, including *Python for Data Science For Dummies,* 2nd Edition, and *Data Science Programming All-in-One For Dummies* (Wiley).

Understanding k-means analysis

The k-means clustering analysis technique helps identify ways in which objects are related. Although k-means can work for any number of features, it is easiest to visualize when comparing two features. You start the k-means process by creating a scatterplot of points, each of which represents one object. For each object, assign one feature's value to the x coordinate and another feature's value to the y coordinate and then plot the point on the graph. Repeat this process until each object in the dataset is represented by a point on the graph.

To show what a well-clustered scatterplot looks like, run the Python code in the genscatterPlot.py file, shown here:

```python
import matplotlib.pyplot as plt
import numpy as np
from sklearn.datasets.samples_generator import make_blobs

X, y_true = make_blobs(n_samples=300, centers=4,
                       cluster_std=0.60, random_state=0)
plt.scatter(X[:, 0], X[:, 1], s=50)
plt.xlabel('Rating')
plt.ylabel('Months as customer')
plt.show()
```

The Python code in genScatterPlot.py generates data that is clearly clustered and then creates a scatterplot of that data, as shown in Figure 9-1.

The data in Figure 9-1 shows clear clusters. In this case, you can infer that a relationship exists between the length of time a customer has been purchasing from the organization and how well that customer rates the organization. However, not all data self-organizes into such clean clusters, which is where clustering techniques come into play. Clustering analysis can help identify groupings that may not be obvious by looking at a scatterplot.

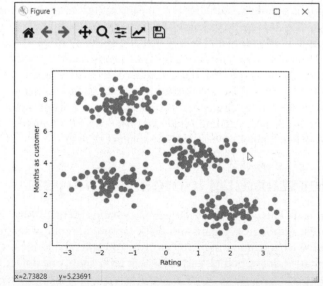

FIGURE 9-1:
Scatterplot showing clustered data.

TECHNICAL STUFF

The k-means algorithm can be implemented in many ways. The approach I explain in this chapter, often called naïve k-means or Lloyd's algorithm, is the simplest and slowest approach. In real analytics, you'll likely use one of the faster k-means algorithm implementations. The results are the same, but you get answers much faster with a more sophisticated k-means implementation.

The most common k-means algorithm is an iterative approach to assigning each point to the best cluster. The process follows these steps:

1. Select a value for *k* (the number of clusters) and randomly select *k* points, each of which will be the center, or *centroid,* of each cluster.

2. Calculate the distance from each point to each centroid and assign each point to the cluster with the closest centroid.

3. Calculate the new centroid of each cluster from Step 2.

4. Repeat Steps 2 and 3 until the positions of the new centroids don't change much from the previous centroid locations.

To see the output of the k-means algorithm for a randomly generated dataset with four clear clusters, run the Python code in the kMeans.py file, shown next:

```python
import matplotlib.pyplot as plt
import numpy as np
from sklearn.datasets.samples_generator import make_blobs
from sklearn.cluster import KMeans

X, y_true = make_blobs(n_samples=300, centers=4,
                       cluster_std=0.60, random_state=0)

kmeans = KMeans(n_clusters=4)
kmeans.fit(X)
y_kmeans = kmeans.predict(X)

plt.scatter(X[:, 0], X[:, 1], c=y_kmeans, s=50, cmap='viridis')
centers = kmeans.cluster_centers_
plt.scatter(centers[:, 0], centers[:, 1], c='black', s=200, alpha=0.5)
plt.xlabel('Rating')
plt.ylabel('Months as customer')
plt.show()
```

Figure 9-2 shows the output from the kMeans.py Python code.

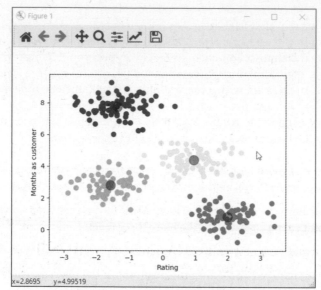

FIGURE 9-2:
The k-means
clustering
algorithm
visualization.

TIP

Note that the `kMeans.py` Python code hardcoded the number of clusters. In the generated data, it's clear to see that the data is organized in four clusters. For real-life datasets, the number and boundaries of clusters aren't always so clear. Real data may not appear to be clustered at all, regardless of the number of clusters.

Before you can use k-means on data, you must determine the number of clusters in your data. If the scatterplot of your data doesn't show clear groups of data, you have to use math to select the best number of proposed clusters. One of the most common methods is to use *within cluster sum of squares (WCSS)* or just *within sum of squares (WSS),* which iteratively carries out the k-means algorithm with different numbers of clusters, *k*. For each iteration, WSS calculates the sum of squared distances from each point to the cluster's centroid. A smaller WSS value indicates a better cluster organization because points don't deviate a lot from their assigned centroid. However, as you increase the number of clusters, you eventually create too many clusters and don't see much value from adding new clusters. The point at which you stop adding more clusters is when *k + 1* clusters don't decrease the WSS value as much as adding the previous cluster.

The following Python code, from the `wss.py` file, applies the k-means algorithm with various values of k ranging from 2 to 8. The code then stores the current k value and corresponding WSS value (`k, km.intertia_`), and then plots the results to show the relative WSS values.

```
from sklearn.cluster import KMeans
k = [2, 3, 4, 5, 6, 7, 8]
```

```
X, y_true = make_blobs(n_samples=300, centers=4,
                       cluster_std=0.60, random_state=0)

wss = []
for i in k:
  km = KMeans(n_clusters=i, max_iter=1000, random_state=47)
  km.fit(X)
  wss.append(km.inertia_)
plt.plot(k, wss)
plt.xlabel("Value for k")
plt.ylabel("WSS")
plt.show()
```

Figure 9-3 shows the inertia, or WSS, plot, which shows that increasing the number of clusters beyond four results in only minor WSS decreases. Therefore, four is the optimal number of clusters for this data.

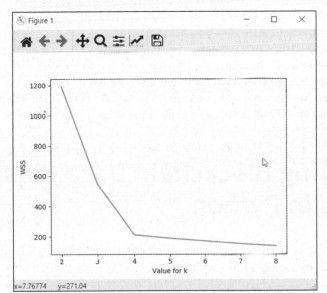

FIGURE 9-3:
WSS plot showing the optimal number of clusters (four).

These preceding examples show the k-means algorithm for generated data, but you probably want to use these techniques on blockchain data. The good news is that data analytics techniques are useful on any type of data, regardless of its origin. The next section steps you through applying the k-means algorithm to blockchain data.

TIP

In most cases, you'll have the easiest time carrying out analytics on a dataset after extracting it from a blockchain. You'll probably find it easier pulling the data you need from a blockchain in one pass and then using the resulting data as input for your analytics scripts.

Evaluating model effectiveness with diagnostics

Some models you'll learn about have specific methods for evaluating their effectiveness. Clustering effectiveness is generally determined visually. After applying the algorithm of choice and creating a visualization, you can judge how well the algorithm worked by looking at it. Although simply looking at a graph may not seem to be an accurate approach, remember that clustering is often an early activity to learn how data may be related.

When you look at a clustering visualization, such as the one in Figure 9-2, ask yourself the following questions:

>> Are the clusters separated enough to appear distinct from one another?

>> Does any cluster have far fewer points than most other clusters?

>> Are any clusters so close to one another that they appear as one bigger cluster?

These questions can help you determine whether the clustering algorithm and parameters you used reveal information about your data. A lack of distinct clusters isn't a failure — it simply means that you should look elsewhere for interesting knowledge from your data. Don't get discouraged if you don't hit gold early in the process. Most analytics projects find more dull results than spectacular findings. But keep at it. Finding valuable knowledge hidden in your data is worth the effort.

Implementing Blockchain Data Clustering Algorithms in Python

You know how to implement k-means on generated data, but now it's time to look at blockchain data. In this section you examine supply chain transfer data. In previous chapters, you find out how to access transaction events and store them in flat files. You can store blockchain data in any repository, but you'll use flat files for simplicity.

You'll use the `transfers.csv` file, a text file with data separated by commas, as your input dataset. If you examine the `transfers.csv` file, you'll see that it includes identifying information that you don't need quite yet. You're most interested in seeing how the activity represented in the data might be related.

Because you don't know yet what you're looking for, a great place to start is to create a scatterplot matrix of your data. A *scatterplot matrix* creates a set of scatterplots, showing how each pair of features is related. Creating a scatterplot matrix is a common first step in selecting the most interesting features.

Look at the Python code in the scatterplotMatrix.py file. This code reads the transfers.csv file, creating a table-like data structure called a dataframe with the features cost, price, qty, year, month, and day. It then creates a scatterplot matrix showing how each pair of features in the dataframe relate to one another:

```
import pandas as pd
import matplotlib.pyplot as plt
from pandas.plotting import scatter_matrix

df = pd.read_csv('transfers.csv', usecols=['cost', 'price', 'qty', 'year',
    'month', 'day'])
scatter_matrix(df, alpha = 0.2, figsize = (6, 6))
plt.show()
```

Figure 9-4 shows the output of the scatterplotMatrix.py script. The scatterplot shows that most of the features don't exhibit interesting relationships. Straight lines of any type imply obvious relationships. The scatterplots for cost or price compared to the day feature are a little more interesting.

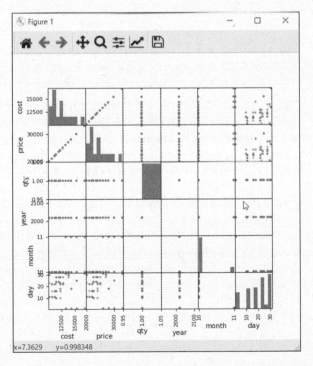

FIGURE 9-4:
Scatterplot matrix of blockchain transfer data.

The relationships between cost and day, as well as price and day, show data points that are more distributed and not linear. From this finding, try k-means on the cost and day features. (Because cost and price have a linear relationship, you would expect clustering to be effectively the same whether you compared cost or price to the day feature.)

The code in the kMeansBlockchain.py file shows how to put all the pieces together. This script assumes that you've extracted the data you need from your blockchain (as described in Chapter 6) and stored that output in the transfers.csv file. The script reads data from the transvers.csv file into a dataframe, and then applies the k-means algorithm to the blockchain data in the dataframe:

```python
from sklearn.cluster import KMeans
import pandas as pd
import matplotlib.pyplot as plt

df = pd.read_csv('transfers.csv', usecols=['cost', 'day'])
kmeans = KMeans(n_clusters=4)
kmeans.fit(df)
y_kmeans = kmeans.predict(df)

df.plot.scatter(0, 1, c=y_kmeans, s=50, cmap='viridis')
centers = kmeans.cluster_centers_
plt.scatter(centers[:, 0], centers[:, 1], c='black', s=200, alpha=0.5)
plt.xlabel('Cost')
plt.ylabel('Day')
plt.show()
```

Figure 9-5 shows the results of the k-means analysis using cost and day data from the supply chain blockchain. Although the analysis identifies four distinct clusters, it doesn't tell you much because the clusters are just vertical partitions. For cluster analysis to be meaningful, it should result in clusters that exhibit limits in all directions, generally conforming to a circular pattern.

WARNING

Stating that clusters should have limits in all directions doesn't mean that all clusters should be circular. Circular clusters are nice, but uneven clusters that are distinct from other clusters can still be valuable. Remember that the idea behind clustering is to reveal hidden ways in which your data may be related.

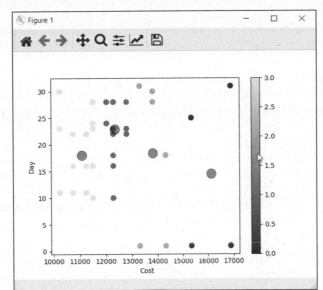

FIGURE 9-5:
The k-means algorithm applied to blockchain supply chain ownership transfers cost and day features.

Discovering Association Rules in Data

In the preceding section, you learned about clustering and how to implement the k-means algorithm. Clustering analysis can show how similar feature values imply relationships between objects. For example, cluster analysis can show that people whose income is between $140,000 and $175,000 annually prefer a certain type of car as opposed to those making under $50,000. Clustering depends on selecting features to compare.

Association rules analysis is a different approach to uncovering relationships among objects. Instead of comparing features of different objects, association rules analysis examines the presence of multiple objects in distinct transactions. This type of analysis is sometimes called *market basket analysis* because it tries to determine how likely specific items appear together in a market basket (either real or online).

Delivering valuable knowledge with association rules analysis

Association rules analysis looks at existing transactions to determine the probability of a new object being added based on the presence of one or more objects. A transaction can be any collection of objects, such as items in a shopping basket or the contents of a box shipped from one location to another. Transaction analysis using association rules makes it possible to examine a transaction and make recommendations for adding additional objects based on the objects present in similar transactions.

Whether you realize it or not, you've been the subject of association rules analysis thousands of times. Recommendation engines depend on association rules to do their work. Every time you see a recommendation to add another product in your online shopping cart, you've seen the result of an association rules analysis. That's how online retailers can make additional purchase recommendations with uncanny accuracy. They aren't reading your mind; they're just using good analytics! Suppose analysis shows that a high percentage of shoppers who purchase a flashlight also purchase batteries in the same transaction. If your shopping cart contains a flashlight but no batteries, it makes sense for the retailer to suggest that you also purchase batteries. In many cases, such a simple suggestion can increase sales.

Describing the apriori association rules algorithm

One of the most common algorithms for detecting association rules is the apriori algorithm. The *apriori* algorithm is a structured way to identify objects that commonly occur together, also called *frequent itemsets*. For example, if a shopping basket in a supermarket contains bread, what is the likelihood that the same basket contains eggs? The apriori algorithm defines the technique for calculating the probabilities of frequent itemsets occurring.

The apriori algorithm is a bottom-up approach to identifying sets of objects that occur more frequently than a desired minimum probability, or *support*. If you have a grocery store transaction dataset and want to find items with a minimum support of 0.25, you would accept all items that are found in 250 or more transactions. If an item is found in only 150 transactions, it falls below the minimum support (150/1000 < 0.25) and will not be included in the results.

Apriori is an iterative algorithm. It first examines all itemsets that contain only a single item to select only those that meet or exceed the minimum support. From the selected candidates, it then considers all two-item itemsets and selects those that meet or exceed the minimum support threshold. The algorithm continues with three-item itemsets, then four-item itemsets, and so on until no itemsets meet or exceed the support threshold.

The following table contains a list of six transactions from a grocery store. Just like real transactions, each market basket can have a different number of items in it. The purpose of analyzing transaction contents is to use an existing basket to make recommendations for additional purchases before checking out:

Eggs, bacon, bread, milk

Eggs, bread, milk

Milk

Bacon

Eggs, bacon, milk

Eggs, bacon, milk

Apriori step 1: Count the frequency of single-item itemsets

The first step in the apriori algorithm is to count the number of times each individual item appears in separate transactions. The results of the first apriori step follow:

Itemset	Frequency (count)
Eggs	4
Bacon	4
Bread	2
Milk	5

Apriori step 2: Prune itemsets based on support threshold

The next step (step 2) is to remove, or *prune*, any itemsets that do not meet the minimum support threshold and then move to the next larger itemset phase. Suppose you define the support threshold to be 50 percent (which is three items for this dataset). To keep any itemset, that itemset must appear in 50 percent of the transactions. Because bread occurs in only two transactions, you'll prune that itemset and proceed to the next step with only eggs, bacon, and milk.

TIP

Pruning is an essential action for apriori's accuracy and performance. After you prune any itemset, future algorithm steps can ignore larger itemsets that include any pruned itemset. For the current example, you can ignore any itemsets that include bread because you just pruned the itemset that contains bread.

Apriori step 3: Count the frequency of two-item itemsets

The third step repeats step 1 with a larger itemset. The preceding step was for single-item itemsets, so this step will be to count the number of times each two-item itemset appears in transactions. You construct the new itemsets by combining each item with each other item to create sets of two items. The following table shows all two-item itemsets and how many times those itemsets appear in the list of transactions:

Itemset	Frequency (count)
Eggs, bacon	3
Eggs, milk	3
Bacon, milk	3

REMEMBER

Remember that you just pruned the itemset that contained bread, so you shouldn't count the {eggs,bread,milk} itemset because it contains a pruned itemset. This approach saves a lot of time.

Apriori step 4: Prune itemsets based on support (again)

All itemsets meet the support threshold, which means you don't need to prune anything in this step (step 4).

Apriori step 5: Count the frequency of three-item itemsets

The next step (step 5) is to increase the size of our itemsets and count the frequency again. The following table shows the results of step 5 in the algorithm:

Itemset	Frequency (count)
Eggs, bacon, milk	3

The only transaction that contains three items exists in three transactions and meets the support threshold. Because the only transactions with more than three items also contains pruned items, the algorithm terminates. You're finished!

The code in the `apriori.py` file shows how to put the steps together. The following Python script defines the transactions in the initial grocery store list and applies the apriori algorithm with a support threshold of 50 percent:

```
from efficient_apriori import apriori
transactions = [('eggs', 'bacon', 'bread','milk'),('eggs', 'bread',
    'milk'),('milk'),
                ('bacon'),('eggs', 'bacon', 'milk'),('eggs', 'bacon', 'milk')]
```

```
itemsets, rules = apriori(transactions, min_support=0.5, min_confidence=1)

print(itemsets)
```

Running the preceding script produces the following output (which corresponds to the itemsets in the previous results):

```
{1: {('bacon',): 3, ('eggs',): 4, ('milk',): 4}, 2: {('bacon', 'eggs'): 3,
    ('bacon', 'milk'): 3, ('eggs', 'milk'): 4}, 3: {('bacon', 'eggs',
    'milk'): 3}}
```

Evaluating model effectiveness with diagnostics

After you have the collection of itemsets from the apriori algorithm, you can build a set of rules and calculate a few additional values to determine which rules best describe the transactions. *Association rules* are stated X –> Y (X implies Y). This rule means that if you observe X (a certain set of items is in a basket), then Y (adding an additional item to the basket) is likely to happen.

You can use rules to make recommendations for likely purchases. Association rules allow retailers to examine items in a customer's current basket, and then make recommendations for potential additional items the customer may want to purchase.

You build a set of candidate rules from each itemset in the results from applying the apriori algorithm. The following table lists the candidate rules from our example:

{eggs} –> {bacon}

{eggs} –>{milk}

{bacon} –> {milk}

{bacon} –> {eggs}

{milk} –> {eggs}

{milk} –> {bacon}

{eggs,bacon} –> {milk}

{eggs,milk} –> {bacon}

{bacon,milk} –>{eggs}

Two primary metrics are used to evaluate association rules: confidence and lift. *Confidence* is a measure of how trustworthy a rule is. In other words, a rule with a high confidence is one that you can count on as a strong recommendation; a weaker rule is one with a low confidence. *Lift* measures how many more times you observe X and Y together than would be expected if they were independent. Put another way, lift helps to determine if X and Y are related and influence one another.

To calculate the confidence of the rule (X -> Y), use this formula:

```
Confidence(X -> Y) = support(X AND Y) / support(X)
```

To calculate the lift of the rule (X -> Y), use this formula:

```
Lift(X -> Y) = support(X AND Y) / support(X) * support(Y)
```

The Python `efficient_apriori` library makes it easy to calculate confidence and lift for association rules. Just add the following three lines of Python code to the `apriori.py` file and run it again:

```
rules_rhs = filter(lambda rule: len(rule.lhs) == 2 and len(rule.rhs) == 1,
    rules)
for rule in sorted(rules_rhs, key=lambda rule: rule.lift):
 print(rule)
```

In addition to the list of itemsets, you'll now also see three-itemset rules with confidence, support, and lift calculated for you:

```
{bacon, milk} -> {eggs} (conf: 1.000, supp: 0.500, lift: 1.500, conv:
    333333333.333)
{bacon, eggs} -> {milk} (conf: 1.000, supp: 0.500, lift: 1.500, conv:
    333333333.333)
```

Determining When to Use Clustering and Association Rules

One of the first phases in any data analytics project is looking at your data to determine where relationships exist. Relationships within data imply an ability to learn about past behavior and even predict future behavior. Clustering is a common early analysis step to learn about relationships between objects that share feature similarities. Although you saw clustering analysis in only two features, using more features to search for relationships is common. Clustering analysis can reveal relationships that aren't evident through visualization alone.

After examining your data for similar feature values among objects, a next logical step is to look for other unexplained relationships. In many cases, objects are related by characteristics not captured in recorded features. For example, even though we know that eggs and milk are common to many meals and recipes, no descriptive data can explain why eggs and milk are often purchased together. The external influence of how objects are consumed can make relationship discovery difficult. Association rules analysis can help identify that relationships exist, even if the cause of the relationship isn't clear.

The primary reasons for clustering and association rules analysis is to learn about the relationships between objects in your data. These relationships may have clear explanations, or they may defy efforts to explain them. Either way, relationships in data describe behavior, and behavior reveals value. Understanding past customer or partner behavior may help to predict future behavior. Such knowledge can be extremely beneficial when planning future business activities. The more you know about expected behavior, the better you can prepare for that behavior.

Every organization should assess its goals and understand which ones have the highest priority. Data analytics efforts should concentrate on understanding and influencing the goals with the highest priority. For example, if the pursuit of profit is most important, understanding how to increase sales and reduce cost should take precedence. On the other hand, if establishing long-term positive relationships with customers is viewed as most important to long-term revenue, you should focus on customer sentiment influences and keeping them happy.

The most effective analytics projects are those that focus on results that directly align with the organization's primary goals. Understand your organization's goals, learn its data, and use analytics to unlock secrets it may contain.

IN THIS CHAPTER

» **Identifying common data characteristics**

» **Assigning labels to data**

» **Choosing the right algorithm for your data**

» **Assessing the value of your model with diagnostics**

» **Writing Python code to label data with classifications**

Chapter **10**

Classifying Blockchain Data

Chapter 9 introduces clustering and association rules analysis, which help analysts uncover patterns and relationships in data. By examining features present in existing data, you can uncover relationships and use those relationships to better understand your data and, more importantly, what that data represents. Understanding your customer data is good, but gaining a clearer understanding of your customers who produce that data is far better. By understanding your customers, you may be able to tailor your service and product offerings to better meet their needs. That approach can lead to more sales, lower costs, or any goals your organization pursues.

Data that represents past behavior is often useful for predicting future behavior. Such analysis is referred to as *predictive analysis.* After you identify general clusters of data based on *feature values* (values of sampled data, such as products purchased), you can look at current data and make a prediction as to which cluster best represents a new object the data represents (such as a customer). By examining features of new objects, it's possible to determine how the new object is similar to other objects you've seen before. *Classification* is based on the idea that objects in the same class, or group, tend to share similar characteristics. *Classification analysis* formalizes this idea to make prediction easier.

In this chapter, you learn about techniques to predict a new object's classification based on your observations of other objects. Correctly predicting an object's classification means you can figure out what group that object belongs in. You then learn how to build models, train those models, and use them to predict expected behavior.

Analyzing Data Classification Using Popular Models

One of the most common uses for analytics is to predict future behavior so you can be better prepared if the predicted behavior occurs. For example, if you expect a surge in sales of generators because your model shows increased sales of generators as a result of an approaching hurricane, you can stock up and be ready for the added demand when a hurricane is expected.

Clustering and association rules models help to identify hidden patterns and relationships in data by grouping objects. Classification models build on prior discovery and help predict an outcome that places an object in an identified group. Classification models are mostly supervised learning models. A *supervised model* is one in which you provide a list of labels, or groups, and the model determines where to place an object.

Delivering valuable knowledge with classification analysis

Classification models must be trained before you can use them to make predictions. But before you can train a classification model, you must define the class labels. *Class labels* are anything that's meaningful for your data and describes different groups of objects. Some class labels are pass and fail; high, middle, and low; and premium, standard, and economy. The feature values should indicate into which class each object should be assigned.

After defining labels for classes, you train a model by providing labeled input data, which includes both the feature values and the correct class label. To train your model, you provide input data that describes some object (such as a customer), along with a class label that tells the model to which class this data belongs. As the model examines input data and associates that data with a class, it "learns" about that data. The more training data you give a model, the more likely it will recognize similar data in the future and assign it to the correct class.

After training the model, you test the model's performance by providing unlabeled input data, which has no assigned class. A perfect model will examine the unlabeled input data and always correctly determine the right class for the data. However, no model is perfect. The goal is to maximize the frequency of correct predictions and adjust the model's parameters when that frequency falls below a desired goal.

Examining popular classification techniques

As with all types of analytics, multiple models are available for carrying out classification, each with its own strengths and weaknesses. In this chapter, you learn about two of the most popular models — decision tree and naïve Bayes — but don't stop there. For information on other models, check out *Python for Data Science For Dummies*, 2nd Edition, and *Data Science Programming All-in-One For Dummies* (Wiley). The best model for any application depends on the type of data available to you, the type of output you need to produce, and how well the technique aligns with your organizational goals. Each time you reach the model building phase, explore multiple models to determine the best for your project.

TIP

Sometimes non-technical goals play a part in model selection. For instance, some models are easier to explain to non-technologists than others. If you're required to explain to a non-technical audience how a model comes up with an answer, choose a simpler model. In that case, a decision tree model might be easier to explain than a support-vector machine.

At a conceptual level, the decision tree and naïve Bayes algorithms are similar. They both look at each object's features and use those values to make a classification prediction based on similarity to other objects. A decision tree approach is easy to visually present and explain, even to non-technical people. It takes a question-based approach to arrive at a prediction. The naïve Bayes technique looks at probabilities of feature values and determines the closest match with similar objects. Both techniques are strongest when the training data provides sufficient coverage for all classifications.

Understanding how the decision tree algorithm works

Decision tree is a classification algorithm that consists of decision nodes and leaf nodes and works much like a flowchart. A *decision node* is a node in the tree that contains decision criteria, such as *weight > 2 oz.* or *color = 'red'*. You work your way down the tree toward a solution (a classification for the object) by answering questions in nodes and following one of the downward facing arrows depending on the answer.

Figure 10-1 shows a decision tree created for the iris dataset, a commonly used dataset that contains descriptive data made available by biologist Ronald Fisher in a paper he published in 1936. The data in the iris dataset describes the variations of three related iris species. You can determine a flower's variety by measuring its petal and sepal length and width and then comparing those measurements to Dr. Fisher's data. It is a good representation of how data can be used to classify objects — in this case, flowers.

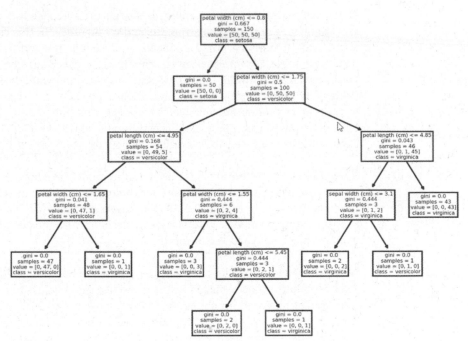

FIGURE 10-1:
Decision tree for the iris dataset.

Generally, at the top of each decision tree is a *root node,* which is a decision node that contains an initial decision based on one or more feature values. You start at the root node, evaluate the decision criteria, and follow the child link that corresponds to your answer. In most cases, true means you take the left link and false means you take the right link.

The Python code in the decisionTree.py file builds a simple decision tree. After you import the necessary libraries and load the iris data into a dataset, set the output resolution of your visualization to 300 dpi, you build the tree by invoking the DecisionTreeClassifier().fit() method. The next four lines of code create the visualization of the decision tree, save it in the `decisiontree.png` file, and then display it. The following Python code generated the output shown in Figure 10-1:

```python
from sklearn.datasets import load_iris
from sklearn import tree
import matplotlib.pyplot as plt

iris = load_iris()
plt.figure(dpi = 300)
clf = tree.DecisionTreeClassifier(random_state=0).fit(iris.data, iris.target)

tree.plot_tree(clf, feature_names=iris.feature_names, class_names=iris.
    target_names)
plt.tight_layout()
plt.savefig('decisiontree.png')
plt.show()
```

TIP

Nodes can have more than one child. In other words, you can construct decision criteria that has more than two answers. For example, you could ask if a value is less than, equal to, or greater than a number. Depending on the feature's value, there could be any of three answers. Each distinct answer (less than, equal, greater than) would have a link to a new child.

Suppose you have a flower that you want to identify. You know it's an iris and you've measured its sepal and petal length and width, but you aren't sure which variety it is. You can use a decision tree to determine what kind of iris you have. In the iris decision tree in Figure 10-1, the root node is level 1 and contains the decision criteria *petal width (cm) <= 0.5*. If the decision criteria is true (the petal width is <= 0.5 cm), you follow the left child arrow. Note that the left child in Figure 10-1 has no decision criteria, which means this node is a leaf node. When you reach a leaf node, you have exhausted the algorithm and accept the class as the predicted class for the current object (that is, the answer).

If the decision criteria is false, you follow the right child link. In Figure 10-1, following the right child link from the root node takes you to another decision node, which is at level 2. Answer that question, *petal width (cm) <= 1.75* and follow the child link based on the answer. Keep repeating this process until you either reach a leaf node or exhaust the number of levels you can explore.

Using a decision tree is easy, but creating it can be hard. Fortunately, Python supports many libraries that can quickly and efficiently build decision trees. Decision tree learning algorithms analyze the test data and use it to create the tree. Learning algorithms select the best splitting features and values (decision criteria) based on rules that discriminate data to the highest degree. (*Discriminating data* simply means that each split in the tree should help you move toward a class label.)

Early decision tree learning algorithms include ID3 (Iterative Dichotomiser 3) and C4.5. The *ID3 decision tree learning algorithm* uses a formula to calculate how much a split decreases randomness in data. This decrease in randomness metric is called *information gain.* Information gain is a simple metric that has limitations. Simply maximizing information gain can result in a feature that is too specific, such as a product number that only stores unique values. The *C4.5 decision tree learning algorithm* extended ID3 to use a gain ratio to smooth out some of the stark decisions of ID3.

A more recent decision tree learning algorithm commonly used today is CART (classification and regression tree). *CART* uses the Gini method to calculate a weighted sum of the *impurity* (a measure of the randomness of data in an attribute) of each split in the tree. The *Gini index* represents this impurity value. The algorithm selects the attribute with the smaller Gini index when comparing the Gini indexes of pairs of candidate splitting attributes. The math behind these techniques is beyond the scope of this book, but it's interesting to look at how the Python libraries you use in your code do their work.

After the decision tree learning algorithm identifies the best split points, it creates the nodes of the tree. After the tree gets built, you make a class prediction by evaluating the feature values of a new object using the decision criteria at each node. Eventually, you should reach a leaf node and assign the object's class to the class in that leaf node.

Understanding how the naïve Bayes algorithm works

Another common classification algorithm is the naïve Bayes algorithm. The *naïve Bayes* algorithm is based on Bayes theorem and is useful in classifying objects such as text and images. Many spam detection engines use the naïve Bayes algorithm or some variation of it. Naïve Bayes is popular because it is simple and fast. The technique determines the conditional probability of an outcome (membership in a class) by considering a prior state (feature values).

Two events are independent if the occurrence of one event has no effect on the occurrence of the other event. For example, if you flip a coin, the probability that the coin will land with the head's side facing up is ½ (0.5). If you flip the coin a second time, the probability that the coin will land with the head's side facing up is still 0.5, regardless of the previous flip result. Each time you flip the coin, the outcome is independent of any other coin flips.

Some events depend on prior events occurring. Suppose you have a toolbox full of screwdrivers, consisting of 10 Phillips-head and 10 slotted-head screwdrivers. If you reach into the toolbox and grab a random screwdriver, the probability you'll grab a slotted-head screwdriver is 10 out of 20, or 0.5. If you need a slotted-head screwdriver but you pulled out a Phillips-head screwdriver on your first attempt, you'll need to reach in and grab another screwdriver. Because now only 19 screwdrivers are left in the toolbox, the new probability of grabbing a slotted-head screwdriver is 10 out of 19, or 0.526. With fewer Phillips-head screwdrivers in the toolbox, your odds of grabbing a slotted-head screwdriver just went up a bit. The second probability is dependent on the prior event.

For large datasets, calculating conditional probabilities can get tedious. Fortunately, some interesting math proposed in the Bayes theorem can help. Figure 10-2 shows the Bayes theorem formula for calculating conditional probabilities.

FIGURE 10-2:
Bayes theorem calculation of conditional probability.

$$P(A|B) = \frac{P(B|A)\, P(A)}{P(B)}$$

To calculate the probability of an event A, given that a prior event B has already occurred (also called the probability of A given B) follow these steps:

1. **Calculate the probability of A (given B) and B both occurring.**

2. **Divide the results of Step 1 by the probability of B.**

The training process counts the instances of each feature value and calculates the probabilities of each one occurring. After all probabilities have been calculated, you can predict the class of a new object by determining the probability that the supplied feature values align to a specific class. In other words, the naïve Bayes algorithm returns the relative probability that an object should be assigned to a specific class.

Implementing naïve Bayes in Python takes a few more steps than implementing decision tree, but those steps are still straightforward. The following code, from the naiveBayes.py file, shows an example of implementing naïve Bayes using the iris dataset:

```
from sklearn import datasets
import matplotlib.pyplot as plt
import pandas as pd
```

```
from sklearn.model_selection import train_test_split
from sklearn.naive_bayes import GaussianNB
from sklearn.metrics import accuracy_score

iris = datasets.load_iris()
class_names = iris.target_names
iris_df=pd.DataFrame(iris.data, columns=iris.feature_names)
iris_df['target']=iris.target

X_train, X_test, y_train, y_test = train_test_split(iris_df[['sepal length
    (cm)', 'sepal width (cm)', 'petal length (cm)', 'petal width (cm)']],
    iris_df['target'], random_state=0)
nbClass = GaussianNB()
nbClass.fit(X_train, y_train)
y_predict = nbClass.predict(X_test)

print("Accuracy: {:.2f}".format(accuracy_score(y_test, y_predict)))
```

After loading the iris dataset, and assigning feature labels, you invoke the `train_test_split()` method to separate the dataset into training and testing partitions. You'll use part of the data to train the model and the rest of the data to test it. After splitting the dataset, you invoke the `GaussianNB()` method, followed by the `fit()` method to create and train the naïve Bayes model. Finally, the `predict()` method uses the test partition of the dataset to test the model. The `score()` method returns the accuracy of the naïve Bayes model you just trained. The output of this Python code is minimal:

```
Accuracy: 1.00
```

The output shows that the naïve Bayes model was correct 100 percent of the time! Unfortunately, very few models will ever be that good in real life. The iris dataset contains only 150 objects (rows), so it isn't a very big dataset. In spite of the small dataset size, this example of a naïve Bayes model does show that very high accuracy is possible.

Evaluating model effectiveness with diagnostics

Decision trees are easy to visualize and present to technical and non-technical people. One of the best ways to evaluate a newly built decision tree is to have a subject matter expert (SME) look at it to see if it makes sense. A good decision tree should be clear and easy to understand, at least by a domain SME. Paths through the tree should be distinct and lead to clearly identified leaf nodes. Ambiguity should be minimized, and any incorrect predictions should be explainable.

No default diagnostic exists for evaluating the naïve Bayes algorithm. Naïve Bayes is a simple and computationally efficient algorithm that works well with continuous or categorical data. Its main weakness is that it relies on each feature being conditionally independent. If two or more features depend on one another, the naïve Bayes algorithm will likely end up double counting the feature's effects, resulting in an overreliance on feature sets. Results will be skewed, and the model's accuracy will suffer. It is important to consider only independent features when using naïve Bayes.

Implementing Blockchain Classification Algorithms in Python

The previous Python model implementations in this chapter were built on the iris dataset. You can easily extend classification models to work with blockchain data. The only real changes you need to make for any analytics model to process blockchain data is to fetch the desired data and provide that data as input to your models. For each new model, you can either fetch blockchain data on demand or extract what you need ahead of time.

For the examples in this book, I assume you've already executed a process that fetches blockchain data and places it in an external repository. For our simple examples, we'll use CSV files for analytics model input. For your projects, you may choose to use a more sophisticated repository, such as a database, to store extracted blockchain data. Regardless of the approach you use, the most important initial step is to understand your blockchain data and identify the input data your models need.

In this section, you learn how to implement the decision tree and naïve Bayes algorithms using your supply chain blockchain data. You'll see that the examples are more complex than what you saw earlier in the chapter but still simple. After you're comfortable with the basics of each model, you should dig into the nuances to learn how to leverage each model's strengths for your organization's goals.

Defining model input data requirements

In every data analytics project, you must first identify and collect input data, and then clean it up. Because classification models are based on supervised learning algorithms, you'll need training data to build your model. Training data includes feature data for objects, along with the object's assigned class. The model learns by examining the supplied training data and how features relate to classification.

A well-trained model will recognize new data that you provide and be able to predict the correct class to which the new object belongs.

Although getting clean data from the start is possible, it isn't the norm. One of the most time-consuming steps in data analytics is cleaning your input data. The data you get may have multiple issues, each of which must be addressed. Here are a few of the most common reasons why input data might be less than perfect:

>> **Missing data:** Feature values or related objects are missing. For example, a participant definition is missing the participant's address, or an entire participant definition that a product references is missing. Either way, dependent data that a model requires is missing.

>> **Duplicate data:** Multiple objects (rows) in a dataset shouldn't refer to a unique entity. Having too much data can skew a model's effectiveness. Many model metrics depend on the model knowing how many unique objects exist in its input dataset.

>> **Errors:** Wrong or inaccurate feature values can negatively affect a model's accuracy. Sometimes it isn't easy to correct data errors, but when possible, you should fix errors or exclude objects with erroneous data.

>> **Out of range:** One subset of data errors is a feature that stores data that falls outside the defined range or list of valid values. All data acquisition software should aggressively validate input data before the data is stored, but this doesn't always happen. For a variety of reasons, invalid data can make its way into data repositories of all types.

>> **Incorrect format:** Data stored in an unsupported format can cause problems for analytics models. One of the most common issues you may encounter in this category is character data stored in features defined to store numeric data. If you encounter this type of issue, you'll need to either map data to a correct format or exclude the object.

>> **Inconsistent format:** A common problem when acquiring data from multiple sources is that each source may store data using different formats. Suppose a date feature has dates stored as eight numeric digits (02042020) and ten-character strings ("02/04/2020"). Although it's easy to see that both values refer to the same date, you'll need to align input data to use a single data format for your models to work correctly.

There are basically two approaches to cleaning data. You can either extract data, clean it, and provide your cleaned data as input to your models, or you can build the cleaning phase into your models. The two examples in the next section show you how to clean input data in your models. Regardless of the approach you use, the goal is to ensure that your models have valid data to provide the highest quality output possible.

Building your classification model dataset

Classification models make predictions based on existing features. For this chapter's examples, you look at information about TVs and try to determine which features buyers want. Because blockchain data isn't free (you have to pay to store data on the blockchain), you often won't find all the information your models need in blockchain blocks, so you'll use the review information for each TV to decide which TVs buyers like best. The classification model will try to determine the buyer's review rating based on TV features.

Many descriptive TV features aren't stored on the blockchain. We'll assume most TV descriptive attributes are stored in an off-chain repository. You'll need to find TV rating information in the blockchain, find the related off-chain TV features data, combine the related data, and store it in a new repository. You've already carried out this preliminary step and stored the combined data in the products. csv file, so you'll use the products.csv file as your input for classification models.

Reading and cleaning input data

An easy way to read data from a csv file into a Pandas dataset is to use the pandas. read_csv() method. However, you must do a little work on the data to get what your model will need. The classification models you use in this chapter need numeric input data. If some of your input data is not numeric, one solution is to map existing data to numeric data. That's the approach you learn in this chapter.

Figure 10-3 shows a portion of the products.csv file. Note that the values in the screenType and resolution columns are character data, not numeric data. You'll need to change the datatype of both columns to numeric before using the data as model input.

	column 14	column 15	column 16	column 17	column 18	column 19
1	dDesc	prodSKU	prodCat	screenSize	screenType	resolution
2	47inch HD LED	106702	TV	47	LED	HD
3	47inch HD LED	106702	TV	47	LED	HD
4	47inch HD LED	106702	TV	47	LED	HD
5	47inch HD LED	106702	TV	47	LED	HD
6	47inch HD LED	106702	TV	47	LED	HD
7	47inch HD LED	106702	TV	47	LED	HD
8	47inch HD LED	106702	TV	47	LED	HD
9	47inch HD LED	106702	TV	47	LED	HD
10	47inch HD LED	106702	TV	47	LED	HD
11	47inch HD LED	106702	TV	47	LED	HD

FIGURE 10-3: TV product data.

One of the easiest ways to handle categorical data type issues is to map alphabetic class labels to numeric indexes. In other words, make a list of all values in the source data and number each value. Then assign the number that corresponds to a specific label to the corresponding object.

For example, suppose each TV in the products.csv file has a value in the screen Type column of LED, QLED, or OLED. To translate the screenType column to a numeric type, you can assign 0 to all TVs with a screenType of LED, 1 to all QLED TVs, and 2 to all OLED TVs.

Python makes it easy to clean your data. To accomplish the tasks of mapping input data to a format your models can use, follow these steps:

1. Read the products.csv file into a temporary dataframe.

2. Convert the screenType and resolution features to Python lists.

3. Define functions to map an alphabetic feature value to an integer.

4. Read the products.csv file into the analytics dataframe, converting the screenType and resolution features to index values.

Here is the Python code, from the decisionTreeBlockchain.py file, to carry out each of the steps to map input data to an analytics dataframe:

```python
import pandas as pd

dfpreprocess = pd.read_csv('products.csv', usecols=['screenType','resolution'])
screenTypeList = dfpreprocess.screenType.unique().tolist()
resolutionList = dfpreprocess.resolution.unique().tolist()

fscreen = lambda x : screenTypeList.index(x)
fresolution = lambda x : resolutionList.index(x)

converter = {'screenType':fscreen,'resolution':fresolution}
df = pd.read_csv('products.csv', usecols=['screenSize','screenType',
    'resolution','hdmiPorts','usbPorts','reviewRating'],converters=converter)
```

After importing the pandas library, you read the products.csv file into the dfpreprocess dataframe. (Because you need only two features, you read only the screenType and resolution columns.) After reading the csv file, convert the input data into two lists, screenTypeList (list of unique screen types) and resolutionList (list of unique TV resolution values). You'll use these two lists to map your input character data to integer values.

Before you're ready to read data into the analytics dataframe, you must define the functions to map the raw character data in the screenType and resolution columns to integer data. You'll define two lambda functions to carry out the simple mapping, and then combine these two functions into a set named `converter`.

TECHNICAL STUFF

Note in the preceding Python code that we use lambda functions to assign `fscreen` and `fresolution`. A *lambda function* is a small anonymous function in Python that has no name, takes multiple input arguments, and consists of a single expression. Lambda functions are useful when you want to evaluate an expression and assign its resulting value without having to define a formal named function. In this program, lambda functions are convenient to call to handle the character-to-integer data mapping as you read data into the `df` dataframe.

The last step is to read the desired features from the `products.csv` file into the dataset, `df`, mapping `screenType` and `resolution` feature values to integers.

Splitting data into training and testing partitions

The next step in preparing your data for the classification model is to split your dataset into training and testing partitions. The training partition will be the data your model will use to learn how your feature data determines the object's classification (`reviewRating`). The testing partition evaluates the model's accuracy. In other words, you build the model using the training dataset partition and then use the testing partition data to see if the model predicts the correct classification. The percentage of correct predictions from the testing partition is the model's accuracy.

Here is the Python code, from the `decisionTreeBlockchain.py` file, to split the `df` dataframe into training and testing partitions:

```
from sklearn.model_selection import train_test_split


y = df.reviewRating
X = df.drop('reviewRating', axis=1)


X_train, X_test, y_train, y_test = train_test_split(X, y,test_size=0.2)
```

The first line imports `train_test_split` from `sklearn.model_selection`. (This line of code would normally be at the top of the Python program.) The next two lines separate the `df` dataframe into a set of input features, `X`, and the feature that contains each object's classification, `y`. The `y` dataframe contains only the `reviewRating` feature, and the `X` dataframe contains all other features.

Finally, the `train_test_split()` method splits the dataframes into four partitions, `X_train`, `X_test`, `y_train`, and `y_test`. The `train_test_split()` method put 20 percent of the original data in the test partitions and 80 percent in the training partitions. Now you're ready to train and test your models.

Developing your classification model code

The Python code I just presented loads blockchain data for either the decision tree or naïve Bayes analytics models. In this section, you learn how to use the data you've loaded to build both types of models and determine which one works best for your supply chain data.

Coding the decision tree model

One of the strengths of the decision tree model is that building the model results in an easy-to-visualize model. For purposes of instruction and documentation, a decision tree makes it easy to convey your model's purpose. The primary methods to build and visualize a decision tree are the `tree.DecisionsTreeClassifier()` and the `tree.plot_tree()` methods, which are both imported from the `sklearn` library. All you need to do in addition to calling these methods is set up the output parameters and render the figure.

Here is the Python code, from the `decisionTreeBlockchain.py` file, to build and visualize a decision tree based on supply chain blockchain data (this code continues the Python program from the preceding section):

```python
from sklearn import tree
import matplotlib.pyplot as plt

plt.figure(dpi = 300)
clf = tree.DecisionTreeClassifier(random_state=0).fit(X_train, y_train)

tree.plot_tree(clf, feature_names=['screenSize','screenType','resolution',
    'hdmiPorts','usbPorts'], filled=True)

plt.tight_layout()
plt.savefig('decisiontree.png', dpi = 300)
plt.show()

score = clf.score(X_test, y_test)
print(score)
```

After importing the required libraries, the first executable code in this segment is the `plt.figure()` method. This method sets the resolution of the generated figure to 300 dpi. Without this method, the library will use a default value of 100 dpi and generate a figure that is difficult to read.

REMEMBER

It's best practice to place all `import` statements at the top of your Python program. I included them here to show which libraries you'll need for this section of your code.

After setting up the figure resolution, the `tree.DecisionTreeClassifier().fit()` method examines the data you pass to the method, `X_train` and `y_train`, and builds a decision tree. After you build the decision tree, `clf`, you can create a visual representation of the tree by invoking the `tree.plot_tree()` method. In the preceding example, you provided the feature labels to make the tree depicted in the figure more readable.

The next three lines of Python code specify the layout type for the figure, save the rendered figure as a PNG file, and then display the decision tree in a window. After dismissing the figure window, the last two lines of code calculate the accuracy of the decision tree you just built and display the calculated score. Figure 10-4 shows the decision tree based on your supply chain blockchain data.

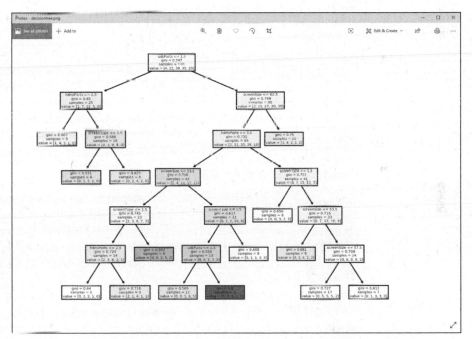

FIGURE 10-4: Decision tree based on supply chain blockchain data.

Figure 10-5 shows the program's output (the decision tree's score). Note that the accuracy (score) is 0.33333333333333, which means the decision tree is correct only one out of three times you use it to make a prediction. An accuracy of 33 percent isn't great. A decision tree can be very accurate, but only when you've selected the right features and have enough data to train it.

TIP

The complete dataset you use for the supply chain blockchain example contains only 150 products. For data that is clearly representative of distinct classes, 150 records may be enough. For example, the iris dataset consists of only 50 samples. For real datasets, you generally want to have many more than 150 entries.

If you want to play around with the decision tree model, drop some of the features it uses to build the tree. Additionally, change the percentage of data reserved for testing. Try those changes and see if your accuracy changes. Making small model changes demonstrates how important it is to explore as many options as possible. Your first choice of features may yield the best accuracy, but it's more likely that you'll have to experiment to get the right mix of features.

Coding the naïve Bayes model

The second classification model you learned about in this chapter is the naïve Bayes model. The purpose of a naïve Bayes model is the same as a decision tree model: accurately predict an object's class based on selected features. However, the naïve Bayes approach is different from the decision tree. Naïve Bayes models use probabilities to calculate predicted outcomes instead of a series of decisions.

The mathematical nature of naïve Bayes models makes rendering visualizations of the model more difficult. You can always create graphs of results, but constructing a figure of the process is harder than it is with a decision tree. Because visualization is not of major concern in a naïve Bayes model, the code to implement the model requires fewer lines than a decision tree. The initial setup and data import are the same as with the decision tree model.

After you load data into the dataframe and create the training and testing datasets, you simply build the model and display its accuracy. Here is the remaining Python code, from the naiveBayesBlockchain.py file, to build a naïve Bayes model on the supply chain blockchain data:

```
from sklearn.naive_bayes import GaussianNB
from sklearn.metrics import accuracy_score

nbClass = GaussianNB()
nbClass.fit(X_train, y_train)
y_predict = nbClass.predict(X_test)

print("Accuracy: {:.2f}".format(accuracy_score(y_test,y_predict)))
```

After importing the required libraries, you instantiate a new GaussianNB object, nbClass. Naïve Bayes can be implemented in multiple ways; I chose to use the implementation based on a *Gaussian*, or normal, distribution. Data that is normally distributed and fits a bell curve is referred to a Gaussian-distributed dataset. Figure 10-6 shows a Gaussian distribution. Note that the highest percentage of data points, 0.4 (40 percent) of all readings, occurs at the middle of the curve. Values that are higher or lower than the middle value occur less frequently as you move away from the middle. If your data maps well to a Gaussian distribution, a Gaussian naïve Bayes model is probably a good choice. If your data isn't distributed normally, a Gaussian naïve Bayes model may struggle to make accurate predictions.

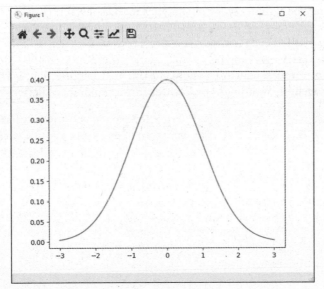

FIGURE 10-6: Gaussian (normal) distribution.

After instantiating the nbClass object, you invoke the nbClass.fit() method to train the model, passing it the X_train and y_train datasets. After you've trained your model, you can build a test dataset by invoking the nbClass.predict() method and passing it the X_test dataset.

The last line of Python code invokes `accuracy_score()` to determine the model's accuracy when tested on your test dataset, `X_test`. When you run the `naiveBayesBlockchain.py` program, notice that the only output is the accuracy value. Using your supply chain blockchain data, the naïve Bayes model is only 20 percent accurate, which is even worse than the decision tree. As with the decision tree model, play around with features and the train and test partitions to see if you can increase the accuracy.

Determining When Classification Fits Your Analytics Needs

Neither model produced very accurate predictions for the supply chain blockchain data. Low accuracy can be due to various reasons. In our case, the data didn't indicate clear classifications. In addition, the blockchain product dataset was small (only 150 TVs) and didn't exhibit clear correlations between features and eventual classifications. In a real project, you would assess correlations between features before the model building phase.

Learning about many types of analytics models, even if they don't all give you 99 percent accuracy, is important. Examining models that aren't clearly the best choices may lead you to discover aspects of your data you wouldn't have seen otherwise. This is part of the overall analytics process. In this case, classification didn't give much valuable insight. In the next chapter, you learn about another type of analysis that might be a better fit for making predictions with your data.

IN THIS CHAPTER

» **Capitalizing on trends**

» **Identifying indicators of future activity**

» **Choosing the right regression method for your data**

» **Determining the accuracy of your model**

» **Writing Python code to predict future outcomes**

Chapter **11**

Predicting the Future with Regression

C hapter 10 presented a couple ways to predict the future with analytics. The techniques you learn in Chapter 10 work well for *categorical outcomes,* which are situations in which the outcome, or result, is one item from a list of options. For example, if your model attempts to predict the best day of the week to purchase an airline ticket, the outcome would be one of the seven days of the week. You could use a decision tree or naïve Bayes approach to build your model.

Sometimes your outcome might not fit into a clean list of options. Suppose your model attempts to predict tomorrow's price for a specific stock. The answer could be any price. Data that represents values in a range is called *continuous data.* Analytics models that work well with continuous data are different than those you normally use for categorical data.

This chapter describes a different type of analytics model called a *regression model,* which examines training data and constructs a mathematical function to represent the data, based on features you supply. Once trained, each model derives an outcome prediction that matches training data outcomes. The resulting model allows you to provide newly sampled feature values and the function will return an outcome prediction.

You can use regression to predict future outcomes based on past behavior. Regression models can predict future prices, costs, or measurements of any type. Although a common use of regression is to predict continuous outcomes, a specific type of regression model works well with categorical data as well. In this chapter, you learn about regression models and how to build them in Python.

Analyzing Predictions and Relationships Using Popular Models

Regression analysis focuses on using statistics to estimate the relationship between independent variables and a dependent variable. In short, regression looks at a set of input feature values, also called *independent variables,* and makes a prediction of the outcome, or *dependent variable* value. A good regression function will accurately predict outcome based on the input feature values you provide.

The advantages of using regression are that your models are easy to use after you train them and visualizing output is generally easy. As with all analytics models, the most challenging parts of the process are determining the best features to use and keeping models current as your dataset changes. As you collect more data, many dataset trends change over time, which change any model's prediction accuracy.

Delivering valuable knowledge with regression analysis

To build a regression model, you start with training data and determine a function that best represents your data. The accuracy of your model directly depends on the quality of your training data. If you use too small a partition of data to build your model, its accuracy can be all over the place. As with other analytics models, a popular technique is to split a training dataset into two partitions, one for training and the other for testing. The training dataset should include a reasonable representation of expected "real" data, along with observed outcomes.

The regression-model-building algorithm will examine the training data and create a function that best represents the relationship between dependent and independent variables. After training, you use the other partition of your data for testing. You run the regression function with input-testing data to compare the prediction with the observed outcome from the testing data. You can use the testing data to evaluate how well (or poorly) your regression model matches observed outcomes in your testing dataset partition.

The accuracy of any regression model depends on a careful balance of selecting features that have the most effect on outcome and basing the model on reasonably distributed data. Regression models tend to work well for data that closely aligns with a normal distribution. Although normal distribution is not a prerequisite for regression model use, datasets that include many outliers and other anomalies can make building models of any type more challenging.

Examining popular regression techniques

The most common types of regression models are linear regression and logistic regression. *Linear regression* is a common model for predicting continuous outcomes. When you have one or more *features,* or independent input variables, a linear regression model can predict an outcome based on the values of your selected features.

For example, suppose you're helping student musicians prepare for honor band tryouts. You've collected historical data on how many hours a week each student practiced, whether the student was accepted in the honor band, and what audition score each student earned. As you would expect, there is a linear correlation between hours of practice and audition score; the more a student practiced each week, the better score that student earned at his or her audition. A linear regression model can predict any student's audition score if you know how many hours that student practices each week.

TIP

The correlation between practice hours and honor band audition score is basic and far too simplistic for use in real life. In a real scenario, other factors, such as experience, talent, quality of education, and even disposition, play a part in the earned audition score. Regression models can take all these factors into account by including them in the regression function. Our simple example has only one dependent and one independent variable, but real models almost always have more independent variables.

The other common type of regression model is logistic regression. Instead of predicting a final audition score (which is a continuous outcome prediction), you may only want to know whether a student is likely to be accepted into the honor band based on the hours of practice each week. That outcome is categorical because the model needs to predict only a yes or no value. *Logistic regression models* are optimized to return results that predict outcome categories. Categorical outcome determination is just another way to describe classification. In the case of yes/no prediction, you're determining into which of two classes a new object is likely to belong.

REMEMBER

You see the naïve Bayes and decision tree classification models in Chapter 10. Logistic regression is another classification model you can use. The best approach is to evaluate multiple types of models and choose the one that gives you the most accurate results.

Visualizing linear data

A linear regression model is built on the concept that as the number of dataset observations increase, the outcomes of dependent variables tend to approach, or regress towards, some relative mean value. A linear relationship exists between dependent and independent values when a plot of the mean values appears on a graph as a line. The mean value in a linear regression model is not a single value but a range of values represented as a line drawn through a set of plotted data that best represents that data. Figure 11-1 shows an example of data that visualizes as a linear relationship between dependent variable, x, and independent variables (features), y.

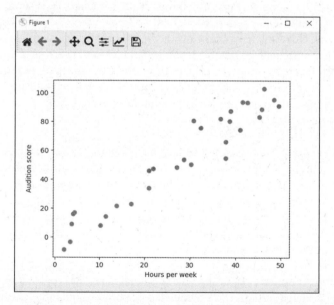

FIGURE 11-1:
Data exhibiting a linear relationship.

Figure 11-1 shows randomly created x and y values that demonstrate a linear relationship. Here is the Python code (linearData.py) to create a random dataset of linearly related data:

```
import numpy as np
import matplotlib.pyplot as plt


x = 50 * np.random.random((30, 1))
y = 0.5 * x + 1.0 + np.random.normal(size=x.shape)


ax = plt.axes()
ax.scatter(x, y)


ax.set_xlabel('x')
ax.set_ylabel('y')


plt.show()
```

The first two lines of the Python code import the `numpy` and `matplotlib.pyplt` libraries. The next two lines populate the x array with random values between 0 and 50 and the y array with corresponding values that include some "noise" that locates each point a small random distance from a perfect line. The remaining lines of code set the axes and labels, and then render the plot.

Looking at the graph in Figure 11-1, it's easy to see that the data is generally organized as a line. The points aren't all on a straight line, but they're close to a line so you can draw through the middle of the data. A linear regression model considers the data points you see in Figure 11-1 and constructs a line, called a *regression line*, that is closest to as many of the points as possible. The result of a linear regression model is the function that represents the regression line.

Visualizing categorical data

A logistic regression model predicts which class an object is most likely to belong to. Suppose the number of hours a student practices each week is a strong indicator of whether that student would pass the audition for honor band. Students who practice more than 25 hours each week get in (category 1), while those who practice fewer than 25 hours per week do not make it (category 0). Figure 11-2 shows a plot of simple categorical data.

Figure 11-2 shows randomly created x values and y values that depend on the generated x values (where y = 1 when x > 25, else x = 0). Here is the Python code (`categoricalData.py`) to create a random dataset of categorical data:

```
import numpy as np
import matplotlib.pyplot as plt
```

```
x = 50 * np.random.random((30, 1))
y = np.where(x<25,0,1)

ax = plt.axes()
ax.scatter(x, y)

ax.set_xlabel('Hours per week')
ax.set_ylabel('Audition score')

plt.show()
```

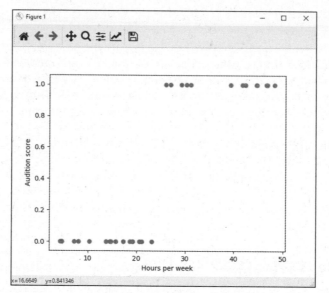

FIGURE 11-2:
Data exhibiting a categorical relationship.

The first two lines of the Python code import the `numpy` and `matplotlib.pyplt` libraries. The next two lines populate the x array with random values between 0 and 50 and the y array with corresponding values based on whether the x value is greater than 25 or not. Calculating the y values based on the x value artificially associated 25 or more hours per week of practice with success and less than 25 hours per week with failure. The remaining lines of code set the axes, set the labels, and then render the plot.

As you can see in Figure 11-2, the data is separated into *levels*, or steps, unlike the linear relationship you see in Figure 11-1. Each level in a logistic regression model visualization (the horizontal lines of data points) represents a classification prediction.

Describing how linear regression works

A *regression line*, which is the visual representation of a linear regression model, represents the average of the minimum distance between observed dependent variable data and the predicted dependent variable data. In other words, your regression model's function, f(x), will return a predicted value for y when you provide a value for x. Each pair of values, (x,y), provides the coordinates of a single point.

Most of the points you plot on a graph should be close to the regression line. Perfect data points will all lie on the regression line, but in real life most data points lie just off the regression line but within a distance to the regression line called the error, or residual. The *residual* is the difference between an observed value (x, y) and the value your model predicts (x, f(x)). The idea is to build a model where the cumulative residuals are as small as possible.

TECHNICAL STUFF

In this book, you concentrate on single values of x. In reality, linear regression models (or any analytics models) can handle multiple values, or features, of x. Models that take into account multiple features are far more useful than those that focus on simple relationships between two features. So, think of x as being an array of values, as opposed to a simple variable that holds only a single feature's value. A regression model based on a single variable is called a *simple linear regression* and results in a regression line. A regression model that includes more than one independent variable is called a *multiple linear regression* and results in a different visualization, such as a parabola.

Because a regression line is just an estimation of data samples, it will rarely be perfect. The best linear regression model will be a line that results in predictions that are overall closer to actual observations than any other line. One of the most common methods used to build a linear regression model is *Ordinary Least Squares (OLS)*, which is an iterative approach that evaluates functions based on supplied independent variables. For each selected function, the process evaluates that function over supplied values of x and compares the result with supplied results (supplied values of y). The process calculates the square of the distance between the observed point and the predicted point (that is, the value of the function, f(x)).

The key to a good regression model is the regression function. In its simplest sense, a regression model is expressed as follows:

$$y = \beta_0 + \beta_1 x + \varepsilon$$

where β is some constant and ε is the error term. This equation may look familiar. If you ignore the error term you can restate the preceding equation as the point-slope form of a line:

$$y = mx + b$$

In the point-slope formula of a line, m is the slope (the same term as β_1 in the linear equation), and b is the y-intercept (the same as the independent constant β_0 in the linear equation). The OLS method will result in a set of points that form a line. After you know at least two points on that line, you can represent the line as an equation that can be expressed in the point-slope form of a line. After you have the point-slope form of your line, you have the regression function. But don't worry — you don't have to do all that work manually. Python libraries will do it for you!

Here is Python code (linearRegression.py) that builds on the code you saw earlier in the chapter (linearData.py) that just showed data in a linear organization. The code in linearRegression.py builds a linear regression model by fitting a line to the data, and then visualizing the regression line:

```python
import numpy as np
import matplotlib.pyplot as plt
from sklearn.linear_model import LinearRegression

x = 50 * np.random.random((30, 1))
y = 2 * x + 10.0 * np.random.normal(size=x.shape)

model = LinearRegression().fit(x, y)

x_new = np.linspace(0, 50, 100)
y_new = model.predict(x_new[:, np.newaxis])

ax = plt.axes()
ax.scatter(x, y)
ax.plot(x_new, y_new)

ax.set_xlabel('Hours per week')
ax.set_ylabel('Audition score')

plt.show()
```

The first three lines of the Python code import the numpy, matplotlib.pyplt, and sklearn.linear_model libraries. The next two lines populate the x array with random values between 0 and 50, and the y array with corresponding values that include some "noise" that locates each point a small random distance from a perfect line.

The next line of code instantiates a new linear regression model named model and fits the regression function to the test data. The code then creates two arrays: One (x_new) contains the numbers 1 to 50, and the other (y_new) contains the predicted scores that correspond to each x_new value. The remaining lines of code set the axes, set the labels, and then render the plot for the x, y, x_new, and y_new data. Figure 11-3 shows the visualization of linear data and the regression line fitted to the supplied data.

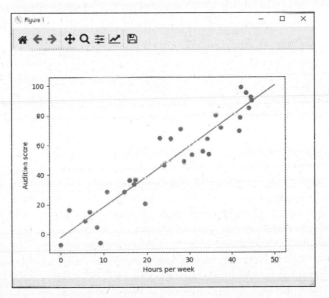

FIGURE 11-3:
Linear regression
model
visualization.

Note that the visualization is little more than adding a line through the data. However, it takes effort to figure out the best line to draw.

The regression equation just shown is for a single independent variable (that is, evaluating the effect of a single feature on some outcome). In real life you'll likely want to examine how multiple features affect an outcome. Linear regression can handle multiple dependent variables. The general form of a multivariable regression equation is as follows:

$$y = \beta_0 + \beta_1 x_1 + \beta_2 x_2 + \ldots + \beta_{p-1} x_{p-1} + \varepsilon$$

Visualizing multiple dependent variables is more difficult than just plotting x and y values. Later in this chapter, you see how to handle assessing multivariate linear regression models without simple visualizations.

Describing how logistic regression works

Whereas the visualization of a simple linear regression is a straight line, the visualization of a logistic model is a curve that looks like stair steps. Each step represents a different class. Logistic regression is a classification method that you can use with the methods in Chapter 10 to predict the class of objects. Unlike linear regression, which can be used for interpolation and limited extrapolation, logistic regression cannot extrapolate beyond the defined classes. A *logistic regression model* predicts the class an object belongs to, along with a relative probability of the prediction.

The simplest implementation of logistic regression predicts class membership in one of two classes. A simple logistic regression model, or binary logistic regression model, predicts the probability of an object belonging to one of two classes and then assigns the object to the class with the higher probability.

Logistic regression involves two main parts: the regression equation and the probability calculation of an event. The regression equation is equivalent to the one used in linear regression:

$$y = \beta_0 + \beta_1 x_1 + \beta_2 x_2 + \ldots + \beta_{p-1} x_{p-1} + \varepsilon$$

The difference is that in linear regression, this equation results in a distinct prediction value. In the case of logistic regression, you don't want output expressed as a value in a continuous range. You want the result to be a class label. To accomplish binary (or other categorical) output, the output of the regression equation is most commonly evaluated under a sigmoid function.

A *sigmoid function* rapidly assumes the value of either 0 or 1, depending on the variance above or below a threshold value. In the general sigmoid function shown in Figure 11-4, an input value > 0.0 returns a class probability of 1.0 (true) and an input value < 0.0 returns a class probability of 0.0 (false). As input values approach 0.0, the sigmoid function returns a class probability indicating the closeness to the most likely class.

Because logistic regression has more fundamental components that linear regression models, building a logistic regression model takes more effort. When you're using libraries or tools to build models, more effort generally means it takes more time to build more complex models.

Another difference between linear and logistic regression models is that with linear regression, you can directly observe outcome values of y. By contrast, outcome values aren't directly observed with logistic regression models. Rather, outcomes are expressed indirectly as the probability that independent variable values will result in a distinct class assignment.

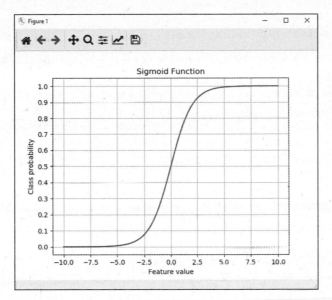

FIGURE 11-4:
Sigmoid function.

Logistic regression model building commonly uses techniques such as maximum likelihood estimation (MLE) to calculate probability outcomes for independent variable values. MLE is interesting to unpack but is beyond the scope of this book.

REMEMBER

Just remember that linear regression returns a predicted value and logistic regression returns the probability that the provided features will align the feature set with a specific class.

Here is Python code (logisticRegression.py) that builds a logistic regression model by fitting a stair-stepped line to the data, and then visualizing the regression line:

```python
import numpy as np
import matplotlib.pyplot as plt
from sklearn.linear_model import LogisticRegression
from sklearn.metrics import confusion_matrix


X = 50 * np.random.random((30, 1))
y = np.where(X<25,0,1)


model = LogisticRegression(solver='lbfgs', random_state=0).fit(X, y.ravel())
X_new = np.linspace(0, 50, 100)
y_new = model.predict(X_new[:, np.newaxis])


ax = plt.axes()
ax.scatter(X, y)
ax.plot(X_new, y_new)
```

```
ax.set_xlabel('Hours per week')
ax.set_ylabel('Audition score')

plt.show()

print('Classes: ',model.classes_)
print ('Coefficient of determination:', model.score(X,y))
print ('Coefficients:', model.coef_)
print ('Intercept:', model.intercept_)
```

The first four lines of the Python code import the `numpy`, `matplotlib.pyplt`, `sklearn.linear_model`, and `sklearn.metrics` libraries. The next two lines populate the x array with random values between 0 and 50 and the y array with corresponding values based on whether the x value is greater than 25 or not. Calculating the y values based on the x value artificially associated 25 or more hours per week of practice with success and less than 25 hours per week with failure.

The next line of code instantiates a new logistic regression model named `model` and fits the regression function to the test data. The code then creates two arrays: one (`X_new`) contains the numbers 1 to 50, and the other (`y_new`) contains the predicted scores that correspond to each `X_new` value. The remaining lines of code set the axes and labels, render the plot for the x, y, x_new, and y_new data, and then display the model diagnostics. Figure 11-5 shows the visualization of logistic data and the regression line fitted to the supplied data.

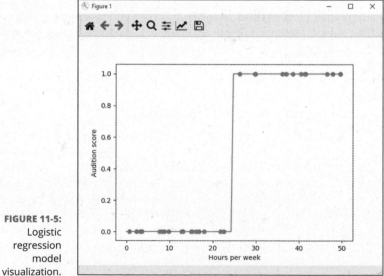

FIGURE 11-5:
Logistic regression model visualization.

Evaluating model effectiveness with diagnostics

Evaluating any model is necessary to determine whether or not its output is meaningful. Relying on inconsequential results always increases organizational risk. Businesses are unlikely to invest for very long in analytics efforts that fall short of expectations. In addition to being able to provide results, you need to be able to defend those results and explain why they're valid.

There are many more diagnostic techniques than the ones I can cover in this book. Instead, you look at a few simple diagnostic techniques to determine whether your models are reliable.

Determining effectiveness of linear regression models

Evaluating linear regression models starts before building any model. Always assess and visualize the data you're planning to analyze to see if it exhibits a linear relationship. If your data doesn't look something Figure 11-1, it might not be a good candidate for a linear regression model.

Even if your data doesn't appear to exhibit a linear relationship, consider re-scaling your data first. Suppose you want to compare temperature readings from different sensors. If some sensors use the Celsius scale and others use the Fahrenheit scale, any linear relationships may be obscured. You'll see this difficulty anytime you incorporate data collected in different scales or bases. It may help to experiment with scales conversions or even alternate presentation. If one axis varies much more than the other axis, you could try converting the former to a log scale. Sometimes you can see interesting relationships just by converting or normalizing input data.

Assuming your data is linearly related, the next step is to evaluate how reliable your model is for your predictions. Another way to state this is to determine how much you can rely on your model's predictions. One metric to measure a model's reliability is the coefficient of determination. The *coefficient of determination*, or *goodness of fit*, provides a number between 0.0 and 1.0 that indicates how well your model fits your data. The closer the coefficient of determination is to 1.0, the better your model. Many Python libraries provide the coefficient of determination by invoking the score() method on the model. You see the score() method used in the next section.

Determining effectiveness of logistic regression models

The coefficient of determinant from the preceding section is an effective diagnostic for logistic regression as well as linear regression. Because logistic regression generally returns a binary class result, four responses are possible:

>> **True positive:** A prediction of true is accurate.

>> **True negative:** A prediction of false is accurate.

>> **False positive:** A prediction of true is incorrect. (The correct classification is false.)

>> **False negative:** A prediction of false is incorrect. (The correct classification is true.)

An easy way to view these four categories of model predictions is to use a confusion matrix. A *confusion matrix* shows a 2x2 matrix of prediction results, with the count of each type of response from the preceding list. The prediction process makes a prediction for each set of features and compares the predicted result with the observed class. A confusion matrix helps determine a model's accuracy (or inaccuracy). You can add a confusion matrix to your Python output with the following single line of code:

```
print ('confusion matrix: ', confusion_matrix(y,model.predict(X)))
```

Figure 11-6 shows the output of the `logisticRegression.py` Python code, including the confusion matrix.

FIGURE 11-6: Logistic regression model visualization including the confusion matrix.

You can see from Figure 11-6 that this model results in no false positive or false negative results, and 13 true positive and 17 true negative results. The lack of any false results makes this a very good model (and one you'd be lucky to find in the real world).

Implementing Regression Algorithms in Python

Applying regression models to blockchain data is easy. All you have to do is identify and extract the data you need from the blockchain, and then use Python libraries to carry out the analytics. In Chapters 9 and 10, you see how to use blockchain data for analytics. Regression models are no different when it comes to input requirements. After you've identified and extracted the data you need, the analytics phase is straightforward.

Defining model input data requirements

In Chapters 9 and 10, you identify blockchain data, extract that data, and clean it to get it ready for your analytics models. Remember that clean and complete data is a prerequisite for any model — not just regression models. The time you spend making sure your data is appropriate for your model will pay tremendous dividends when interpreting analytics model output.

Pay close attention to the data input requirements discussion from Chapter 10. The checklist items will help you determine if your data is ready for analysis or needs some preprocessing. The accuracy of your models depends on the cleanliness of your data. Although this may seem redundant, its importance can't be understated.

Building your regression model dataset

To evaluate regression models on blockchain data, you'll use the product dataset generated in Chapter 5, which contains both continuous and categorical outcomes. The dataset will be used for linear regression to predict the best manufacturer's suggested retail price (MSRP) based on product criteria, and again for logistic regression to predict a customer satisfaction rating based on product features.

Developing your regression model code

You've already learned how to create linear and logistic regression models using generated data. In this section, you find out how to use Python to build linear and logistic regression models on your product dataset.

Coding the linear regression model

One of the strengths of the simple linear regression model is that it results in an easy-to-visualize model. For purposes of instruction and documentation, a simple linear regression model makes it easy to convey your model's intent and use. The primary methods to build and visualize a simple linear regression model are the LinearRegression(), predict() and plot() methods. All you need to do in addition to calling these methods is set up the output parameters and render the figure.

Here is the Python code (linearRegressionBlockchain.py) to build and visualize a linear regression model based on supply chain blockchain data. This code continues the Python program from the previous section:

```python
from sklearn.linear_model import LinearRegression
import pandas as pd
import numpy as np
import matplotlib.pyplot as plt

df = pd.read_csv('products.csv', usecols=['screenSize','msrp'])

y = df.msrp
X = df.drop('msrp', axis=1)

model = LinearRegression().fit(X, y)

X_new = np.linspace(40, 70, 60)
y_new = model.predict(X_new[:, np.newaxis])

ax = plt.axes()
ax.scatter(X, y)
ax.plot(X_new, y_new)

ax.set_xlabel('Screen Size')
ax.set_ylabel('MSRP')

plt.show()
```

```
print ('Coefficient of determination:', model.score(X,y))
print ('Coefficients:', model.coef_)
print ('Intercept:', model.intercept_)
```

The first four lines of the Python code import the libraries you need for this model. The next line reads the products.csv dataset file (only the 'screenSize' and 'msrp' features) into a dataframe. The next two lines separate the features into X and y arrays. The next line of code instantiates a new linear regression model named model and fits the regression function to the data.

The following two lines of the code create two arrays: X_new contains the numbers 40 through 70, and y_new contains the predicted scores that correspond to each X_new value. The remaining lines of code set the axes and labels, render the plot for the x, y, x_now, and y_new data, and display the model diagnostics.

Figure 11-7 shows the visualization of linear data and the regression line fitted to the supplied data.

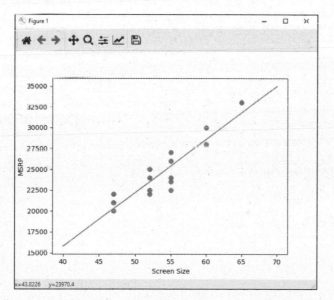

FIGURE 11-7:
Linear regression model visualization based on supply chain blockchain data.

Coding the logistic regression model

Logistic regression models provide an easy to interpret visualization, much like its close cousin, the linear regression model. For purposes of instruction and documentation, a logistic regression model also makes it easy to convey your model's intent and use. The primary methods to build and visualize a logistic regression model are the LogisticRegression(), predict() and plot() methods. All you need to do in addition to calling these methods is set up the output parameters and render the figure.

Here is the Python code (logisticRegressionBlockchain.py) to build and visualize a logistic regression model based on supply chain blockchain data. This code continues the Python program from the preceding section:

```python
from sklearn.linear_model import LogisticRegression
from sklearn.metrics import confusion_matrix
import pandas as pd
import numpy as np
import matplotlib.pyplot as plt

dfpreprocess = pd.read_csv('products.csv', usecols=['screenType','resolution'])

screenTypeList = dfpreprocess.screenType.unique().tolist()
fscreen = lambda x : screenTypeList.index(x)
converter = {'screenType':fscreen}

df = pd.read_csv('products.csv', usecols=['screenType','reviewRating'],
    converters=converter)

y = df.reviewRating
X = df.drop('reviewRating', axis=1)

model = LogisticRegression(solver='lbfgs', random_state=0).fit(X, y)

X_new = np.linspace(40, 70, 60)
y_new = model.predict(X_new[:, np.newaxis])

ax = plt.axes()
ax.scatter(X, y)
ax.plot(X_new, y_new)

ax.set_xlabel('Screen Type')
ax.set_ylabel('review Rating')

plt.show()

print ('Coefficient of determination:', model.score(X,y))
print ('Coefficients:', model.coef_)
print ('Intercept:', model.intercept_)
```

The first five lines of the Python code import the libraries you need for this model. The next line reads the 'productscsv' dataset file (only the 'screenSize' and 'resolution' features) into a dataframe. The next five lines define converter functionality to map 'resolution' labels to integer values. The following three lines read the product.csv data into a dataframe, converting the resolution data in the process, and then separate the dataframe into two arrays, X and y.

The next line of code instantiates a new logistic regression model named model and fits the regression function to the data. The following two lines of the code then create two arrays: One (X_new) contains the numbers 40 through 70, and the other (y_new) contains the predicted scores that correspond to each X_new value. The remaining lines of code set the axes, set the labels, render the plot for the x, y, x_new, and y_new data, and then display the model diagnostics.

Figure 11-8 shows the visualization of categorical data and the regression line fitted to the supplied data.

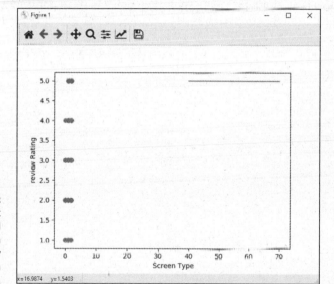

FIGURE 11-8:
Logistic regression model visualization based on supply chain blockchain data.

Determining When Regression Fits Your Analytics Needs

Regression models can provide rich predictions under the right circumstances. It's important that you evaluate your models on your existing data and periodically test your assertions. *Fluid accuracy* (accuracy that may change as input data changes) can exist for various reasons. In a real-life project, you would assess correlations between features before proceeding to the model-building phase, and then again as frequently as is feasible. The goal is to assess your models frequently enough to demonstrate zero, or minimal, changes in your model's accuracy as input data changes. As long as you assess frequently enough to demonstrate minimal accuracy differences, you're monitoring changes well.

It's important to learn about many types of analytics models, even if they don't all give you 99 percent accuracy. Examining models that aren't clearly the best choices sometimes leads you to discover aspects of your data you wouldn't have seen otherwise. Exploring alternative models is part of the overall analytics process. In this case, classification didn't provide much valuable insight. In the next chapter, you learn about another type of analysis that might be a better fit for making predictions with your data.

REMEMBER

The preceding paragraph should seem familiar. It's similar to the text that ends Chapter 10. It's as pertinent here as it is in the other chapter. Remember that data analytics is all about providing value. You don't have to reinvent the wheel — you just have to show how well it rolls.

IN THIS CHAPTER

» **Examining how behavior changes over time**

» **Looking beyond seasonal trends**

» **Learning from data cycles**

» **Identifying trends despite fluctuations**

» **Writing Python code to analyze time series data**

Chapter **12**

Analyzing Blockchain Data over Time

You learn about identifying clusters of data in Chapter 9, how to predict an object's classification in Chapter 10, and how to predict future activity with regression in Chapter 11. All three chapters examine data as monolithic datasets. That's not bad but looking at data as being the same doesn't always help to tell the whole story. In many cases, your data depends on time. For example, sales occur at specific times on specific days. Each transaction's timestamp may be hiding its own keys to understanding your data.

If you've ever used a coffee shop as an alternate office, you've probably noticed that sometimes it's busy and other times it's not. In the case of any retail business, time affects employee workload and should affect a business's capacity planning. If you don't take date and time into account, you could miss important information in your data. For example, what day and time is best for receiving products and restocking a store? In most cases, receiving and restocking should correspond with known times of low customer activity. Visualizing activity over time as activity cycles can help with staffing for busy and slack times.

On the other hand, examining time-based activity and its associated variations can make trend identification more difficult. To model data in which observations are collected over time, you can use *time series analysis*. This type of analysis attempts to predict future behavior even though features are dependent on time and seasonal variations exist. In this chapter, you learn about time series analysis techniques and how to implement them in Python.

Analyzing Time Series Data Using Popular Models

A *time series* is an ordered sequence of data points (feature values) separated by equal amounts of time. The standard representation of a time series is the equation

$$Y = a + bX$$

REMEMBER

If you think this equation looks familiar to the regression equation in Chapter 11, you're right! This equation is the same as a simple regression equation, except time is now the dependent variable.

The primary difference between time series and regression analysis is the inclusion of a time feature. Outcomes for a time series analysis model are dependent on time and potentially other features. Time dependency has the effect of spreading out observations chronologically, potentially obscuring trend or seasonality aspects of the data. Time series analysis helps you see through the time effects to get to the meaningful information in your data.

One of the more difficult aspects of analyzing time series data is isolating the various components of your data. Time series data is made up of four main components:

>> **Trend:** The consistent movement of dependent feature values over time. Trends indicate steady movement in a single direction, such as increasing sales or decreasing costs.

>> **Seasonality:** Any periodic fluctuations in related data that occurs in regular patterns. Seasonality commonly occurs annually, monthly, weekly, or with some other easily identifiable regularity.

>> **Cyclic:** Periodic fluctuation that can't be explained as a periodic variance. Cyclic variations generally result from unforeseen events, such as economic changes or natural disasters.

>> **Random:** Remaining behavior after trends, seasonality, and other cyclic variations are filtered out. The goal of time series analysis is to clear out any noise and make it easier to visualize and analyze random influences.

Analyzing time series data follows the same basic steps as other analytics approaches, with the addition of flattening non-random influences before selecting the best model.

Delivering valuable knowledge with time series analysis

To build a time series model, you start with raw data and examine it to identify any trends, seasonality, and cyclic variations. In most cases, you'll look for any variations in the specific order just listed. After smoothing your data by removing the effects of variations, your results will likely look like basic regression model input.

At this point you follow a process similar to building a regression model by determining a function that best represents your data. To best assess your model's accuracy, you should split your dataset into training and testing partitions. The accuracy of your model directly depends on the quality of your training data and the way you choose to smooth out any variations.

As with building regression models (see Chapter 11), in the process of building a time series model, you examine your training data and create a function that best represents the relationship between dependent and independent variables. After training, you use the other partition of your data for testing. You run the time series function with input-testing data to compare the prediction with the observed outcome from the testing data. You can use the testing data to evaluate how well (or poorly) your time series model matches observed outcomes in your testing dataset partition.

The usefulness of any time series model depends on a careful balance of selecting the features that have the most effect on results (outcomes), providing your model with reasonably distributed data, and applying smoothing techniques to address known variations. Although normal distribution is not a prerequisite for regression model use, datasets that include many outliers and other anomalies can make building models of any type more challenging.

Examining popular time series techniques

Most time series analysis techniques are based on the *ARIMA (autoregressive integrated moving average)* model. ARIMA has multiple parts, and a complete dive into the model's foundation is beyond the scope of this book. Because you're learning how to build and use analytics models, we'll focus on the basics.

If you want to learn more about the ARIMA model or time series models in general, take a look at *Python for Data Science For Dummies,* 2nd Edition, and *Data Science Programming All-in-One For Dummies* (Wiley).

Three main ideas are bundled into ARIMA: differencing, autoregression, and moving average. *Differencing* means to subtract one or more previous values from the current value to flatten your results. *Autoregression* refers to the idea that in a series of data points, any point (observed data) is dependent on previous data and some defined modifier. Autoregression implies that you can describe a sequence of observations as a linear trend that varies as some variable changes, such as time. Another way to look at autoregression is that it maps data to a linear regression model that uses time as its primary horizontal axis for visualization.

The other main idea in ARIMA is the moving average. A *moving average* helps to smooth cyclic variances that occur often in time series data. For example, Figure 12-1 shows the AXP (American Express) closing stock prices in the first seven months of 2011.

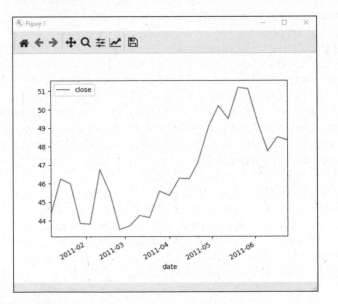

FIGURE 12-1: AXP closing stock prices.

Many datasets that you can use for your own projects are available online. Go to your favorite Internet search engine and search for *free datasets.* You can get the dataset with historical stock prices that I used for Figure 12-1 at `https://archive.ics.uci.edu/ml/datasets/Dow+Jones+Index`.

When you build an ARIMA model later in the chapter, you'll need to provide three parameters:

>> **p:** Autoregression term

>> **d:** Differencing value required to make the time sequence stationary

>> **q:** Moving average term

Each of these terms may be different for each dataset and feature selection. You'll often have to experiment to find the right values.

You can see in Figure 12-1 a trend toward higher stock prices, but considerable variation exists. You might be wondering if the upward trend will continue. One way to help answer this question is to look at an autocorrelation plot.

The Pandas Python library provides an easy way to create an autocorrelation visualization. Figure 12-2 shows a simple autocorrelation plot of the AXP stock prices for the first seven months of 2011.

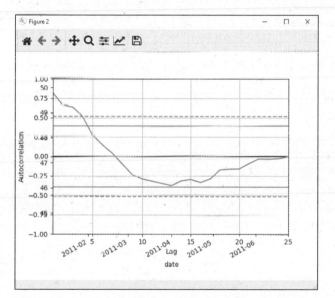

FIGURE 12-2:
AXP stock price
autocorrelation.

The two sets of parallel lines in Figure 12-2 indicate how well the closing stock price is correlated with the date. An autocorrelation plot is useful to determine how random your data appears to be after you address the time factor. The two dotted lines show the boundaries for a 99 percent confidence level. The two solid lines show the boundaries for the 95 percent confidence level. If the plotted line stays within either of the two parallel lines, your underlying data is random, which is good. Autocorrelation near 0 means the raw plot's variances can be largely explained by the passing of time.

On the other hand, if much of your autocorrelation plot falls outside the confidence bands, something else is probably affecting your outcomes. In the case of Figure 12-2, observations after February 2011 appear to be well correlated with dates. In fact, the closing price data gets more stable as time goes on.

Visualizing time series results

You've already seen two visualizations of time series data, but you haven't seen much about differencing. Visualization is one of the best techniques to find the best ARIMA parameter values for p, q, and d. The second parameter, the d parameter, is the differencing value. The easiest way to find the best differencing value is to visualize increasing orders of differencing until the autocorrelation corresponding to a chosen differencing order starts to thrash. *Thrashing* is a condition in which values frequently oscillate between positive and negative values.

Figures 12-1 and 12-2 show the original data series and its autocorrelation. Figure 12-3 shows the plot of the difference of each observed data point and its previous data point, previous minus two data points, and previous minus three data points. The three different plot lines show how each differencing value affects the output. As you can see in Figure 12-3, each differencing value appears to be nearly superimposed on the others, which indicates that an increasing differencing level doesn't materially change the results. So in this case, a differencing value (d) of 0 should be optimal.

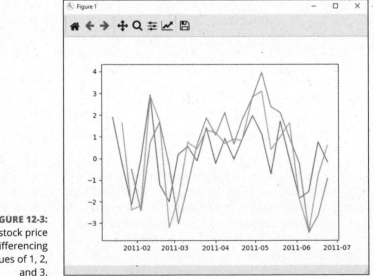

FIGURE 12-3: AXP stock price differencing values of 1, 2, and 3.

The remaining values (p and q) require tuning as well to find the right ones. In many cases, values of p = 1 and q = 3 provide decent starting results. Try building models with different p, q, and d values and test each one to see which values provide the most accurate results.

Figure 12-4 shows the results of building an ARIMA model with the input parameters of p = 1, d = 0, and q = 3. This model gives you the initial prediction platform to determine future outcomes.

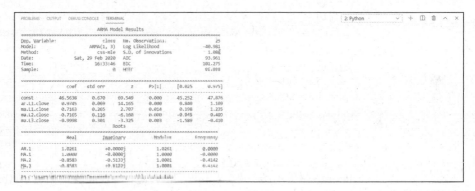

FIGURE 12-4: ARIMA Model build results.

This summary contains a lot of information, so we'll focus on only one column, P>|z| data. The data in the P>|z| column shows the p-value of each coefficient. If any of these values is larger than 0.05, that coefficient could provide unreliable results, and your model will probably not be useful. Time series ARIMA models often involve multiple features, so the P>|v| column can help determine if dropping a feature may improve accuracy. Figure 12-4 shows that the moving average of the close feature (at 1, 2, and 3 lags) shows acceptable p-values (< 0.05). The p-values give us confidence that this model is worth pursuing.

If it were easy to predict future outcomes with high accuracy, it would be easy to predict future stock prices and every data analyst would be rich! Unfortunately, prediction models are subject to many more influences in the real world than any mathematical model can realistically predict. In the best case, all analysts can do is simulate some of the difficult-to-measure inputs that affect real-world decisions.

Implementing Time Series Algorithms in Python

Now that you've learned a little bit about time series analysis, you're ready to use Python to implement a simple times series analysis model. The first step in building any model is to import the necessary libraries and load your data. You'll use the Dow Jones data used to create Figures 12-1, 12-2, and 12-3.

Navigate to https://archive.ics.uci.edu/ml/datasets/Dow+Jones+Index. From the UCI Machine Learning Repository page, click or tap the Data Folder link to open the download data files list. Click or tap dow_jones_index.zip to download the zip file. The file you just downloaded contains two files: dow_jones_index.data and dow_jones_index.names. Extract the dow_jones_index.data file to your workspace project folder. (On my computer, my folder is C:\Users\micha\Dropbox\Documents\workspace\blockchainlab; yours will be different. Just make sure the dow_jones_index.data file gets copied to the same folder where your Python code resides.)

Here is the Python code (importTimeSeriesData.py) that imports the libraries you'll need and initially reads the Dow Jones data:

```python
import matplotlib.pyplot as plt
import pandas as pd
from statsmodels.tsa.arima_model import ARIMA

# Dataset source: https://archive.ics.uci.edu/ml/datasets/Dow+Jones+Index

def convert_currency(val):
  new_val = val.replace(',','').replace('$', '')
  return float(new_val)

# Import data
df = pd.read_csv('dow_jones_index.data', usecols=['stock','date','close'],
    index_col='date', header=0, parse_dates=True)

print(df.head())
print(df.dtypes)
```

Figure 12-5 shows the output from this code. The Python code print(df.head()) lists the first five rows of the df dataframe, and the code print(df.dtypes) shows the datatype of each column in the df dataframe. Note that the closing prices have dollar signs, and the close column is of type object. The dollar signs indicate that the data in the close column isn't numeric, and the datatype of the `close` column confirms that. Although the data looks okay, you'll need to convert the `close` column data to a numeric datatype to analyze closing price values.

FIGURE 12-5: Initial Dow Jones dataframe after loading from file.

```
PROBLEMS   OUTPUT   DEBUG CONSOLE   TERMINAL                                                    2: Python        + ⬚ ⬚ ∧ ×

AttributeError: 'DataFrame' object has no attribute 'type'
PS C:\Users\micha\Dropbox\Documents\workspace\blockchainlab> & C:/Users/micha/Anaconda3/python.exe c:/Users/micha/Dropbox/Documents/workspace/blockchainlab/chap
12_build.py
              stock   close
date
2011-01-07      AA   $16.42
2011-01-14      AA   $15.97
2011-01-21      AA   $15.79
2011-01-28      AA   $16.13
2011-02-04      AA   $17.14
stock    object
close    object
dtype: object
PS C:\Users\micha\Dropbox\Documents\workspace\blockchainlab>
```

Defining model input data requirements

Quite often you'll find that the data available to you isn't quite what your models need. In the case of building a time series model, you'll need a dataset that consists of dates and closing prices for a specific stock, AXP (American Express). If you look at the Dow Jones data text file, you'll see that the price data is stored as a string, the file contains many more stocks than AXP, and you don't need most of the columns.

One important early step in data analytics is to clearly define the data you need. After you can describe what your models need, you can develop the code and procedures to convert the data you have into what you need. Some solutions aren't as simple as they may seem. For example, your time series model doesn't need the `stock` column. At first glance, you might plan to simply not read any data from your input file — that is, not include the `stock` column in the `read_csv()` method. However, you need the value of the stock to determine which prices correspond to AXP. After you filter the stock data, you can remove the `stock` column.

You may wonder why you should go to the trouble of converting price data to a numeric data format. The reason is that comparing strings and numbers gives different results. It's easy to see that $12 > 4$ when you consider 12 and 4 as numbers, but if you compare the strings "12" and "4", you might as well be comparing the strings "hello" and "world". Although we do have a notion of alphabetic order, comparing strings is less intuitive than comparing numbers. To make matters worse, carrying out arithmetic on strings doesn't have the same meaning as on numbers. If you want to analyze numeric data, you have to make sure your data is numeric.

The `read_csv()` method includes an option to carry out conversion functions as you read data. Converting data as you read it into a dataframe is often the easiest way to preprocess input data to ensure that your data is in the format your models require. Two steps are required to convert data as it is read using the read_csv() method. First, you define a conversion function and then you bind that function to an input data item. The read_csv() method executes the conversion function each time it reads a new row.

Here is a simple Python function, convert_currency(), to remove the dollar sign and any commas from a price string, convert the stripped string to a decimal value, and then return the numeric value:

```
def convert_currency(val):
  new_val = val.replace(',','').replace('$', '')
  return float(new_val)
```

After you define the conversion function, add the converters option to the read_csv() method. The updated read_csv() method will look like the following. (Note that you define a dataframe named raw_df to store your temporary data because you still have some more data cleansing work to do.)

```
raw_df = pd.read_csv('dow_jones_index.data', usecols=['stock','date','close'],
    index_col='date', header=0, parse_dates=True, converters={'close':
    convert_currency})
```

The read_csv() method in the preceding code runs the convert_currency() function for every new row that is read, and then passes the value of the close data item input to the function. The read_csv() method then stores the value returned by the convert_currency() function in the close column for the current dataframe row. Figure 12-6 shows the output of the Python program (importTimeSeriesConverted.py) to import and convert Dow Jones data. The close values no longer have dollar signs and their datatype is float64.

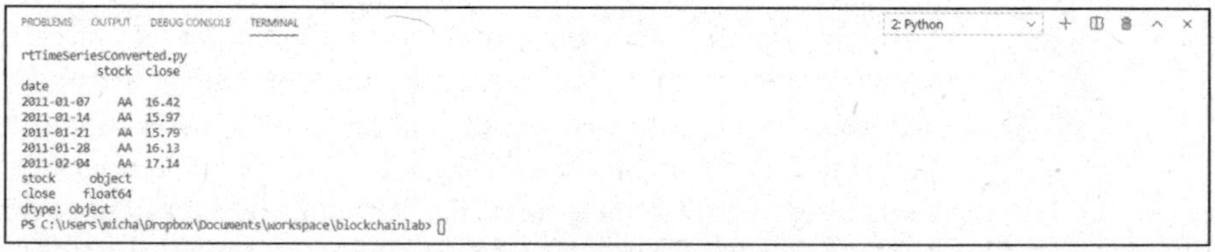

FIGURE 12-6: Imported and converted Dow Jones data.

The two remaining steps in cleansing the Dow Jones data are to filter out data (rows) and remove any columns the analysis doesn't need. You'll filter out all rows except the data for the AXP (American Express) stock. Then you'll remove the stock column from the dataframe. That will leave you with a dataframe of AXP stock data that includes only the date and close columns. To accomplish these tasks, all you have to do is add the following two lines of code after reading the data from the external text file. (The updated code is in importTimeSeries Filtered.py.)

```
df = raw_df[(raw_df['stock'] == 'AXP')]
del df['stock']
```

The first line of code extracts all dataframe rows from `raw_df` that have values in the `stock` column of AXP and stores those rows in a new dataframe, `df`. The second line of code removes the `stock` column from the `df` dataframe, leaving only the `date` and `close` columns. Figure 12-7 shows the output of the Python program (`importTimeSeriesFiltered.py`) that imports, converts, and filters Dow Jones data.

```
                  close
date
2011-01-07   44.36
2011-01-14   46.25
2011-01-21   46.00
2011-01-28   43.86
2011-02-04   42.02
close      float64
dtype: object
PS C:\Users\micha\Dropbox\Documents\workspace\blockchainlab>
```

Developing your time series model code

After you have the data your model needs in a dataset, you can start to build your time series model. First, you explore your chosen model's build parameters to build the most accurate model for your data. The build process for an ARIMA model consists of determining values for p (autocorrelation), d (differencing), and q (moving average), and then fitting the model to your data.

In Figure 12-2 you see the results of autocorrelation on the Dow Jones AXP stock closing price data. In Figure 12-3 you see the results of using differencing values of 1, 2, and 3. After looking at each of the visualizations, I chose to build the model with values of p = 1, d = 0, and q = 2. The following Python code comes from the complete file (`timeSeries.py`), and shows the statements to create each of the plots for Figures 12-2, 12-3, and 12-4.

Here is the Python code used for Figure 12-2:

```
# Step 2 Autocorrelation: Figure 12-2
df_ar = pd.plotting.autocorrelation_plot(df);
```

Following is the Python code used for Figure 12-3:

```
# Step 3 Differencing: Figure 12-3
diff = df.diff(1)
plt.plot(diff)
```

```
diff2 = df.diff(2)
plt.plot(diff2)

diff3 = df.diff(3)
plt.plot(diff3)
```

You haven't seen a plot of the moving average compared to the raw data. Figure 12-8 shows how the moving average smooths variations in raw data and makes trends easier to see. The following Python code plots the raw data and then adds a moving average line in red:

```
df.plot()

rollmean = df.rolling(6).mean()
plt.plot(rollmean, color='red', label='Rolling Mean')

plt.show()
```

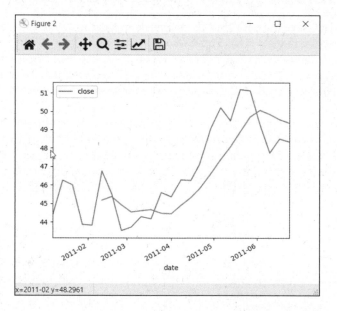

FIGURE 12-8: Dow Jones dataset raw data and moving average.

After looking at various views of your data and selecting the ARIMA parameter values you'd like to use, the last step is to build the model. Here is the Python code to build the ARIMA model summarized in Figure 12-4 (and display the ARIMA model along with the raw data and rolling mean):

```
# 1,0,3 ARIMA Model
model = ARIMA(df.close, order=(1,0,3))
model_fit = model.fit(disp=0)
plt.plot(model_fit.fittedvalues, color='green')
print(model_fit.summary())
```

Figure 12-9 shows the plot of the raw Dow Jones data, the calculated moving average, and the ARIMA time series model built on the Dow Jones dataset.

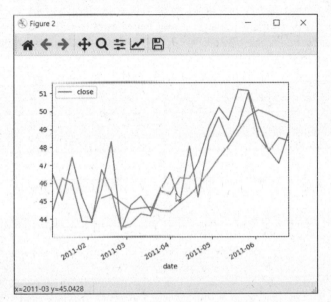

FIGURE 12-9: Dow Jones dataset raw data, moving average, and ARIMA model.

Determining When Time Series Fits Your Analytics Needs

Time series analysis is the most complex type of analysis I cover in this book, and I haven't touched on many aspects of it. My goal is to introduce you to this type of analysis and provide the basic skills to start using it.

Whenever your data includes a date or time feature, time series analysis might be a good place to start. Remember that the real strength of this analysis model class is in removing seasonality and other cyclic fluctuations from your data, which enables you to examine the true trends that occur over time.

Although you didn't use any time series analysis techniques directly on blockchain data in this chapter, the techniques are data source agnostic. After you acquire your blockchain data, the analytics techniques work in the same way as when using downloaded data.

As with all types of blockchain analytics activities, the initial effort will focus on identifying and acquiring the data your models need. In the case of time series analysis, blockchain data automatically includes a timestamp for each block and transaction. Regardless of whether you read data directly from storage, through smart contract functions, or via event logs, each data artifact will have an accompanying timestamp. You can use that timestamp to order data in a chronological fashion to assess the effect of time on trends. Blockchain is tailor-made for time series analysis.

4

Implementing Blockchain Analysis Models

IN THIS CHAPTER

» **Connecting to a blockchain and reading data**

» **Updating datasets from new blockchain data**

» **Choosing a blockchain language**

» **Planning for blockchain development**

» **Managing blockchain software development**

Chapter **13**

Writing Models from Scratch

Chapters 9 through 12 cover how to build clustering, classification, regression, and time series models using the Python language. Although you need to know how to write code in Python, you rely heavily on libraries to do most of the heavy lifting. Have you ever wondered whether you could just build models from scratch? The answer is yes, you can. It takes a lot more time (at least the first time) to build an analytics model from scratch, but the payoff is maximum flexibility. If you write a model, you can make it behave any way you want.

Of course, if you over-tweak a model to make it work well, you risk making it so customized that it won't work with any other data. Whether you use generic libraries, write everything from scratch, or land somewhere in the middle, you'll need to learn how to implement several primary tasks. You need to identify the data you'll need and then fetch it. Fetching data means you'll have to connect to one or more datastores, include blockchain(s), and then locate and extract the data. Then you can feed that data to your models. If you store any of the data in off-chain repositories, you'll need to be able to update your local data when new blocks are added to the blockchain.

In this chapter, you discover how to carry out the tasks of writing code to build, train, and execute analytics models. You learn about several programming language options and how to choose the best one for your needs. And finally, I provide guidelines on deciding whether to keep things simple or write everything from scratch.

Interacting with Blockchains

Blockchain technology supports only two data activities: append and read. You can add new blocks to a blockchain, and you can read from existing blocks. Unlike traditional database systems, you can't modify or delete data stored in a blockchain. In most current blockchain implementations, adding data to a block occurs only via smart contracts. As a data analyst, you'll only use smart contracts to access data — in most cases, you won't write your own smart contracts.

REMEMBER

Smart contracts define the data a blockchain stores and the actions necessary to access it. Although you can read raw blockchain data, using smart contracts to describe and access data is far easier. You'll find accessing blockchain data is simpler if you have access to the smart contract source code.

Your main interest in building analytics models is to identify and extract, or fetch, data for your models. You'll need to use a host language to connect to your blockchain and read the desired data from it.

In the unlikely situation that you're analyzing data from a static blockchain, you need to only connect to it and read its data once. In almost all real-life scenarios, however, your blockchain is a living, breathing (well, sort of) data repository that grows continually. In this case, you'll need to revisit the blockchain at some point after the initial data read to update your models with new data.

In the following section, you learn how to connect and read blockchain data to use in your analytics models.

Connecting to a Blockchain

Connecting to a blockchain is little more than invoking a function to set up a connection or instantiating an object that provides the connection. You can establish a direct connection, use a third-party API, or use a general-purpose library, such as web3.py. Instead of actually connecting to the blockchain, you are connecting to a blockchain node. Although each blockchain implementation handles connection and data I/O a little differently, the concept is the same. Let's look at each connection method.

Connecting directly to a blockchain node

The most straightforward method of connecting to a blockchain node is to establish a basic network connection to the node's running process. In the Ethereum environment, the node software is called the Ethereum virtual machine (EVM). EVMs, and similar blockchain nodes for non-Ethereum blockchains, monitor one or more ports for connection requests. When the process receives a request, it sets up a connection and exchanges messages with the remote process.

TIP

This description of setting up a remote connection is oversimplified. Security controls will likely prevent you from connecting to a blockchain node. However, many public blockchain nodes allow connections with few prerequisites.

For example, if you want to connect to a Bitcoin node, you could use code that looks like the following. Note that this is only a sample of Python code to demonstrate the concept of connecting to a Bitcoin node:

```python
import http.client
import base64


def connect(self):
    hostName = '127.0.0.1'
    portNumber = 8332
    authCredentials = "%s:%s" % ('myUsername', 'myPassword')
    self.authhdr = b"Basic %s" % (base64.b64encode(authCredentials.
    encode('utf-8')))
    self.conn = http.client.HTTPConnection(hostName, portNumber, False, 30)
```

After you import the two required libraries, the connect() function assigns the hostname to your local computer, the portNumber to Bitcoin's default port of 8332, and builds the authCredentials string with a supplied user name and password. The last two lines of Python code encode and build the authhdr (authorization header) and establish a connection with a local Bitcoin node.

The basic steps are similar for setting up a direct connection with other blockchain implementation nodes. It isn't difficult to connect to nodes, as long as you have the necessary access permissions. The complexity comes after you connect. If you set up your own connection, you have to manage all communication with the node, which involves building messages, sending them to the node, and then interpreting each response.

Many current blockchain implementations use JavaScript Object Notation (JSON). JSON is an open standard format used to exchange data between programs. JSON data is easy for humans to read and easy for programs to use, regardless of what type of program created the data. Because the JSON format makes it easy to exchange self-documenting data between dissimilar programs, it has become a favorite for distributed and decentralized systems, including many blockchain implementations.

Although JSON is easy to learn and use, you still have a lot of manual work to do. Your program must construct each JSON message you want to send to a blockchain client, and then decode and respond to all JSON messages the blockchain clients send back to you. Although directly interacting with a blockchain node gives you complete flexibility to do what you want, leveraging that flexibility requires a lot of work.

Using an application programming interface to interact with a blockchain

If you decide against setting up a direct blockchain node connection and handling communication manually, other options are available. One option for accessing blockchains is to use a third-party application programming interface (API). An *API* is similar to a published library of code that provides services and functionality without having to write everything from scratch. The primary difference between a library and an API is that an API provides the ability to invoke functionality from remote entities, while libraries provide code that you include in your own programs.

You'll generally find APIs provided by organizations that realize value in having their customers utilize their API calls. In other words, you're likely to pay for the convenience of using APIs one way or another. APIs provide an easy way to access data or carry out some functionality. Some APIs carry usage charges, and others are "free" for customers. Many organizations provide API access as a benefit of being a customer.

For example, the Coinbase digital currency exchange (www.coinbase.com/) includes access to its own API for its customers to query multiple blockchains and even create transactions to exchange cryptocurrencies. You can find out more about the Coinbase API at https://developers.coinbase.com/. To access a wider range of blockchain information across multiple exchanges, you can use the CoinMarketCap API. The CoinMarketCap API uses a subscription-based model in which customers pay a monthly fee for using API resources. For more about the CoinMarketCap API, go to https://coinmarketcap.com/api/.

TIP

If you want to see how you can use an API to interact with the Bitcoin blockchain, look at `https://realpython.com/python-bitcoin-ifttt/` for a nice introduction to Bitcoin price notifications in Python.

Using an API may seem to be the easiest choice for interacting with a blockchain. In many cases, APIs are easy. Most APIs provide lots of documentation and examples (and support from the providing organization). However, APIs offer only the functionality and access to the data that the provider organization is willing to expose. If an API gives you everything you need, that's great! However, if you find that API functionality leaves something out, you may have to pursue another option to get the data you need.

Letting a library do most of the work

The last main category of connection options is using libraries, which provides a balance between direct connections and APIs. Libraries provide prewritten software to carry out many tasks you need without having to write all the code yourself. If you can identify and acquire a library that includes all the functionality you need, you may have to write only a minimal amount of code.

In Chapter 5, you learn how to connect to an Ethereum blockchain node using `web3.py`. I chose that library for this book because it provided everything I wanted to present and is written in Python. The `web3.py` library isn't the only option — and it's not the best library option for every environment. Before deciding on an access option, explore several options to ensure that you're selecting the best fit for your projects.

The advantage of using libraries is that they provide simple, language-familiar techniques to carry out common tasks. A good approach to identifying a library is to start with your chosen host language. If you plan to write code mostly in Python, search for libraries available for Python. I chose Python for examples in this book because Python is a popular language for data analytics models and several libraries already exist for blockchain access.

Using the `web3.py` library, it takes only two lines to import the web3 library and assign a variable to hold the EVM host and port. Setting up the connection requires a single line of code:

```
from web3 import Web3

ganache_url = "http://127.0.0.1:7545"
web3 = Web3(Web3.HTTPProvider(ganache_url))
```

TIP

You've seen examples for connecting to only Bitcoin and Ethereum blockchain nodes, but many more options are available. Every blockchain implementation provides techniques to connect and interact with its stored data. A basic Internet search for accessing data for your chosen blockchain will likely return lots of options.

Although `web3.py` is a popular library for the Ethereum blockchain, it isn't the only option available. Other popular options include `web3.js` and `ethers.js` for the JavaScript language, `web3j` for Java, and `web3.php` and Ethereum-php for PHP. Because the web3 approach to accessing blockchain is so popular, you'll even find libraries such as `fab3.js`, a JavaScript library for accessing a Hyperledger Fabric blockchain using the web3 specification. Libraries exist for many popular languages and blockchains, making accessing blockchains through libraries a popular option with developers.

Reading from a blockchain

In the preceding section, you learn about different ways to connect to blockchains. After you choose an option and connect to a blockchain, you can do only two things: Read existing data and create new transactions. Because you're interested in analytics in this book, you don't care about creating new transactions. So all you need to learn is how to read existing blockchain data.

In Chapter 3, you find out about the different types of data a blockchain stores. Depending on the needs of your analytics models, you may need to read blockchain state data, event log data, or even raw block data. Each type of data requires a slightly different approach to fetching data and decoding the returned results. In this section, you learn about each type of data and how to fetch the data you need.

Fetching blockchain state data

Smart contract source code is a great place to start when you're searching for analytics model input data. With the exception of transaction information (from account, to account, amount, timestamp), nearly all data of interest to you will be stored as contract state data. *Contract state data* is the data a smart contract stores in blocks on the blockchain. You can ask for the latest value of any contract date variable (which some implementations store in an off-chain repository) or the variable's value for any block. The capability to explore variable values by block means it's easy to see all historical values of any state variable.

You can fetch state variables in two easy ways. In Ethereum, the compiler automatically creates a function to return the variable's current value for any state variable defined as `public`. If the state variable isn't defined as `public`, you'll have to rely on a function provided by the smart contract developer to return the value you want. Consider the following excerpt from the `SupplyChain.sol` smart contract (written in the Solidity language):

```solidity
pragma solidity >=0.4.21 <0.6.0;

contract supplyChain {
    uint32 public participant_id = 0; // Participant ID

    struct participant {
        string UUID;
        string userName;
        string password;
        string participantType;
        address participantAddress;
    }
    mapping(uint32 => participant) public participants;

    function getParticipant(uint32 _participant_id) public view returns (string
            memory,string memory,string memory,address) {
        return (participants[_participant_id].UUID, participants[_participant_
                id].userName,
                participants[_participant_id].participantType,participants
                [_participant_id].participantAddress);
    }
}
```

This code segment defines the `participant_id` state variable, `participant` state structure, `participants` mapping, and `getParticipant()` function. Because `participant_id`, `participants`, and `getParticipant()` are defined as `public`, you can access them from your client through the `web3.py` library (or any other library that provides Ethereum blockchain access). Each state data item automatically gets an accessor function (a function that returns the current value) of the same name. If you want to get the current value of the `participant_id` state variable, you can just call the `participant_id()` function in the `supplyChain` smart contract. You can use Python and the `web3.py` library to display the connect value of the `participant_id` with this code:

```python
print('Participants: ',contract.functions.participant_id().call())
```

Likewise, you can get an element in a mapping by providing the mapping key to the mapping's named function. If you want the second participant, `participants(1)`, this code will return and display it:

```python
print(contract.functions.participant(1).call())
```

Another way to get state variable contents is to invoke smart contract functions that return the data you need. In the `SupplyChain.sol` smart contract, the `getParticipant()` function is provided to return participant information. In some smart contracts, state variables are not public, but other accessor functions are provided to give access to state variables. You can use the following Python code to use the `getParticipant()` function the return the second participant's information:

```
print(contract.functions.getParticipant(1).call())
```

TIP

That's two ways to get participant data from your blockchain. In this case, you get to choose which approach you'd like to use. In many real-life situations, you'll have to use provided functions because important state variables aren't exposed as public variables.

Although getting data from a blockchain is easy, the real work is in identifying what you really need. Take the time to understand what data a smart contact stores and how you can get to the data your models need.

Parsing logs of events

Many times, you want more than just the final state of variables. Even though you can trace the changes to any state value through multiple blocks, the process isn't easy (or fast). If you really want to see how a value changes over time, look for a defined event in the smart contract source code. In Ethereum, smart contract programmers use events to create logging messages of activities. Due to the way in which Ethereum stores logs and state variables, event logs are cheaper to use for storage and are sometimes used to store state data at a discounted price (that is, it costs less cryptocurrency to store event logs than it does to store state variables).

As you examine smart contract source code, pay close attention to defined events and how the developers use those events. In smart contracts written in Solidity, you can find the events in a smart contract by looking for lines that start with the `event` keyword. Solidity smart contracts trigger events, thereby causing a log entry to be written to the blockchain, by executing the `emit eventName()` statement. The following Solidity code segment from `SupplyChain.sol` shows the `TransferOwnership()` event definition and how the smart contract triggers the event:

```
event TransferOwnership(uint32 productId, address fromOwner, address toOwner);

function newOwner(uint32 _prodId, uint32 _user1Id, uint32 _user2Id, uint32 _
            cost, uint32 _price, uint32 _qty, uint32 _timestamp)
```

```
        // Code to transfer owndership here
        emit TransferOwnership(_prodId, p1.participantAddress,
        p2.participantAddress);
        return (true);
    }
```

The first line of code defines the TransferOwnership() event. Note that events accept parameters. The parameters you provide when the code triggers an event are written to the event log file in the blockchain. In the newOwner() function, after the function carries out the transfer of ownership process, it triggers the TransferOwnership() event and passes the product ID for the product that was transferred, the previous owner's address, and the new owner's address, which logs the event (transfer of ownership) that just occurred.

Fetching event logs is easy. After you know the event name you want and connect to the blockchain, you define the event you want and fetch entries for that event log. The following Python code (showEvents.py) shows the complete program to fetch all logged occurrences for the TransferOwnership() event. Don't forget to replace the contract address with the address to which you deployed your SupplyChain.sol contract for your Ganache blockchain:

```
import json
from web3 import Web3

ganache_url = "http://127.0.0.1:7545"
web3 = Web3(Web3.HTTPProvider(ganache_url))

with open('SupplyChain.abi') as f:
    abi = json.load(f)

address = web3.toChecksumAddress('0xE9D226EC619D087Ac76E76Fc89094ac8aBe34a5dyou
                just ') # FILL ME IN
contract = web3.eth.contract(address=address, abi=abi)

myfilter = contract.events.TransferOwnership.createFilter(fromBlock=0,
                toBlock='latest')
eventlist = myfilter.get_all_entries()

print(eventlist)
```

After you fetch the desired event log entries, you can parse the list for event data, including the block and transaction hashed for each event. You can use the block and transaction information to fetch time/date information and create a granular chronological log of events.

Examining contract storage without the ABI

The last source of blockchain data will likely be your last resort. Instead of fetching blockchain data via smart contracts or event logs, you can fetch raw contract storage and attempt to decode the data. In most cases, fetching raw contract storage requires far more work than using other methods.

The techniques you've seen so far in this chapter assume that you have access to smart contact source code (or at least the ABI). Without the source code or ABI, you won't be able to fetch state data easily, invoke smart contract functions, or access event logs. However, you can still fetch contract storage and you might find that the information is usable enough to be helpful.

The setup for fetching raw contract storage requires that you know only the address of the deployed contract. After you know the contract address, you can iterate through the 16-byte storage entries to see how the state data is stored. It's up to you to decode and interpret that data. Reading raw contract storage data is an advanced topic, so I won't cover it here. However, the following code, from the file contractStoratge.py, will give you a peek at the getStorageAt() function that returns raw storage data:

```
from web3 import Web3

ganache_url = "http://127.0.0.1:7545"
web3 = Web3(Web3.HTTPProvider(ganache_url))

web3.eth.defaultAccount = web3.eth.accounts[0]

# supplyChain contract address - convert to checksum address
address = web3.toChecksumAddress('0xE9D226EC619D087Ac76E76Fc89094ac8aBe34a5d') #
    FILL ME IN

for i in range (0, 10):
    print('i: ',web3.eth.getStorageAt(address, i))
```

Because accessing needed data is far easier if you have the smart contract source code or ABI or both, start with known smart contracts. Only dig into the unknown if you really need to.

Updating previously read blockchain data

The last operation in reading blockchain data is concerned with subsequent reads. The two main approaches to reading blockchain data for analytics are parsing the blockchain each time to populate a model and extracting blockchain data to an off-chain repository in a single pass. Unless you plan to execute a model only once, it generally makes sense to extract blockchain data to an off-chain repository in a single pass and use the off-chain data for your analytics models. You can rerun models more quickly using off-chain storage versus parsing the blockchain every time.

The first time you read the data stored in a blockchain, you essentially take a snapshot of the data at a point in time. Because blockchains grow over time, each new block added to the blockchain means the dataset you extracted at a previous point in time is increasingly out of date. Fortunately, a relatively easy fix can determine what has happened since your last extract to help keep your off-chain repository more current.

You can query any blockchain to find its last block at any time. For Ethereum, you can use the web3.eth.getBlock() method to return the current (latest) block number. The following Python code, from the file currentBlockNumber.py, displays the current block number:

```
from web3 import Web3

ganache_url = "http://127.0.0.1:7545"
web3 = Web3(Web3.HTTPProvider(ganache_url))

print('Current block number: ',web3.eth.blockNumber)
```

When you run an initial (or any) blockchain extraction process, recording the current blockchain block number is easy. Then you can filter event logs to return only events that have occurred in a range. To get the events that have occurred since your last data extraction, use the filter {fromBlock: lastExtract, toBlock: 'latest; }. Assuming the showEvents.py Python code from the preceding section stored the current block number in a variable named lastExtract, you have to change only one line of code to filter out old (already read) events and return only events that have occurred since the last extract process:

```
myfilter = contract.events.TransferOwnership.createFilter(fromBlock=lastExtract
        + 1, toBlock='latest')
```

This line of code starts at the block right after the last block you initially read and continues to the latest block in the blockchain. This technique works only for events. You can't directly filter state data by block range. However, you can query the value of any state value for a specific block, which is the same as querying a state variable value as of a specific point in time.

The process of querying state data and providing the latest block number is the same as asking for the latest value of that state variable. Querying state variables as of the latest block makes it easy to update your off-chain date to reflect the latest blockchain data. Here is the Python code (showStateDataByBlock.py) to return the latest values of product_id, participant_id, and owner_id:

```python
import json
from web3 import Web3

ganache_url = "http://127.0.0.1:7545"
web3 = Web3(Web3.HTTPProvider(ganache_url))

with open('SupplyChain.abi') as f:
    abi = json.load(f)

address = web3.toChecksumAddress('0xE9D226EC619D087Ac76E76Fc89094ac8aBe34a5d') #
                    FILL ME IN
contract = web3.eth.contract(address=address, abi=abi)

latestBlock = web3.eth.blockNumber
print('Current block number: ',latestBlock)

print(contract.functions.product_id().call(block_identifier=latestBlock))
print(contract.functions.participant_id().call(block_identifier=latestBlock))
print(contract.functions.owner_id().call(block_identifier=latestBlock))
```

Instead of just displaying these values, you could use them to update your off-chain repository to freshen your analytics model input data.

Examining Blockchain Client Languages and Approaches

Many times, when you search for blockchain languages, you end up with a list of languages to write smart contracts. The most popular languages in use today are Solidity for writing Ethereum contracts and Golang for writing smart contracts for Hyperledger Fabric. (The Bitcoin blockchain isn't included here because Bitcoin doesn't support smart contracts.) Smart contract programs run on each blockchain node and control what data gets added to the blockchain.

Data analytics is a client function. As a data analyst, you aren't concerned with adding data to the blockchain — you just want to read and analyze what is there. Although you'll likely use existing smart contracts, you won't generally write smart contract code to build models.

TIP

It's possible to write new smart contract functionality or extend what's already there to support extended analytics. If your organization has control over smart contract source code you may participate in smart contract development. However, creating or modifying smart contracts is beyond the scope of this book. I focus on building models that read from blockchains.

When building analytics models yourself, you aren't limited to a specific language. As long as your language of choice supports connecting and interacting with your blockchain, you can use it to build models. In this section, you learn about a few languages that you can use to build analytics models of all types.

Introducing popular blockchain client programming languages

Most developers and analysts have a favorite language. In most cases, the favorite language is the one that is most familiar and comfortable. There's a lot to be said for selecting a familiar language. As you explore the languages listed in this section, choose the one that works best for you. In many cases, it will be a language you already know.

Although virtually any programming language could be a candidate for building analytics models for blockchain environments, three languages are used most frequently. The following main features are required:

>> The language easily supports analytics libraries.

>> The language supports easy blockchain interaction.

With these two simple criteria in mind, the languages that are most commonly used for blockchain clients are as follows:

>> **C++:** The oldest of the three languages covered in this section. C++ is an object-oriented extension to the wildly popular C language. C++ supports very low-level control and fast execution.

>> **JavaScript:** A high-level scripting language often used in web content creation. JavaScript became popular with web developers as the web grew and needed a language that was easy to learn, easy to use, and flexible enough to adapt to changing user needs.

>> **Python:** The newest language of the three covered in this section. Python is a language designed to be simple, extensible, and functional in many types of environments.

You can develop analytics models in other languages, but choosing one of the three languages listed here will allow you to get up to speed faster and take advantage of a large body of existing models and templates.

Comparing popular language pros and cons

Each language has its own advantages and disadvantages. Table 13-1 lists the most prominent strengths and weaknesses of the three languages mentioned in the preceding section.

Deciding on the right language

There is no one right language for every situation. The best language for your organization and analytics project depends on your existing proficiency in a specific language and its capability to get the job done. If your analysts like one of the languages listed in Table 13-1, that may be the best choice. If you have no preference, try Python. Python isn't the best choice for all situations, but it's a great choice if you're just getting started with blockchain analytics.

TABLE 13-1   **Pros and Cons of Popular Blockchain Client Languages**

Language	Pros	Cons
C++	Has very fast execution	Requires compilation and linking
	Supports procedural and object-oriented models	Has a steep learning curve
	Includes many data types	Code can be difficult to transport code across platforms
	Provides memory allocation control	
JavaScript	Front-end code is easy to write	Has no procedural model support
	Provides cross-platform support	Is weakly typed
		Has limited data types
Python	Provides support for procedural and object-oriented models	Executes slowly
	Is easy to learn and code	Is not compiled, so most errors are detected at runtime
	Is strongly typed	
	Includes multiple data types	
	Provides cross-platform support	
	Has extensive libraries	

Chapter **14**

Calling on Existing Frameworks

I n Chapter 13, you learn about writing analytics models from scratch. Although I focus only on the Python language in this book, I cover several other languages you can use to develop effective data analytics models that interact with blockchain data.

Building models from scratch isn't your only option. You can build models also by using one of the growing number of analytics frameworks. Instead of just using libraries to carry out model-specific calculations, a framework can abstract away many of the decisions you have to make when building models manually. A *framework* is essentially a collection of libraries and services that provide prebuilt analytics functionality. You provide the data and some configuration parameters, and the framework does all the rest.

The main differences between writing models yourself and using a framework are that using a framework is easier and requires less code, but writing from scratch gives you much more flexibility. Depending on what is most important to you, a framework could be a great choice or an obstacle.

In this chapter, you learn about some of the advantages and disadvantages of using third-party frameworks for building analytics models. You discover the main advantages of frameworks and even some of the reasons not to choose a framework. Whether using an analytics framework makes sense depends on your organization's goals and resource availability. A good framework can be a force multiplier or a source of frustration. It is crucial to understand your organization's goals and capabilities before choosing to rely on any framework.

Benefitting from Standardization

When you call on a framework to build a model, you rely on a library of code and initial decisions to return a model that meets design criteria. Although a framework may limit choices, it also enforces a standard set of choices. Without specific examples, you may wonder what the difference is between a framework and a library. The quick answer is that a library provides you with a large number of low-level functions whereas a framework provides a smaller number of complex capabilities.

For example, in Chapter 11, you learn about building a linear regression model. In the examples in Chapter 11 you use the `LinearRegression` library (imported from `sklearn.linear_model`). That library provides the *primitives* (basic functions) to create a Python object based on the linear regression model. You create the model, then invoke other Python library functionality to display the model's attributes and visualize the model's output. The library does most of the computational work, but you still have to interpret, output, and visualize the model yourself.

A framework, on the other hand, encapsulates many of the display and visualization functions into the model-building process. When you use a framework, you generally call a function to build a model and automatically get the model's output and visualization returned. You don't have to do as much work to, for example, display output parameters or plot graphs.

One of the drawbacks of using frameworks is that they implement a limited number of models and options. However, limited options provide more standard output. Limited output enforces standardization of results, which makes assessment and auditing easier.

Easing the burden of compliance

Compliance has long been a concern for all IT endeavors. IT supports business operations and manipulates data to provide critical organizational support.

IT's access to, and effect on, your organization's data means that the policies and procedures governing IT and related activities are often subject to a number of compliance requirements.

For example, any software development that affects financial data in a publicly owned organization may be subject to the Sarbanes-Oxley (SOX) Act, even if your models only read (and don't write) data. In a more general sense, you must review all your analytics models for privacy gaps. Because the main idea behind analytics is to aggregate and examine data, you might reidentify individuals as part of your data-linking process. Reidentification is just one area that could get you into trouble with compliance requirements such as the European Union's General Data Protection Regulation (GDPR) or California's Consumer Privacy Act (CCPA). SOX, GDPR, and CCPA are only samples of the various compliance requirements that may affect your analytics projects.

Using an analytics framework won't automatically make you compliant, but frameworks do provide structure and the capability to repeat tasks in a defined manner. Because frameworks provide more limited entry points for building analytics models, it's easier to demonstrate model-building consistency if auditors require you to justify your approach.

Additionally, general frameworks will likely be used by a community of organizations. Communities of framework users often communicate via social media or framework-provider-supported resources in a supportive spirit in which sharing experiences is encouraged. If you want to find out how others are staying compliant, you can just ask.

A first step in exploring compliance is assessing the requirements in place for your organization that affect data analytics projects. Assembling a list of in-force requirements can be an intensive task, but one that can help you avoid costly infractions later. Each organization falls under a different set of requirements, due to the organization's nature, the software it uses, the type of data it processes, and the type of analytics it pursues.

Here is a list of general categories that can affect compliance activities:

>> **Organization type:** Enterprises and government agencies each have very different management structures, reporting requirements, and oversight structures that affect the compliance requirements in place. Even within enterprises, publicly and privately-owned organizations have different requirements. And small- and medium-sized business (as well as non-profits) must comply with completely different requirement sets.

>> **Organization jurisdiction:** Although the global economy has made some jurisdictional boundaries translucent, location still matters. Organizations in

the state of California have more compliance regulations than those in other U.S. states. Plus, a regulation's jurisdiction may be defined by the customer's location, and not the organization's location, as in the case of GDPR.

>> **Software licensing:** Software licenses set the terms for appropriate use of the covered software. Before rushing into a data analytics project, review the licenses for the software you'll use to ensure that extracting, cleaning, aggregating, and analyzing data is within the scope and don't violate license limits.

>> **Presence of protected data:** Many of the regulations in force today that will affect data analytics projects relate to privacy and the handling of protected data. Every organization should conduct a data audit to identify all personally identifiable information (PII) and personal health information (PHI). Understanding the protected data you deal with (and the specific compliance requirement that governs that data) will help you better prepare to stay compliant.

>> **Analytics results recipients:** Identifying the recipients of your analytics results will affect compliance. Internal results distribution within an organization generally is of less concern than publicly available results. Clearly define the target audience of each analytics project.

Frameworks help standardize the analytics process, making it more repeatable and easier to document. Good documentation is a basic need to provide evidence of compliance. Because frameworks can help you pass a compliance audit, it's worth the time to explore whether a framework is a good option for your organization. You learn about several popular analytics frameworks in Chapter 15.

Avoiding inefficient code

If you've ever written software that someone else has to use, you know how easy it is to write ugly code that doesn't run well. All developers do it at one time or another. In most cases, the worst code comes when you're new to a language or environment. You learn by making mistakes — and then figuring out how to correct them.

One of the best ways to avoid writing code that is messy or doesn't run well is to leverage other peoples' experience. Because it isn't possible to be an expert at everything, it makes sense to incorporate into your own projects the hard-won experience of other architects, designers, and developers. One convenient way to do this is by using frameworks.

A good framework will include libraries (you've already used these), templates, documentation, and examples to help you get started. Framework resources provide not only a great way to learn about a new environment but also a prescriptive approach to analytics. If you follow the recommendations of your chosen framework, you don't have to develop an analytics model completely from scratch. You can start with recommended core models and extend them as needed for your environment.

Although it's a stretch to imply that all framework code is more efficient than anything you could write, there are some assurances to that effect. Any framework in general use has multiple (sometimes many) people using it. A framework's users commonly report bugs or other issues to the framework's provider. Especially in the case of an open source product, contributions for bug fixes and functionality enhancements may come from contributors all around the world.

In nearly all cases, software utilities and frameworks used by multiple organizations and users undergo more testing than any analytics model an organization builds. Software has to work for every organization that implements it, so formal testing (including regression testing of all features, I hope) gets carried out to ensure that things work as advertised.

In addition to formal testing by the framework provider, each organization that uses a framework essentially tests it on a regular basis. Software defects and performance issues that get through prerelease testing are commonly reported by users. Those defect reports end up being issues or requests that the framework provider can fix in a subsequent release. Although not all defects and performance issues are fixed immediately, such problems are usually addressed and mitigated.

Having a provider constantly evaluate the software it releases almost always results in code becoming more efficient over time. Inefficient frameworks are more of a hinderance than a benefit and will eventually fall out of use. One of the most compelling advantages of using someone else's framework over building all your models from scratch is that the framework you use is the result of far more experience than your organization possesses. Even for organizations with very experienced analytics personnel, teams that focus on building analytics frameworks are likely to have more overall experience creating efficient methods for building models.

Although you can still write inefficient code while using an analytics framework, the framework tends to encapsulate the intensive parts of analytics and insulates you from "doing it wrong." Operations that involve aggregating lots of data, oftentimes iteratively, can be carried out slowly or cleverly. The clever implementations result in efficient models. Frameworks generally do a good job of making sure that their techniques are clever and efficient.

Raising the bar on quality

In addition to the arguments in the previous two sections for using a framework to build analytics models, one of the most compelling reasons to use a framework is that it makes high quality easier to achieve. Frameworks are built on libraries and prescribed methods of using them to produce models. The main idea of a framework is to wrap complex functionality in easier-to-consume packages. A well-designed framework should allow analysts to build models more easily than writing the code themselves.

One way frameworks make model development easier is by reducing the number of choices available to model builders. The framework may simply limit choices or determine other options based on context. Either way, framework use has the effect of reducing the variability in the way models are built.

Whenever you can reduce variability in any process, you can focus on eliminating the parts of the process that don't work well and invest more in the parts that do work well. The pursuit of refocusing effort on aspects of models that produce better output is simply the pursuit of quality. Don't think that just dropping an analytics framework on your system and using it to build models will magically increase quality — it probably won't. But using a framework allows your organization to put more effort into the process of creating models as opposed to writing the code.

Focusing on the process of any series of tasks makes it easier to measure how well (or poorly) you're doing at those tasks. When your primary attention is on low-level steps in a task, it's hard to keep an eye on overall quality. As any effort becomes more granular, you spend more time making the pieces work individually as well as together. Using a framework that provides bundled functionality to carry out many of the low-level operations give you the ability to focus on the quality of the overall process.

Classic project management defines three main constraints for each project: schedule, budget, and quality. The traditional response is that you can manage only two constraints simultaneously, so choose your favorite two. (Of course, project managers are expected to manage all three.) One way you can manage the quality constraint is to rely on dependable components that you don't have to assess and test every time you use them. Frameworks can provide the assurance of dependable code that has been tested and evaluated for correctness and efficiency.

Focusing on Analytics, Not Utilities

Frameworks exist to make things easier. Specifically, a good framework makes it easier to carry out repetitive tasks. One of the many benefits of a good framework is that it should provide the basic functionality required to carry out tasks using a simple interface. The interface is the way in which you interact with a framework component. In our context, a framework will likely look a lot like a library. You import its functionality into your code and then call its functions to build and interact with analytics models.

The main difference between a framework and a library is the scope of a framework's components and what those components do. Libraries generally consist of functions to carry out low-level actions. Frameworks tend to provide functions and data structures intended to carry out high-level tasks that are often aggregations of multiple lower-level tasks. For example, a library would require separate steps to partition a dataset for training and testing, fit a model to the dataset, calculate predictions and diagnostics, and finally visualize the model. In contrast, a framework is more likely to provide the same functionality of a library with fewer steps, perhaps even doing them all with a single call.

Avoiding feature bloat

One of the advantages of using standard techniques and framework offerings is to limit the range of available options. Although limiting options may be perceived as negative, it can help overall productivity by eliminating time spent on evaluating a long list of alternatives. An efficient approach to any series of tasks is to avoid spending too much time evaluating every potential option. Although fully exploring all options might be tempting, doing so is rarely worth the time invested. Limiting choices speeds up the decision-making process.

TIP

Sometimes none of the limited available options are good enough for your analytics goals. In these cases, it's fine to explore beyond what any framework provides. You may end up building the model from scratch. That's okay. Having a small number of models built from scratch while the others adhere to standards is still better than building every model from scratch.

Another reason why limiting options is beneficial is that it helps control scope creep and feature bloat. *Scope creep* refers to the situation in any project where you decide to add "just this little extra feature" because doing so is easy. If adding one feature is easy, adding another one should be okay too, and so on. Scope creep always starts slowly and innocently but frequently ends up derailing a good schedule.

Feature bloat is related to scope creep but happens near the beginning of a project. If your options list for building a model is extensive, the tendency is to ask for everything you can get — which makes your model more complex than it needs to be. Frameworks and standard model offerings help to limit options and reduce the risk of scope creep and feature bloat.

TIP

One way to look at feature bloat is to look at fast food restaurants and how they do business. In the late 1940s, Dick and Mac McDonald streamlined their operations and removed all menu items except hamburgers, French fries, and milkshakes because they determined that all other menu items were wasting time and money. They developed a novel process for efficiently producing their core products and ended up revolutionizing food service delivery worldwide. Using frameworks for analytics models lets you streamline your analytics project like the McDonald brothers did. It's all about focusing on what returns value.

As with all points in this chapter, using a framework won't magically eradicate feature bloat. Frameworks simply provide a mechanism you can use to control how complex your models become.

Setting granular goals

Choosing to use an analytics framework can help resolve many of the low-level issues encountered when building models from scratch. A structured approach to model building is not only possible but easier than starting from scratch each time. You can focus on higher-level aspects of your analytics projects. Instead of investing time into how you're going to code a regression model or determine how many clusters your data represents, for example, you can use a framework to do most of the heavy lifting for you and instead concentrate on each model's desired results.

The ability to implement overall model standards without having to manage how each model is built can have a huge effect on development activities. Instead of spending time setting coding standards and reviewing models for adherence to standards, architects, designers, developers, and managers can focus on the analytics, as opposed to the techniques used to build models.

Although I've combined all types of model building from scratch into one big bucket, two distinct techniques are in common use. The first technique is what you learn about in Chapters 9 to 12, where you build models from scratch but have the help of libraries for lower-level analytics tasks. The other approach to building models from scratch is to skip the analytics libraries and code everything yourself. Instead of calling on a function from a library to build a naïve Bayes model, you could build one yourself in Python (or another language). I presented libraries to demonstrate one way to code your own models.

If you find that the available libraries are insufficient, you can always write the low-level code to construct any type of model you want. Building a model completely from scratch requires a lot more work but also gives you complete control over the entire process. Of course, writing your own code means that you are responsible for the design and its correctness, testing the code to ensure accuracy and efficiency, and fixing any issues encounter during testing or after deployment. In other words, you can't rely on anyone else to provide quality.

Regardless of the approach you choose in building models from scratch, you'll spend more time focusing on getting the models right than you would using a framework. A framework provides a foundation that allows you to focus on analytic goals, not software development quality. Focusing on your analytics objectives allows you to more clearly define granular goals (that is, what each model should provide) and align results with business needs.

Managing post-operational models

In the preceding section I mention the need to manage models after deployment. After you build, train, and test a model, the next logical step in most cases is to operationalize it. *Operationalizing* a model means releasing it to a wider user community for their use. Releasing, or deploying, a model to operations means the model is ready for general use and has met the quality and efficiency goals you set.

In spite of how meticulous you may have been during your testing, operationalizing a model subjects it to a variety of data and input that may differ from the artificial environment during development. The operational world is often less forgiving than development, and software defects are not uncommon. Part of the development life cycle for any software product is to monitor post-deployment (operational) performance and respond to any deficiencies.

Deficiencies generally fall into one of two categories: accuracy and efficiency. Models that fail to provide results that meet or exceed accuracy requirements have limited value. Likewise, models that provide sufficient accuracy but take too long to run aren't providing their full value. In both cases, the development team will likely get involved to explore the reasons for the lack of accuracy or reasonable performance.

TIP

The use of the word *performance* here is tricky. Performance can refer to how fast a model executes or how well the model meets its design goals. In the context of this discussion, both definitions are valid. In most cases, performance with respect to a software program refers to how quickly it responds to user input, but be aware of that other meaning of the word *performance* as well.

Searching for the root cause of any deficiency can be an art form. The task requires patience, familiarity with your data and the tools used to build the model, and familiarity with the theoretical basis of the model in question. Some deficiencies are related to data quality while others are rooted in programming issues.

The use of libraries or a comprehensive framework lightens the load of root cause analysis. Instead of spending the majority of your time sifting through source code, libraries and frameworks enable you to look at your data and the methods chosen to build your model instead of having to debug every part of your model code. Using imported code components makes managing deployed models much easier. You can find deficiencies easier and make necessary code changes faster in response to issues or changing user requirements.

Leveraging the Efforts of Others

The main decision when considering using an analytics framework is balancing the loss of control and flexibility with the advantages of capitalizing on someone else's efforts. Basing your models on libraries of frameworks means you can rely on the efforts of another developer to provide low-level functions that you can use to build models to meet your analytics requirements.

As you learned in the preceding section, libraries and frameworks allow your organization to benefit from others' development, testing, and maintenance efforts. Leveraging others' efforts can act as a force multiplier. Using libraries and frameworks can free up your analysts and developers to spend their time on higher-level analytics model implementation instead of coding each type of model you plan to use. In short, frameworks can keep you from reinventing the wheel over and over again.

Deciding between make or buy

Manufacturers often must decide how to acquire the parts necessary to create their finished goods. For example, a toaster consists of many parts, including a dial to select the desired temperature for the device. An organization that manufactures toasters can either buy the temperature dials from a supplier or make it themselves. The right answer depends on the cost of each option and the benefits of making versus buying the part. Each piece of the final product undergoes this "make-or-buy" analysis.

Data analytics projects must also consider the same options as the toaster manufacturer. The make-or-buy decision refers to libraries and frameworks that you'll use to build analytics models. The decision process boils down to whether it is more effective to write models from scratch or build them using purchased or acquired libraries and frameworks.

Building your own models completely from scratch gives your organization the most control. However, you must balance this control with the cost of enjoying the control. The cost of making anything yourself goes far beyond the cost directly associated with the physical production process. In the case of building analytics models from scratch, you'll invest far more than just the time to write the code.

Your developers will have to invest time and effort to ensure that the model implementation meets the minimum standards even before you start populating the model with data. In other words, you have to ensure that your model does what it's supposed to do in a generic sense. If you're building a naïve Bayes model, you must first demonstrate that your code actually implements a naïve Bayes model. After you demonstrate its capability to do what a model of its class can do, you can start populating it with data and using it for your organization's purposes.

Using libraries and frameworks allows you to omit the basic model-building assessment phase. The main purpose of using other peoples' code is to avoid having to do it all yourself. The flipside is that you have to use the model as provided by your libraries or framework. If you don't like the way a model is implemented, you either have to live with it or modify it yourself. But in most cases, analytics models are well documented and generic across toolsets. You generally don't gain much functionality by writing it yourself — others have already done it.

Scoping your testing efforts

Analytics model testing is an extension of the discussion introduced in the preceding section. One of the major implications of writing your own model code is that you must also test the code you write. Software testing is iterative, time consuming, and necessary. And, to make matters worse, testing is rarely done well for smaller software projects.

TIP

Note that I referred to *software projects*, not *software products*, when I said that testing is rarely done well. Software products that generate revenue stream rely on mature testing to ensure the quality of the product. Software projects, including analytics projects, often do not have the luxury of time or budget to include the expansive testing activities necessary to validate the software's alignment with design goals. Testing for smaller projects is often minimal, which results in more buggy code.

The more code you write, the more code you must test. That may sound obvious, but too many organizations fail to recognize this basic requirement of software development. Testing is all too often a hurried activity carried out simply to check a box. If your organization chooses to build analytics models completely from scratch, your testing requirements will be far more extensive than if you incorporate third-party libraries and frameworks. You'll still have to test the code you write, regardless of how much or little you write, but the scope of your testing can be dramatically smaller if you don't write everything yourself.

It's a mistake to assume that you don't have to test third-party libraries and frameworks. However, you don't have to test with the same vigor as code you write from scratch.

I have used the term *from scratch* several times throughout this chapter. The reason writing code from scratch is such an important facet of software development is that the developer takes on all the responsibility for quality. Purchased or acquired software products come with some level of assurance from the producer that the software meets stated quality standards. When you develop code based on your own specification, you, or more specifically your organization, takes on the responsibility to ensure quality. Accepting such responsibility should never be done casually because it comes with non-trivial costs.

Aligning personnel expertise with tasks

The last main category of consideration when deciding whether to use third-party libraries and frameworks is your organization's personnel expertise. If the only people available to build models are analysts with limited programming skills, you will probably benefit from selecting a framework that abstracts as much programming as possible. When avoiding writing lots of code is appealing, frameworks and extensive libraries can help reduce the amount of coding required to create analytics models.

If, on the other hand, your analytics project staff includes several experienced software developers who enjoy writing code to implement analytics models, it may be worth considering writing everything from scratch. Experienced developers most likely will have access to at least some of their past source code on which they can draw, so they probably won't technically write everything from scratch. And experienced software developers should be well versed in the software development life cycle and prepared to carry out each phase, including testing and post-deployment maintenance.

The decision to make or buy analytics models depends on your organization's culture, resources, and goals. This chapter introduced you to some of the more important aspects to consider when choosing the right basis for your models. You aren't limited to a single choice. The best choice for you and your organization might be a hybrid approach. Regardless of which way you decide to go, working through the process of choosing will help you learn more about what it takes to build effective analytics models.

Chapter **15**

Using Third-Party Toolsets and Frameworks

I n Chapter 14, you learn several reasons why frameworks and other third-party tools can help your analytics models. You also learn some reasons why you might still need to build models from scratch. If you choose to use third-party toolsets to jumpstart your model-building process, you have several alternatives available. As with nearly all choices in the model-building process, there is no best choice for all organizations and projects.

I use the terms *toolset, library,* and *framework* somewhat interchangeably. Although the terms are distinct, they also overlap quite a bit. All three terms can refer to prewritten code that you include in your programs, along with utilities that make it easier to integrate prewritten code with what you've written. For this discussion, I focus on using the term *framework.*

The key to choosing the right third-party framework for your unique situation starts with an awareness of what is available. However, don't make the mistake of selecting a toolset and sticking with it forever. Brand loyalty is a good thing, but always be open to reevaluating toolset decisions with each new project.

Switching from one framework to another will require time to learn about new or different functionality but may not be onerous. As you survey different third-party offerings, you'll find areas of commonality that could make replacing one product with another a reasonable decision. Being familiar with what's out there means you're ready to respond to new project requirements.

Surveying Toolsets and Frameworks

In Chapters 7 and 9 through 12, you use several libraries that provide functions to help you build models. When using libraries in the Python language, you import them into your code to make the functions they provide available to your programs. For example, in Chapter 7, you import the `pandas` library and use its `read_table()` function to read data from a text file. In Chapter 10, you import the `tree` package from the `sklearn` library to build a decision tree model. Libraries make it easy to group related functions into packages that your Python programs can easily use without having to write all the code yourself.

A framework is kind of a super library. In many cases, you simply import the framework like a library. The primary difference is that a framework focuses on higher-level functionality than many libraries. It isn't hard to argue that a framework is just a comprehensive library, and that a library that meets a lot of analytics needs is really a lightweight framework. The distinction isn't important here. The point is that you can use repositories of prewritten (and pretested) code to build your models.

Here is a list of the most commonly used analytics frameworks:

>> **TensorFlow,** originating from Google, is a family of open-source products that support scalable machine-learning model development focused on high performance.

>> **Keras** is a high-level framework written in Python that insulates developers from TensorFlow's low-level functionality, providing an easy-to-use interface for TensorFlow.

>> **PyTorch** is a Python implementation of the popular Torch machine-learning library. PyTorch provides Python programmers with high-performance machine-learning models.

>> **fast.ai** provides an easy-to-use interface on top of PyTorch, making it easier for Python programmers to leverage PyTorch's benefits. (PyTorch offers developers extreme performance and flexibility, at the expense of complexity.)

>> **MXNet** is a Python-based framework with support for many platforms and languages. MXNet has established a reputation as a solid framework and has been adopted as the framework of choice for Amazon Web Services.

>> **Caffe** is a special-purpose framework for high performance image processing developed as part of a Ph.D. project at UC Berkeley.

>> **Deeplearning4j** is a machine-learning framework for Java environments. Deeplearning4j provides many of the capabilities of other frameworks but is specifically for Java developers and environments.

You should familiarize yourself with the basics of each of these frameworks. Knowing what is out there is the first step toward choosing the right framework for your project. In the next sections, you learn about each framework's features and why analysts use it.

Describing TensorFlow

Google is the king of data, with tremendous amounts of data on nearly everything and everyone imaginable. As their massive data repository began to grow faster than they could digest it, the Google Brain team developed a library of machine learning algorithms to support neural network models. Google's main goal was to provide accurate results but also produce models that could handle their vast data. Scalability was a central design feature.

Google's proprietary product, DistBelief, was a great success that quickly found its way into machine-learning projects across multiple business units throughout Google's parent company, the Alphabet corporation. Google recognized the library's value and transformed DistBelief into an open-source, improved, and expanded general-purpose machine-learning framework renamed TensorFlow (www.tensorflow.org). Models were added as part of this transformation, making TensorFlow a powerful general-purpose machine-learning framework.

TensorFlow was designed from the beginning to be scalable and run on multiple CPUs and GPUs. Figure 15-1 shows the TensorFlow web page, which contains product documentation, learning resources, and ways to connect with the Tensor-Flow community. The product got its name from how it works. TensorFlow executes an ordered list of operations, called a Graph, operating on its input stored as a type of multidimensional array, formally called a *tensor*. TensorFlow is one of the most popular frameworks I cover in this chapter, due in large part to the fact that it comes from and is used by Google.

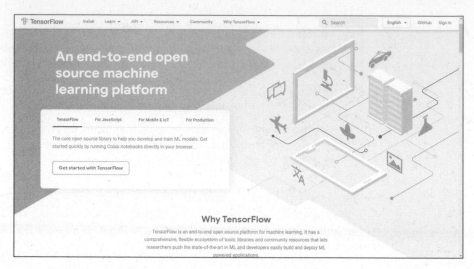

FIGURE 15-1:
The TensorFlow
website.

TIP

Other Python libraries support multidimensional arrays, such as the `ndarray` in the `numpy` library. Tensors are different because they support operations that execute on GPUs. With tensors, you can build models that are capable of extremely fast performance.

TensorFlow exists in multiple flavors, allowing it to run on traditional computers, in the cloud, or even on mobile devices. Its platform flexibility, along with its support of multiple model types, allows TensorFlow to support a wide range of applications. TensorFlow libraries exist for Python and JavaScript, and support is provided for C++ and R as well, making it easy to build analytics models in multiple languages.

TensorFlow is a granular framework, which means you'll write at least a couple dozen lines of code to build a model. The framework is very flexible and able to support a wide variety of requirements. Other frameworks lead to more compact code, but few can rival TensorFlow's scalability and flexibility.

Most programs that you build using TensorFlow follow a common structure:

1. Build the graph. Add sequential TensorFlow operations that carry out your desired algorithm.

2. Feed data to your model. Populate the model with training and testing data.

3. Run the graph. Execute the operations you defined in Step 1.

4. Update and return results. Capture graph output, update internal graph data, and return the results.

Because TensorFlow is currently the most popular machine-learning framework available, lots of tutorials and examples are available online to help you get started.

Examining Keras

Some programmers new to machine learning and analytics may find TensorFlow a big bite to take all at once. Its granular nature results in a steep initial learning curve. In other words, TensorFlow takes effort to learn and requires that you provide specific input at each step to build and use the advanced models it supports. If your main focus is building neural network models, the Keras (https://keras. io/) framework can provide the advantages of TensorFlow but in a much simpler interface. Figure 15-2 shows the Keras website, where you can learn about Keras and how to install it in your environment.

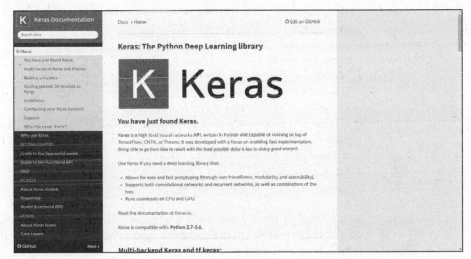

FIGURE 15-2:
The Keras website.

Keras is an open-source library of neural network model-building components written in Python. Keras is a high-level library that runs on top of other products such as TensorFlow, Microsoft Cognitive Toolkit, R, Theano, and PlaidML. Keras makes neural network models more easily accessible to analysts and developers than TensorFlow or other lower-level libraries.

Keras was designed by a Google engineer as an interface, not a stand-alone model-building tool. One design goal was to make building neural networks (a specific class of machine-learning models) easier with fewer lines of code. To make building models easier, Keras offers easy-to-use functions that assume default values for many model parameters. You can override many Keras defaults, or you can build models with minimal input.

Keras's simplicity and its capability to work with multiple underlying products makes it a great tool for prototyping. It also makes it easier to evaluate different models without writing a lot of code. Here is an example Python program that uses Keras to build a neural network model:

```python
from numpy import loadtxt
from keras.models import Sequential
from keras.layers import Dense
# load your data
mydata = loadtxt('your-data.csv', delimiter=',')
# partition data into input (X) and output (y)
X = mydata[:,0:8]
y = mydata[:,8]
# define the neural network model and layers
nn = Sequential()
nn.add(Dense(12, input_dim=8, activation='relu'))
nn.add(Dense(8, activation='relu'))
nn.add(Dense(1, activation='sigmoid'))
# compile the model
nn.compile(loss='binary_crossentropy', optimizer='adam', metrics=['accuracy'])
# fit the model to your data
nn.fit(X, y, epochs=150, batch_size=10, verbose=0)
# predict classes using your model
predict = nn.predict_classes(X)
# summarize the first 5 cases
for i in range(5):
    print('%s => %d (predicted %d)' % (X[i].tolist(), predict[i], y[i]))
```

TIP

Don't worry if the Python code using Keras doesn't make sense. As mentioned, this example builds a neural network model, which I don't cover in this book. This is one type of model you should investigate after you are comfortable with the basic models I cover in Chapters 9–12.

I won't go over the code in this example. The point is that if you used TensorFlow rather than Keras to develop the same neural network, you'd use at least twice the number of lines of code. While that isn't bad, getting things done in fewer lines of code is desirable when prototyping or exploring models. Keras can help you get up to speed and compare models quickly.

Looking at PyTorch

Google isn't the only huge organization interested in analytics and advanced machine-learning models. Facebook's AI Research lab developed their own framework for internal model development. That product matured into PyTorch (https://pytorch.org/), an open-source framework for Python developers targeted for building machine-learning models. PyTorch, like TensorFlow and Keras, focuses on neural network models, but it also supports many multidimensional array functions useful for analytics. Figure 15-3 shows the PyTorch website, where you can learn how to get started using the framework and find many resources to help you learn about PyTorch's features and best practices.

FIGURE 15-3:
PyTorch website.

PyTorch is an adaptation of the classic Torch library. Torch is written in the Lua language and was introduced in 2002, so it has been in use for quite a while. Torch is no longer being developed, but its offshoot, PyTorch (written in the Python language), is currently being enhanced with new functionality.

PyTorch's main data structure is the tensor, allowing many operations to run on GPUs as well as CPUs. Some of the more common uses of PyTorch are image processing and natural language processing. Neural networks are common models used in image and natural language processing, so PyTorch is a natural choice for many organizations. It isn't hard to see Facebook's focus when you look at what PyTorch does so well.

PyTorch implements several distinct modules to support building models. Although neural networks are the core model types you'll use in PyTorch, you can use those to implement other types of models as well. Here are the main modules you'll find in PyTorch:

>> **Autograd module:** The Autograd module implements automatic differentiation, which keeps track of operations you have performed, and automatically

replays them in reverse order to calculate gradients for you. (Gradients are used to estimate errors and train a model.) The Autograd module performs a lot of work that used to be done manually.

>> **Optim module:** The Optim module provides a collection of optimization algorithms that help to build scalable models for many platforms.

>> **nn module:** The nn module, can be thought of as a wrapper library, provides a higher-level interface for programmers to build models without having to explicitly call multiple Autograd functions. The nn module encapsulates many lower-level functions into a simpler interface.

Building neural networks can be complex and tedious. I won't show a complete Python program here, but looking at how PyTorch can be used is interesting. Here is a segment of a Python program that uses PyTorch to define a linear regression model:

```python
import torch

# define linear regression model
regressModel = torch.nn.Sequential(
 torch.nn.Linear(inputUnits, hiddenUnits),
 torch.nn.ReLU(),
 torch.nn.Linear(hiddenUnits, outputUnits),
)
loss_fn = torch.nn.CrossEntropyLoss()

# define optimization algorithm
optimizer = torch.optim.Adam(regressModel.parameters(), lr=learning_rate)
```

In this code, you can see how you can use the nn and optim models to invoke PyTorch's functionality.

Supercharging PyTorch with fast.ai

If you thought that PyTorch syntax was a little too complex, you have an alternative. Just as Keras makes using TensorFlow easier, fast.ai (www.fast.ai) makes PyTorch easier and more accessible. fast.ai is much more than just a machine-learning framework. It is a research lab that created an easy-to-use framework and courses to teach you about analytics, data science, and how to use the fast.ai resources to become a better analyst.

Figure 15-4 shows the fast.ai website. You may notice that the web page looks more like a blog than a software product website. You'll soon see that fast.ai is as much of a movement and educational project as it is a software product. The fast.

ai creators want machine learning to be as accessible as possible. Many great courses and resources on the fast.ai website will help you learn about machine learning and analytics.

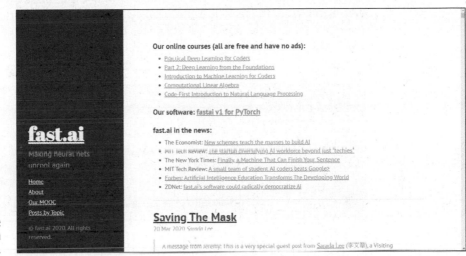

FIGURE 15-4:
The fast.ai
website.

The fast.ai library (they call it a library, but I still classify it as a framework) is built on PyTorch using the Python language. PyTorch provides the speed, flexibility, and horsepower, while fast.ai makes PyTorch's capabilities accessible to all. The fast.ai library excels at image classification and natural language processing, but it can do more. You can essentially do anything PyTorch can do, with fewer lines of code.

To give you an idea of what fast.ai lets you do, here is a sample Python program that uses fast.ai to build an image classifier model:

```
import fastai

PATH = 'directoryOf/imagesToTrain'
arch = resnet34
data = ImageClassifierData.from_paths(PATH, tfms=tfms_from_model(arch, sz))
learn = ConvLearner.pretrained(arch, data, precompute=True)
learn.fit(0.01, 3)
```

You can do a lot in just a few lines of code with fast.ai. As great as its library is, the best part of fast.ai is its extensive community and free courses. The fast.ai courses do a great job of teaching machine-learning and analytics concepts, as well as showing good coding practices for building models. The learning resources make fast.ai a valuable part of any analyst's toolbox.

Presenting Apache MXNet

Yet another machine-learning framework is Apache's MXNet (https://mxnet.incubator.apache.org/). It's an open-source framework used to develop, train, and deploy a wide variety of analytics models. MXNet has been adopted by Amazon Web Services as its deep-learning framework of choice. Figure 15-5 shows the main MXNet website, which has resources to help you get started and effectively use MXNet.

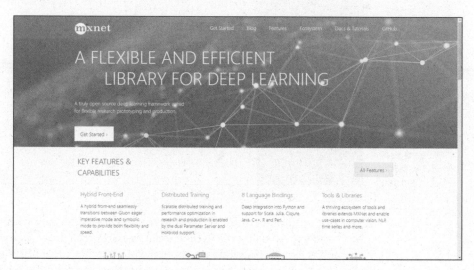

FIGURE 15-5:
The MXNet
website.

Although MXNet's primary supported language is Python, MXNet (like other frameworks covered in this chapter) supports other languages as well. In fact, MXNet supports nine languages. You can build models using MXNet in Python, C++, JavaScript, Go, R, Scala, Perl, Wolfram, or MATLAB. The range of supported languages means that you write code in a familiar language while the MXNet back end runs consistently with exceptional performance.

The language diversity, the fact that MXNet is a member of the Apache family, and MXNet's inclusion in the AWS environment makes this framework a strong contender for enterprise framework choices.

Two of the primary features that MXNet offers are scalability and portability. Models built using MXNet can run on many types of hardware, ranging from lightweight processors such as smartphones and Raspberry Pi devices, up to servers with high-performance GPUs and cloud platforms. MXNet focuses on the entire model life cycle, including deployment. You can quickly prototype a model and then operationalize it with the same framework.

Another strong feature of MXNet is its Gluon API. The Gluon API provides a high-level interface for many rich MXNet features, from prototyping through deployment. Although you can invoke MXNet's functionality directly, the Gluon API makes interacting with MXNet easier.

MXNet models require more lines of Python code than most other frameworks introduced in this chapter. However, the support of multiple languages and its portability may be worth it. If your main goals are to deploy models to a wide variety of devices and support, MXNet is a good option to consider.

Introducing Caffe

If your main analytics goal is to examine and learn from images, the Caffe framework may be of interest. Caffe (http://caffe.berkeleyvision.org/) is an open-source deep-learning framework that allows analysts to build and use models that can process images at an astounding rate. According to the Caffe website, Caffe can process "over 60M images per day with a single NVIDIA K40 GPU," and newer versions of the framework are even faster.

Figure 15-6 shows the Caffe website, which provides a simple access point for installing and using Caffe.

FIGURE 15-6: The Caffe website.

The Caffe framework was developed, and is maintained, by the Berkeley AI Research (BAIR) group, along with a well-established number of community contributors. Caffe started when its creator, Yangqing Jia, developed the initial framework as part of his work toward a PhD at UC Berkeley. Caffe's active contributor community resulted in many features being added to the framework in its first year of release. The framework continues to mature to meet the needs of ongoing and new deep-learning projects around the world.

Caffe supports high throughput with an expressive syntax that allows for architectural changes via configuration as opposed to recoding. For example, you can move an algorithm from a CPU to a GPU by changing a configuration flag instead of writing code to move the target processor.

When you do write code to build models using Caffe, you can use Python, C, C++, or MATLAB. For prototyping and initial model comparisons, you can also build models quickly using a traditional command line.

One valuable aspect of Caffe that is a direct result of the contributor community is the Caffe Model Zoo framework, which is a collection or pretrained models from multiple sources. BAIR provides several model repositories, and community contributors maintain a wiki page where you can download and use any of a growing number of pretrained models. The availability of pretrained models means you can learn Caffe and use it productively faster than most other frameworks.

To show how easy interacting with models can be, here is a simple example from the Caffe website of training a model using the command line in Caffe:

```
# train LeNet
caffe train -solver examples/mnist/lenet_solver.prototxt
# train on GPU 2
caffe train -solver examples/mnist/lenet_solver.prototxt -gpu 2
# resume training from the half-way point snapshot
caffe train -solver examples/mnist/lenet_solver.prototxt -snapshot examples/
              mnist/lenet_iter_5000.solverstate
```

When using the command line, Caffe relies on model settings and many configuration settings stored in files. Although you can't see the model details in this example, you can see how easy it is to train a model using a GPU. All you have to do is provide a command-line parameter. If you want to enjoy extremely high throughput for image processing, Caffe is a good choice for your next project.

Describing Deeplearning4j

The frameworks I've covered so far in this chapter support the Python language, and most support additional languages too. Although Python is extremely popular for building analytics models, Java is another extremely popular general-purpose language. Because so many developers have Java experience, it makes sense for them to want a framework based on the language they know best.

The Deeplearning4j framework is an open-source machine-learning framework written for the Java and Scala languages. Deeplearning4j (`https://deeplearn ing4j.org/`) integrates with other frameworks and libraries, including ND4J (a tensor library), Hadoop, and Apache Spark. Utilizing other libraries and frameworks makes it possible for Deeplearning4j to provide a simplified, high-level Java interface while offering high-performance, portable analytics models.

Figure 15-7 shows the Deeplearning4j website, with resources on getting started and using the Deeplearning4j Java deep learning framework.

![Deeplearning4j website screenshot showing "Deep Learning for Java" with QUICKSTART and LEARN MORE buttons, and "Join the Eclipse Deeplearning4j community forums." with a JOIN NOW button.]

TIP

If you're a Python developer and like what Deeplearning4j offers, don't worry! The Keras framework works with Deeplearning4j and serves as its Python API. Deeplearning4j brings together Java and Python developers in a single framework.

Deeplearning4j was developed by an independent deep-learning group, who contributed it to the Eclipse Foundation in 2017. Because Deeplearning4j was built on top of existing high-performance frameworks, it leverages distributed and parallel capabilities. Training models happens in the context of a cluster, and cluster-based computation makes distributing and parallelizing algorithms easier. In addition, the framework handles all the details of distributing and parallelizing computations among cluster participants and hardware (such as CPUs and GPUs).

Here is a skeleton of a Java classifier using the iris dataset. (Note that the original Java program was a total of 81 lines, but I've reduced the number of lines of code shown here.)

```
public class IrisClassifier {

    public static void main(String[] args) throws IOException,
            InterruptedException {

        DataSet allData;
        try (RecordReader recordReader = new CSVRecordReader(0, ',')) {
            recordReader.initialize(new FileSplit(new ClassPathResource("iris.
                txt").getFile()));
            DataSetIterator iterator = new RecordReaderDataSetIterator(record
                Reader, 150, FEATURES_COUNT, CLASSES_COUNT);
            allData = iterator.next();
        }

        SplitTestAndTrain testAndTrain = allData.splitTestAndTrain(0.65);
        DataSet trainingData = testAndTrain.getTrain();
        DataSet testData = testAndTrain.getTest();

        MultiLayerConfiguration configuration = new NeuralNetConfiguration.
            Builder();
        MultiLayerNetwork model = new MultiLayerNetwork(configuration);
        model.init();
        model.fit(trainingData);

        INDArray output = model.output(testData.getFeatures());

        Evaluation eval = new Evaluation(CLASSES_COUNT);
        eval.eval(testData.getLabels(), output);
        System.out.println(eval.stats());
    }
}
```

If you're an experienced Java developer, Deeplearning4j could be a great choice for your analytics framework.

Comparing Toolsets and Frameworks

You've seen seven frameworks to help you build analytics models in a structured and repeatable way. More frameworks are available today, and likely even more will become available in the future. Deciding on the best analytics model framework can be difficult. You need to ask lots of questions and take into consideration many features.

Table 15-1 lists each of the frameworks you've seen in this chapter. Use this table as a starting point when deciding which framework is best for your organization and product.

In this chapter, you learn about just a few of the analytics model frameworks available to help you build better models. As mentioned, no one choice is best for all situations. Assess the needs and capabilities of your organization and project, and then use that information to identify two or three frameworks. Then create a small model using each of the frameworks to get a good feel for how well that framework works for you.

Don't hesitate to reevaluate in the future. Using the right framework for your organization can improve the chances of project success.

TABLE 15-1   **Comparing Data Analytics Frameworks**

Framework	Year Released	Languages Supported	Strengths	Weaknesses
TensorFlow	2015	C++, JavaScript, Python, R	Most popular framework; used by Google	Complex to learn
Keras	2015	Python	Easier interface for TensorFlow; focused on results not model details	Less direct access to model details
PyTorch	2016	C, Python	More intuitive than TensorFlow; supports fast experimentation	No dedicated visualization tool
fast.ai	2018	Python	Easier interface for PyTorch; lots of free courses	Little direct model control for experienced coders
Caffe	2013	C++	Exceptionally fast image processing	Limited language or model options beyond its main purpose
MXNet	2017	C++, Python, JavaScript, Go, R, Perl	Lean and scalable across many device types, including the cloud; includes easy-to-use interface	Training and deployment flexibility can make model building more complex
Deeplearning4j	2014	C++, Java	Supports Java developers and environments; supports many models	Limited to Java development environments

IN THIS CHAPTER

» Assessing your needs

» Aligning analytics with your organization

» Solving problems with blockchain data

» Determining the best approach to building models

» Managing your analytics project

Chapter **16**

Putting It All Together

Throughout this book, you discover many aspects of blockchain analytics. Learning about any interdisciplinary topic means that you have to understand lots of concepts and techniques, and sometimes it may seem as though the individual components just don't fit together. However, whether you realize it or not, you've already learned most of the concepts and skills you'll need to launch and manage a blockchain analytics project. All that's left is to pull back from the details and look at your project from a more general perspective.

Rolling up your sleeves and building models isn't the best place to begin your blockchain analytics projects. Instead, you identify blockchain data of interest (see Chapter 3) and then get to that data (see Chapter 5). But starting with blockchain data is starting too far in. The most successful analytics projects, regardless of the data source, start with asking questions related to the business not the data.

In this chapter, you take what you've covered in previous chapters and pull it all together into a cohesive plan of action. No cookie-cutter analytics plan works for every organization. To enjoy the greatest level of success, your organization must assess its own needs — which is the topic of this chapter. You look at a blockchain analytics project from the perspective of what your organization needs and then make the choice that will give you the best results.

Assessing Your Analytics Needs

A common mistake for projects of any type is to skip the early stages and jump right into doing the work. However, to get the best results, you have to start at the beginning. The beginning for any project, data analytics project included, is to first define the need for the project and then plan the project. A structured approach will be necessary to manage your analytics projects, but for now you'll learn how to assess your needs and define the goals that your blockchain analytics project should meet.

Assessing project needs isn't hard. You just need to set aside time to think about the problems and ways to solve them. When your organization takes the time to discuss problems and potential solutions in depth, sometimes you'll find simple solutions and other times you might determine that the solution isn't worth it. In either situation, the process of looking at problems and solutions saves your organization time and money.

The goal is to find solutions to your problems that make sense and provide a positive return on investment (ROI). Let's look at ways to start analyzing needs that a blockchain analytics project might solve.

Describing the project's purpose

Before you can decide what to do, you need to decide why you're thinking about data analytics in the first place. In other words, it's important to define the purpose for your project. Every data analytics project — blockchain oriented or not — exists only to answer some questions. If you don't know what questions you're trying to answer, you'll never be able to come up with the right solutions. Although extracting and analyzing lots of data can be fun, unless it's done to satisfy a business requirement and results in a return on the investment, you're basically wasting your time.

The first step in defining your project's purpose is to document the need for data analytics and list the questions you're trying to answer. Those questions could include asking why things happened in the past, what is happening in the present, and what will happen in the future. After you know the questions you're trying to answer, you can start working on a solution or an answer to those questions.

TIP

It's also helpful to know why your results will be valuable to your organization. Sometimes just knowing the questions you're going to answer isn't enough. Knowing how your results will be used can often affect the way in which you conduct your analysis and subsequently present your results.

After clarifying the questions you want to answer, a next logical step is to ask to whom your results will be presented. Presenting analytics results to executives is different than presenting those results to technical people. An executive summary will likely focus on summary data that directly affects an organization's core goals. Technical presentations will likely include more detail and an explanation of nuances. Regardless of the audience, you need to understand how that audience defines ROI. Each audience group may have a different definition of value and how your results can be used to achieve that value. Your audience's perception of ROI should always drive the way in which you present your results.

And lastly, you must also understand how your results are intended to be used. The intended use of analytics results can drive the models you choose to build, the metrics you use in your models, the type of output your models produce, and the way in which you present those results to your audience. Some examples of analytics use include an explanation of events, a prediction of events, and an analysis of the root cause of one or more events. Understanding what the sponsors of your analytics efforts are after makes your job far easier and increases the probability of the project's success.

A task dedicated to discovering your project's purpose is also a good place to start looking at high-level potential obstacles to your project. The earlier you identify potential obstacles, the easier it is to address them. One surefire way to derail a project is to encounter obstacles late in the game that you didn't expect. Although many types of obstacles exist, here are just a few you should examine at the beginning of any new project:

>> **Lack of executive confidence:** Unless your organization's executives as a whole embrace data analytics, even impressive results may have little value to them.

>> **Weak collaboration:** All analytics projects, especially those involving blockchain technology, rely on collaboration among team members with different skill sets. A lack of collaboration will almost always result in more difficulties encountered throughout your project.

>> **Lack of commitment:** To have a reasonable chance of success, all levels of management must be committed to seeing the project through. Your sponsor, the organization's leadership, the managers associated with the project, and the stakeholders at all levels must be committed to seeing that the project succeeds. A lack of commitment at any level is a common cause of project difficulties.

>> **Low data quality:** All data analytics efforts are based on quality data. Although it's common to encounter missing data or data that requires cleansing, large-scale data quality issues can make it difficult for an analytics project to produce quality results.

If you foresee encountering any of the constraints listed here, try to work with your project sponsor and other leadership to resolve the issues before proceeding. By this point, you should have an idea of why the project exists, what you need to do to produce the analytics results your organization requires, and how the audience will use your results to pursue a positive ROI. After you have this clear high-level picture of your blockchain data analytics project, you're ready to start defining what that project really looks like.

Defining the process

In the preceding section, you learned how to find the purpose of your blockchain analytics project. After you know the reason why you're thinking about analytics, you're ready to start defining the process required to fulfill that purpose. At its simplest level, any data analytics project consists of acquiring data, analyzing data, and then reporting the results. As you see throughout this book, however, the real process is far more complex than a simple three-item list. As you move through the process-building phase of your analytics project, never lose sight of the overall project's purpose and the questions you need to answer.

As you keep the high-level goals in mind, you'll need to start considering the low-level components that make up the pieces of the analytics puzzle. The first piece of your analytics puzzle is your data. Inventorying and assessing data is one of the early steps in the analytics process that can have a great effect on the quality of your results. You learn in Chapter 6 how to identify and extract data from a blockchain to use in your models. One thing I didn't discuss is the special categories of data that you may encounter. For example, will any of the data you'll need for your models be protected data, such as personally identifiable information (PII) and personal health information (PHI)? If any of your data is in a protected data category, you must adjust your models and potentially your results reporting to avoid violating privacy laws and regulations.

TIP

I mention privacy in a section on process due to the importance of any process handling private data properly. Privacy is about the individual, whereas confidentiality is about the data. You might be able to enforce confidentiality with controls such as encryption, but privacy is more of a process control issue. To protect privacy, you may need to use slightly different methods for acquiring and analyzing your data. Privacy preserving analytics is beyond the scope of this book but is a fascinating topic worth additional research.

After you have a handle on whether you expect to be working with protected data, you have to start taking inventory of the data currently available to you. The results of your data inventory will help you determine the size of the task of acquiring additional data. In this part of your process definition, you need to ask yourself and your team several questions. Here are a few questions to get you started:

>> How much required data is currently available?

>> Will we require additional external data?

>> Will we need to store any data in new, off-chain repositories?

>> Who will develop ETL code (code to extract, transform, and load data for our models)?

>> After the model is deployed, who will update and maintain it?

These questions are just a starting point of things to consider when planning the process for building your models. In Chapters 9 through 12, you learn how to build different types of analytics models. However, when putting all the pieces together, you need to pay attention to the process of building those models in addition to simply following the steps to build an individual model.

The real key to building a solid process is for that process to be a bridge between the initial requirements and the delivered product. Throughout the entire process-planning phase, pay attention to your business goals. As you build a roadmap of how you're going to get from goals to results, always tie analytics back to your business goals. In other words, all the results that you report at the end of your analytics project should support one or more business goals directly. Make that association clear. When you can show how your results support business goals, your audience will understand the value you're providing through data analytics.

Taking inventory of resources

After carefully examining the purpose for your analytics project and taking the time to consider the process that your project will take to produce results, start looking for the resources you will require to produce those results. However, before you start building your project team, consider the financial stability and political culture of your organization.

For example, if your organization is very profitable and things are good, you'll likely have an easier time getting the resources you need. On the other hand, if your organization is going through a lean time and cutbacks are imminent, you'll have to be careful about asking for resources for a new project.

TIP

Paying attention to your organization's stability may seem obvious, but too many project managers forge ahead the same way on all projects, regardless of environmental changes. Look around to determine the best way to proceed. Understanding limitations positions you to make requests that have a better chance of being fulfilled.

The political landscape is another area that can help or hinder any project. Some organizations operate without overt political overtones, while others encourage those with more political clout than others. You may not be able to do much about your sponsor's or other team members' political standing, but being aware of its potential effect (positive or negative) on your project is helpful during planning. Understanding the current state of your organization is crucial to the success of getting the resources your project needs.

Earlier in this chapter, I mention the audience for your results presentation. Your audience is closely related to your project stakeholders. A stakeholder is any individual or group of people who are affected by, or affect, your project. You need to pay attention to your stakeholders throughout any project because they can help your project move along nicely or become obstacles that threaten to derail your project. Start by identifying all your stakeholders on a piece of paper or in a spreadsheet, and describing them and their effect on the project. Knowing which stakeholders are likely to affect your project more than others is important to ensuring that your results meet the stated goals.

TIP

In formal project management, stakeholder management is a separate process. Knowing your stakeholders and ensuring that their needs are met are important to successful project completion. Stakeholder management includes identifying stakeholders, analyzing the effect each stakeholder has in your project, communicating with stakeholders, and ensuring that stakeholders are kept happy.

After you know who your stakeholders are and which ones will require more active management, you can start to think about your project team. Unless you plan to acquire all the data and build all the models yourself, you'll need other teammates to help. Building your team involves identifying likely resources, determining their availability, and getting approval for those resources to be assigned to your team. Team members can be full-time or part-time resources. They can also be external resources.

The key here is to simply come up with a list of resources you will need for your blockchain analytics project. And don't forget that resources may be more than people. In addition to team members, you may need access to infrastructure, such as computers, online accounts, and other service offerings to acquire data. Understanding your project resource requirements is necessary to provide a realistic budget for approval.

Another part of resource analysis is aligning the capabilities of known resources with project requirements. For example, if your project requires models be built in the Python language, you'll want to have resources on your team who understand Python. The process of aligning capabilities with project requirements can sometimes be bidirectional.

Suppose three highly experienced data analysts are available for your project. One of these resources has experience with blockchain technology and the other two have some familiarity with it. None of these resources know Python, but all are experienced in the R language. This doesn't have to be a problem. In this case, the availability of resources with specific skill sets may influence your decisions for tools to use for your project. As long as the R language allows your project to meet its goals, the proposed resources may be the best fit for your analytics project. The key isn't to find the perfect resources, but to find the ones that can best help fulfill project goals.

Choosing the Best Fit

In Chapter 15, you learn about different frameworks that are helpful in building analytics models. After your project has a purpose and a defined process, it's time to start putting together the toolset that your team will need to build models. Choosing the best fit of tools for your specific team can sometimes be a challenge. It requires that you understand a great deal about your project, its goals, your organization, and your team. As I state in Chapter 15, no best solution exists for all situations. Each project is different, and each team brings different expertise to the table.

Regardless of how much you may like the framework and toolset you chose for your last project, revisit your decision-making process for each new project. You don't have to start the process from scratch, but you should at least review the decisions made for previous projects. Most importantly, note the lessons learned from those projects. If a framework or toolset works well, perhaps you should stay with it. On the other hand, if something didn't fit as well, look at another framework. Whether you stick with a known solution or use something new, take the time to ensure that your choices represent a good fit for your project.

Understanding personnel skills and affinity

Before you can effectively determine which framework, toolsets, and environmental components are the best fit for your project, you should understand the resources for your project. Resources include both personnel and infrastructure components. From an infrastructure component perspective, if your organization is exclusively based on the Windows operating system, your solutions should work in Windows. If you have access to Linux and Windows computers, you may have more options.

Personnel capabilities are not as easy to assess as infrastructure capabilities. After you assemble your project team, try to determine each team member's skill set. Because skills change over time, freshen your personnel information for each project. And don't make decisions based solely on existing skill sets. Instead, ask what each team member likes to do as well. You'll often find that when you assign responsibilities based on team members' affinity as well as skill set, you foster higher productivity.

Two of the most important deciding factors when choosing development tools in analytics frameworks are the operating system in which the framework runs and the language on which the framework is based. The easiest choice for frameworks is likely to be the language common to most development team members. If all team members are comfortable with the Python language, a framework that supports Python is likely the best fit. However, if your key development team members are becoming proficient with the R language and want to gain more experience in that area, perhaps a solution based on R would be a good solution. Of course, affinity without skills may won't provide the most efficient results. You want to balance your team members skill sets with the areas that interest them.

When possible, engage your team members in the decisions that will affect them directly. The choice of toolset and frameworks will directly affect the day-to-day operation of your development-related team members. When appropriate, ask for input as to the best toolset and framework to use. Also, allow personal choices when appropriate. Although your project may dictate a specific framework, you may allow individual developers to write code in their own choice of editors. Some developers may prefer Eclipse, while others may prefer Visual Studio Code (or another integrated development environment).

WARNING

Be careful about giving developers too much choice. Although it is nice to choose your own code development environment, you must ensure that organizational and project requirements are met. One common example of this is source code management. As long as each developer's choice for IDE integrates into the organization's code versioning and management requirements, you should be fine. Avoid allowing developers to build their own isolated sandbox. When that happens, you lose the ability to manage the project.

After taking into account your team members skill sets and affinities, use that information to choose the components for your development environment that most closely align with your team.

Leveraging infrastructure

An equal component of considering your team's skills and affinities is understanding your organization's infrastructure. The infrastructure in which you must operate may be a constraint, but it may also provide a rich environment for your project. For example, if your project relies on a large amount of off-chain stored data, you'll have to store that data somewhere. If your organization already has an enterprise license for a commercial database management system and has in-house expertise in that database, choosing the familiar database is likely a better choice than acquiring, installing, configuring, and using a new database management system.

Likewise, explore how your organization supports existing development activities. Do your developers work isolated on their own computers? Or do they work in shared, cloud-based environments? Or is another method used to provide developers with a development environment? These are all questions you'll need to ask to better understand development support for your organization. Answers will likely provide direction for your own project. You may not be bound by your organization's existing development environments, but awareness of what is already in place can save you a lot of time.

In addition to needing infrastructure to develop extraction and model code as well as data repository software to store extracted data, you'll need computing resources to execute your models. An important aspect of resource planning for your project is acquiring computing resources. You need to determine where your models will execute. Your models may execute in a data center, in a cloud environment, or even on a local computing platform.

TIP

If you read through some of the product descriptions for frameworks presented in Chapter 15, you may have noticed that several platforms highlight the fact that their models can run on low-powered hardware. However, that doesn't mean you should orient your project to run on a low-cost laptop. Although models may run on low-power hardware, they are restricted in the volume of data they can analyze and the speed at which they can return results.

After you understand what your project needs and what personnel resources are available, explore what your organizational infrastructure provides today and can provide in the future. Understanding what you have to start with will help you match the right framework, toolset, and development environment to your project.

Integrating into organizational culture

Regardless of how you build your project team and what software choices you make, your project and its results must integrate into the culture of your organization. It is unwise to build a project team that clashes with your existing culture. If your organization focuses on functional management, which means management is typically at a department level, you should avoid pulling resources from multiple departments in a way that frustrates management. Likewise, if your organization's philosophy is to rely on open workspaces, don't lease a new workspace with closed offices for your project team. Lots of other examples of expressions of corporate culture exist. The idea is not to embrace one culture and reject another, but rather to embrace your organization's culture and not try to change it.

REMEMBER

Paying attention to an organization's culture isn't something you should do just when building your team. That team will eventually have to reintegrate into the organization. A project is a temporary endeavor. It has a starting date and an ending date. And an ending date means that at some point the project team will stop working on the project and return to a previous assignment or move on to a new assignment. Either way, all team members will eventually move on. If your project in any way clashes with your organization's culture, you will make it more difficult for your team members to reintegrate with the rest of the organization. Working on a project should never be a sacrifice. It should always be an opportunity. Pay attention to how well the project team operates in the context of your organization's culture, and avoid friction and tension between your project team, its sponsor, and the sponsoring organization.

Embracing iteration

I have focused on initiating the analytics project, building the team, and choosing frameworks and toolsets, but choosing the right process is just as important. You should consider all data analytics tasks to be iterative — not linear. A *linear process* is one that starts at the beginning, moves through a prescribed set of steps, and ends at a known termination point. An *iterative process*, on the other hand, is one in which steps get repeated multiple times. That's the way data analytics works.

Although experienced data analysts may need to iterate fewer times, nearly every analytics project is one of frequent iterations. You examine your data, build a model, assess the model, and then go back to cleanse the data further or fine-tune your model based on that assessment. The first time you work through the cycle, your results are likely to be coarse and unreliable. As you assess your previous results and cleanse your data if necessary or fine-tune your model, your data should become more and more accurate.

Remember that the purpose of iteration is not to pursue perfection but rather to make your output useful. Useful data is data that your audience can use to make decisions that satisfy business goals. If your output does not empower individuals to meet business goals, it's hard to consider that output as useful. Always keep your eye on this goal.

Managing the Blockchain Project

I have talked a lot about projects in this chapter, and want to wrap up the discussion by considering how to manage your project. For project management advice, there is no place better than PMI (Project Management Institute), an international organization dedicated to advancing the practice of project management.

PMI introduced and maintains the project management professional certification. PMI also publishes PMBOK (project management body of knowledge). PMBOK is considered by many project managers to be the definitive resource for project management knowledge and practice. Although competing philosophies exist, I will focus on the PMBOK prescribed method of managing projects.

The most important aspect of project management is managing each project seamlessly within the sponsoring organization. Seamless project management just means that you adopt and enact the organization's project management philosophy into your projects. Managing a project isn't complex, but it can be difficult. You will increase your chances of success by adhering to a tried and tested methodology.

PMBOK breaks out projects into five distinct phases. Each phase is separate from other phases, and some phases are iterative. But each phase includes specific activities that make it unique from other project phases.

PMI defines the following five project phases.

1. **Initiating:** Processes that initially define a project and formally authorize its activities. This phase generally includes developing the project charter, a high-level document that describes the project goals.

2. **Planning:** Processes that result in detailed plans for resources, budget, schedule, and tasks. Deliverables from the planning phase provide a detailed blueprint of all project planned activities.

3. **Executing:** Processes that carry out the plans from the planning phase.

4. **Monitoring and controlling:** Processes that compare actual performance to planned activities to identify any variances. Variances are addressed, with the hopes of bringing project performance back in line with planned expectations.

5. **Closing:** Processes that manage bringing a project, or project phase, to an orderly end. Activities may include formally handing over activities to customers or operational units, completing agreements with external entities, and collecting lessons learned data.

It isn't necessary to hold the PMP certification to follow PMBOK's guidance for managing projects. PMI publishes a large number of resources available for project managers of all experience levels. Visit PMI's website at www.pmi.org for more information on project management resources.

TIP

You may be wondering why I haven't mentioned agile project management in this chapter. Although PMBOK was developed using legacy waterfall methods, it has been aligned to the agile method and maps quite well to a short sprint iteration method. Comparing and contrasting project management methods is an interesting topic but is beyond the scope of this book. For more information, look at PMI's resources page on its website for traditional and agile project management. You might also want to check out *Agile Project Management For Dummies*, 2nd Edition (Wiley).

Now that you have seen how to interact with blockchains, extract and analyze data, and organize all the activities into a repeatable project, you're ready to start your own blockchain data analytics endeavor. Happy hunting!

5

The Part of Tens

IN THIS CHAPTER

» Discovering productivity tools

» Exploring IDEs for developing models

» Accessing and extracting blockchain data at scale

» Examining blockchain data for analysis

» Protecting the privacy of individuals

Chapter **17**

Ten Tools for Developing Blockchain Analytics Models

Knowing how to access blockchain data and use it in analytics models are only the first steps toward creating useful results. The next step is to actually do these tasks. Although you can develop models using a simple text editor, having the right tools will speed the process and make you far more productive. The right tool for each part of the analytics project can dramatically increase the probability that your results will have value to your organization.

As you learn in Chapters 14 and 15, no single tool, framework, or package works well in every situation. You must define your project's requirements, consider the resources available to you, and then select the best collection of tools for your analytics project toolbox. In this chapter, you learn about ten common tools that analysts use for blockchain analytics projects. I include an assortment of tools that address a wide range of requirements. These tools will help you get a jump-start toward delivering quality blockchain analytics results.

Developing Analytics Models with Anaconda

In Chapter 5, I recommend that you download and install the Anaconda environment because of its value in any analytics project. Anaconda (www.anaconda.com) is the first tool I recommend because of the many ways it makes analytics easier.

I present the Anaconda Individual edition in Chapter 5, but you can also get Anaconda for small teams or for enterprise analytics development and deployment. The team and enterprise Anaconda licenses aren't free, but in exchange for the licensing fee you get lots of collaboration capabilities that will make team analytics development easier, including tools to extract and organize data, prototype models, develop analytics solutions, and deploy those solutions.

The Anaconda environment promotes "an integrated, end-to-end data experience," where analytics project team members can easily collaborate and share project artifacts. Anaconda Navigator, shown in Figure 17-1, is the default user interface, but you can use the conda command-line interface if you prefer a text-based interface.

TIP

In Figure 17-1, note that only some tools are installed. When you install Anaconda, the install process searches your computer to see if any tools in Anaconda Navigator are already installed. Any tools that are recommended as part of Anaconda environment haven't been installed have an Install button under their icons. To install any new tool, just click or tap the Install button.

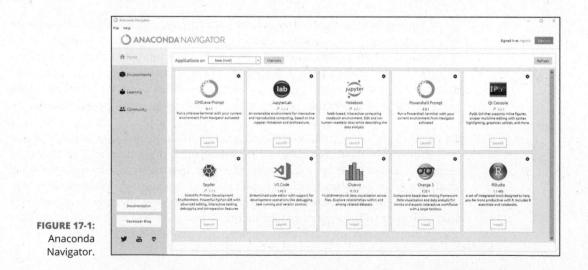

FIGURE 17-1:
Anaconda
Navigator.

Anaconda is far more than just a collection of tools. One of the most valuable aspects of Anaconda is that it automatically installs many of the analytics libraries you'll use when building models. For example, you didn't have to install many of the libraries you used in Chapters 9–12 because Anaconda already did that for you.

And if highly productive tools and preinstalled libraries aren't enough, Anaconda also provides lots of entry points for product documentation and tutorials to help you get up to speed in record time. If you choose only one tool to install to supercharge your analytics projects, choose Anaconda.

Writing Code in Visual Studio Code

When writing software for nearly any environment (in nearly any language), I recommend Visual Studio Code Integrated Development Environment (IDE) (https://code.visualstudio.com/). Visual Studio Code, commonly called VS Code, is a freely available code editor and IDE from Microsoft that includes support for debugging, task execution, and version control. Microsoft provides VS Code for Windows, Linux, and MacOS.

Although technically a lightweight alternative to the flagship product, Visual Studio IDE, VS Code brings a ton of functionality to the table. VS Code is free for private and commercial use and gives developers a great environment for developing code.

In addition to being free, VS Code is extremely functional and developer friendly. VS Code has its own marketplace with hundreds of free extensions. VS Code extensions provide support for multiple languages (syntax checking and inline help), handling different types of file formats, and integration with many other tools. If you use VS Code and want some additional feature, there's a good chance you can find an extension that does what you want.

Figure 17-2 shows VS Code with the buildSupplyChain.py code from Chapter 5 in the editor window. My version of VS Code includes a Python extension, so VS Code automatically checks any Python code for syntax errors. Because you don't see any red squiggly underlines in Figure 17-2, the code you see is syntactically correct.

Although other good IDEs for code development are available, VS Code is one of the most popular choices for software developers, which is why it's one of the default tools in the Anaconda Navigator.

FIGURE 17-2:
Visual Studio
Code.

Prototyping Analytics Models with Jupyter

Jupyter Notebook and JupyterLab are popular products from Project Jupyter (`https://jupyter.org/`), an open-source and open-standards group dedicated to providing interactive programming support for many languages. Jupyter Notebook and JupyterLab are both included in the default Anaconda Navigator due to their popularity with data analysts and machine-learning model developers. Both tools are web applications that allow developers and analysts to build and populate models in a shared environment.

Jupyter tools are popular choices when learning about data analytics and machine learning because the online design of the tools makes it easy to share code and data, called *notebooks*, with others. Anyone who wants to share a model, data, or any examples can just share a notebook. Figure 17-3 shows the kmeans.py Python program from Chapter 9 in Jupyter Notebook.

Building on the popularity of Jupyter Notebook, JupyterLab is the next generation of Jupyter's web interface for notebooks, code, and data. Figure 17-4 shows the kmeans.py Python program from Chapter 9 in JupyterLab. Although you see only Python code in Figures 17-3 and 17-4, Jupyter products support over 40 languages.

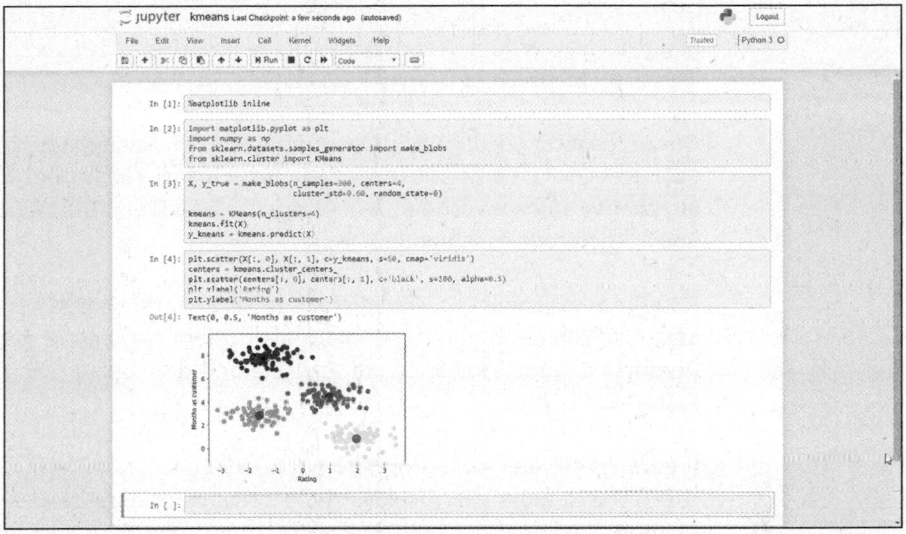

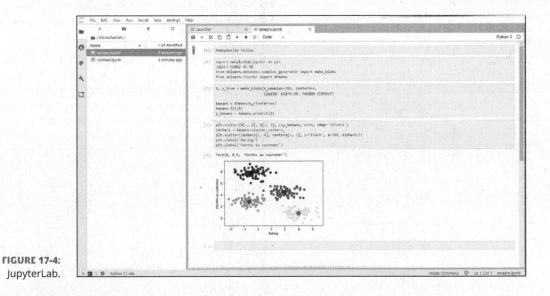

FIGURE 17-3.
Jupyter
Notebook.

FIGURE 17-4:
JupyterLab.

Developing Models in the R Language with RStudio

Throughout this book, you learn about building analytics models with the Python language. But Python isn't the only language commonly used to build analytics models. The R language is another popular language for data modeling and analysis. Like Python, R can import many libraries, called *packages* in R, to provide access to hundreds of analytics functions.

One of the most popular IDEs for working with the R language is RStudio (`https://rstudio.com/`). You can use VS Code for R development, but RStudio is a strong alternative and a favorite of R developers. In fact, you can use RStudio for both R and Python code development.

RStudio is available as a stand-alone IDE and a web-based server interface. Both are open-source products. RStudio also offers a range of professional for-fee products designed for teams of analysts and developers who need collaboration features.

Figure 17-5 shows an R program that analyzes a dataset of income records by zip code. The RStudio IDE displays the R code, console messages, a list of items in memory, and the final visual output.

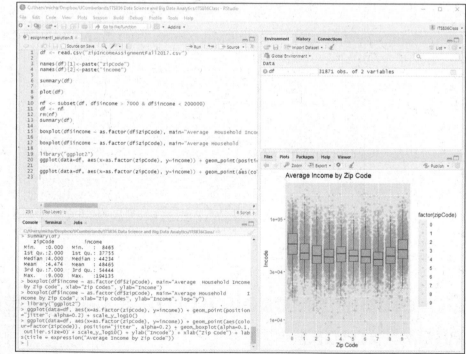

FIGURE 17-5: RStudio IDE.

TIP

Before you install RStudio, you must install the R language from `https://cran.r-project.org/bin/windows/base/`. If you try to install and then launch RStudio and get a message that R needs to be installed, you forgot to install the R language first.

Interacting with Blockchain Data with web3.py

You need a blockchain client to interact with data stored in your blockchain. In this book, I focus on the Ethereum blockchain. Each blockchain implementation is different, but the overall concepts are similar. After you learn how to access and analyze data from one blockchain implementation, mapping that knowledge to another environment is relatively easy.

In Chapter 5, you learn how to install and start using the web3.py Ethereum blockchain client (`https://pypi.org/project/web3/`) to access blockchain data. You'll need this critical library to examine and extract the blockchain data required by your analytics models.

Figure 17-6 shows the web3.py project website and several options you can use to install the web3.py library.

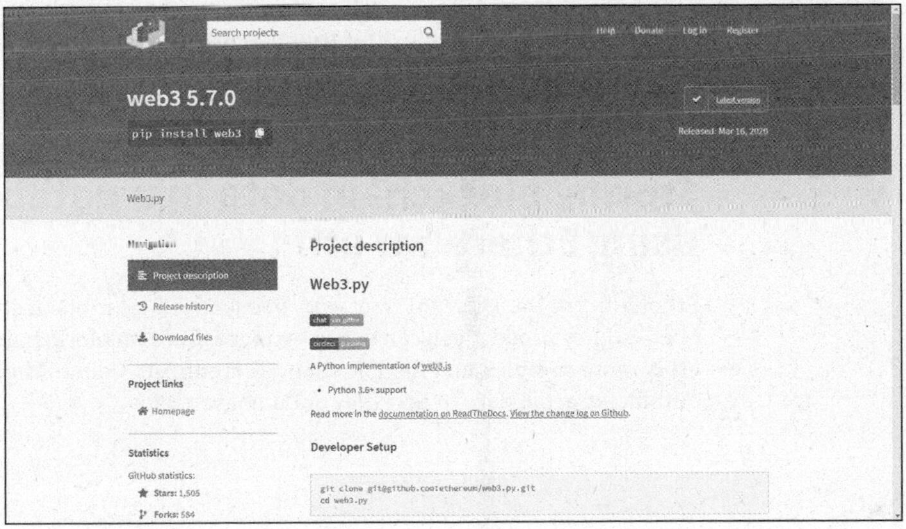

![web3.py website screenshot showing project page]

FIGURE 17-6: The web3.py website.

But web3.py isn't the only option. Chapter 5 lists a few options for the Ethereum blockchain, and a quick Internet search will show you multiple options for other blockchains.

Extract Blockchain Data to a Database

Throughout this book you learn how to identify blockchain data of interest and extract that data for use in analytics models. In some cases, you might need to extract blockchain data first and explore it later. Because you may not know what data you'll need up front, you may find it more efficient to extract blockchain data to an off-chain repository for later analysis. By extracting blockchain data and storing it in a high-performance database management system, you can decrease data access times.

You can write your own extraction code, but several generic products are already available to extract blockchain data and store it in a database.

Extracting blockchain data with EthereumDB

EthereumDB (https://github.com/validitylabs/EthereumDB) is an open-source product that extracts Ethereum blockchain data and stores it in a SQLite database. EthereumDB is a quick and simple method for extracting summary data, transaction details, and block information into separate relational database tables. You can use EthereumDB as-is or as a tutorial on how to extract Ethereum blockchain data.

Storing blockchain data in a database using Ethereum-etl

Ethereum-etl (https://github.com/blockchain-etl/ethereum-etl) is another open-source product you can use to extract Ethereum blockchain data. Ethereum-etl is more complex and flexible than EthereumDB. Using Ethereum-etl, you can output extracted data to text files or database tables.

You also have a wider range of blockchain data you can extract, including block data, token transfers, and event logs. If you want to be able to tailor the data you extract from an Ethereum blockchain, Ethereum-etl is a good option to explore.

Accessing Ethereum Networks at Scale with Infura

All examples in this book use local blockchains provided by Ganache. Although Ganache is a great tool for learning blockchain concepts and developing your own blockchain code, it isn't a live blockchain network. Real analytics projects will need to interact with real blockchain networks. Your organization may implement its own blockchain network; if not, you'll need to interact with Ethereum's mainnet or some other public blockchain.

Interacting with a public blockchain comes with some constraints and obstacles. First, to get to all of a blockchain's data, you need to connect to a full node. Running a full blockchain node requires an investment of infrastructure. Specifically, you need to dedicate disk space to store the blockchain data, a device to run the blockchain client, and sufficient network access to initially download all the blockchain data and then to process new blocks.

Interacting with one blockchain may be feasible, but as you add more public blockchains to your data universe, the infrastructure requirements may become untenable. One common solution to increasing infrastructure investment is to use someone else's infrastructure, and one of the most popular services for Ethereum blockchain access is Infura (https://infura.io/).

An Infura account provides API access over HTTPS and WebSockets to multiple Ethereum networks and InterPlanetary File System (IPFS) resources as well. Using Infura can take one large obstacle (setting up your own Ethereum node) off the table and let you focus on building analytics models. Figure 17-7 shows Infura's architecture for accessing Ethereum and IPFS resources.

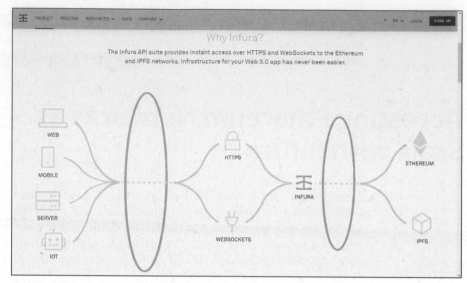

Why Infura?

The Infura API suite provides instant access over HTTPS and WebSockets to the Ethereum and IPFS networks. Infrastructure for your Web 3.0 app has never been easier.

WEB

MOBILE

SERVER

IOT

HTTPS

WEBSOCKETS

INFURA

ETHEREUM

IPFS

FIGURE 17-7: Infura's architecture.

Analyzing Very Large Datasets in Python with Vaex

Regardless where you get your data, there is likely to be lots of it. One common obstacle to operationalizing data analytics models is the size of datasets you need to analyze. Most model types increase accuracy with more data. But at some point, datasets become so large that they become difficult to manage. Even though your organization's infrastructure may have lots of servers with lots of memory, you may not always be able to provision huge amounts of resources every time you need to run a model.

To scale models to available hardware, many developers or analysts run models on partitions of their data or employ distributed processing. Partitioning your data can cut out important information and distributing analytics can take a lot of work. However, another choice is available.

Vaex (https://github.com/vaexio/vaex) is an open-source library that implements out-of-core dataframes, which allows you to write code that explores and visualizes datasets far bigger than your computer's memory. With Vaex, shown in Figure 17-8, you can run analytics models on datasets hundreds of gigabytes in size, even on a laptop computer!

Examining Blockchain Data

One of the most important early steps in any analytics project is to identify the data your models need. You must take inventory of the data available to you and then explore sources for other data that your models require. When working in blockchain environments, the most common tool used to examine available data is a *blockchain explorer*. Most blockchain explorers are web applications that provide an easy interface for accessing data stored in a blockchain.

Many blockchain explorer options are available, and each blockchain implementation has its own options. In this section, I describe three popular options for exploring data on Ethereum and Bitcoin blockchains.

Exploring Ethereum with Etherscan.io

Etherscan.io (https://etherscan.io/) is the most popular blockchain explorer for Ethereum networks. Using Etherescan.io, you can explore blockchain data from Ethereum's mainnet or any of the most popular test Ethereum networks. You can look at blocks, transactions, event logs, or any data related to your selected network.

Etherescan.io makes it easy to examine your blockchain data to identify the source data your models require. Figure 17-9 show the main Etherescan.io web page.

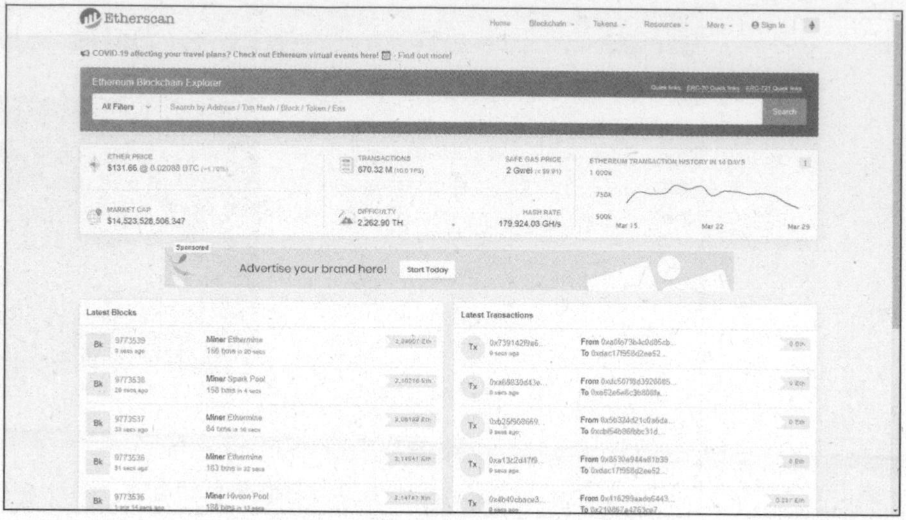

FIGURE 17-9:
Etherescan.io.

Perusing multiple blockchains with Blockchain.com

Some blockchain explorers support access to multiple blockchain networks. For example, Block Explorer from Blockchain.com (`https://www.blockchain.com/explorer?view=btc_blocks`) implements similar visibility as Etherscan.io but to more blockchain network types.

Block Explorer provides an interface to block data from the mainnets of Bitcoin, Bitcoin Cash, and Ethereum, as well as the testnets for Bitcoin and Bitcoin Cash. Figure 17-10 shows the main Block Explorer interface for the Bitcoin network.

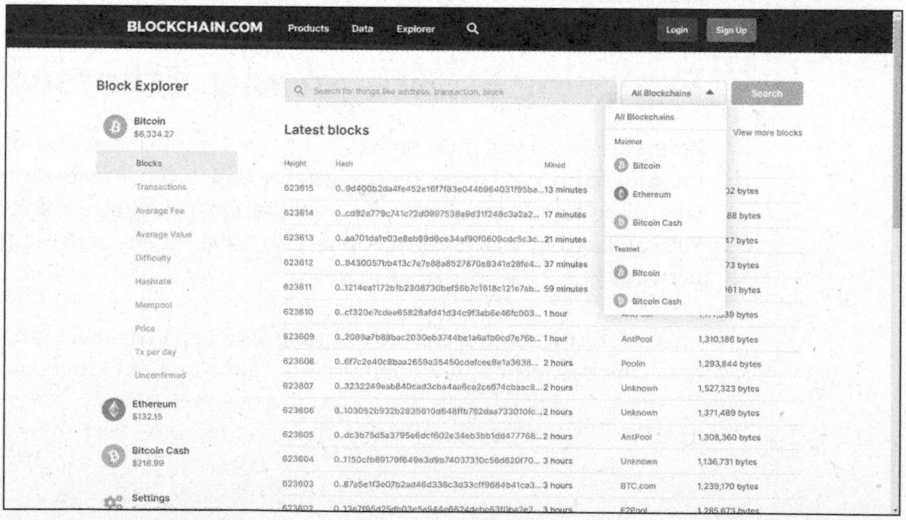

FIGURE 17-10:
Blockchain.com
Block Explorer.

Viewing cryptocurrency details with ColossusXT

Some blockchain explorers, such as ColossusXT (`https://chainz.cryptoid.info/colx/`), focus on cryptocurrency transactions. Instead of providing generic block access, ColossusXT identifies blocks that contain specific cryptocurrency transactions. If your analytics queries focus on cryptocurrency transactions, ColossusXT may help you find the data you need. Figure 17-11 shows the ColossusXT main interface for Bitcoin cryptocurrency transactions.

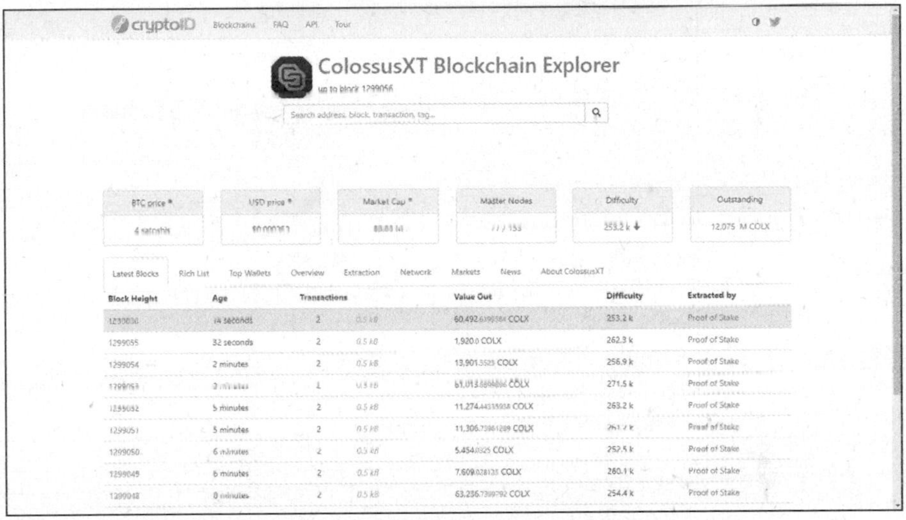

FIGURE 17-11: ColussusXT cryptocurrency Block Explorer.

Preserving Privacy in Blockchain Analytics with MADANA

A core concern for handling data, including in the context of analytics projects, is maintaining compliance with privacy regulations. Privacy is a growing concern with governing bodies. The old, naive perception that encryption enforces privacy has been shown to be false. Privacy isn't about the data — privacy is about the individual. Data analytics queries often provide aggregate results that simplify classification or prediction. If your models enable the audience to associate an individual with its results, you've violated that individual's privacy.

To avoid publishing any data that might inadvertently leak granular data that could be used to identify an individual, you have two main options. The first option is to apply good privacy-preserving techniques to your models. You'll have to learn about k-anonymity, l-diversity, t-closeness, and differential privacy. Or you can use a framework such as MADANA (`www.madana.io`), which does it for you.

MADANA provides a framework that helps you protect confidentiality and privacy. If compliance is a concern for your organization, a framework like MADANA can help you stay compliant without having to design privacy-preserving models yourself. Figure 17-12 shows the MADANA website, with some of its benefits.

FIGURE 17-12: The MADANA website.

IN THIS CHAPTER

» **Considering your environment and resources**

» **Evaluating your data's story**

» **Choosing the right scope and scale**

» **Staying compliant**

» **Having the biggest effect**

Chapter **18**

Ten Tips for Visualizing Data

The main purpose of data analytics is to uncover hidden meaning in data. If it were easy to look at raw data and interpret what it means, there wouldn't be a need for sophisticated data analytics. Although a well-trained analyst can look at a model's mathematical output and make inferences about the data, those inferences aren't always easy to explain to others. To clearly explain the results of most models' output, you need to draw a picture.

Visualizing data isn't just a nice thing to know; it's critical to conveying meaning to other people. Technical and non-technical people alike benefit from a good data visualization. Sometimes a bar chart most clearly explains data visually; other times a pie chart is better. Knowing how to visualize your data for the biggest effect is an important skill that improves with experience.

One of the most critical parts of any analytics project is presenting the results. Choosing the right visualizations for presenting your results can make or break your presentation. In this chapter, you discover ten tips for visualizing data. These tips will help you assess your data and choose a visualization technique that will most clearly convey the story your data wants to tell.

Checking the Landscape around You

Just like the great scientists of our age stand on the shoulders of the giants who came before them, you should take the opportunity to learn from existing visualizations. A quick Internet search on *visualizing data* will give you many ideas on what kinds of visualizations others have used, pointers on how they were done, and even some potential pitfalls. In many cases, you can visualize a specific type of data in several ways, and seeing how others have done it might give you some ideas. And if you've already created visualizations of your data, seeing someone else's approach might inspire you to improve your work.

To get started, look at an example from the king of data, Google. Figure 18-1 shows a visualization of the Ethereum blockchain from BigQuery, Google's big data analytics platform.

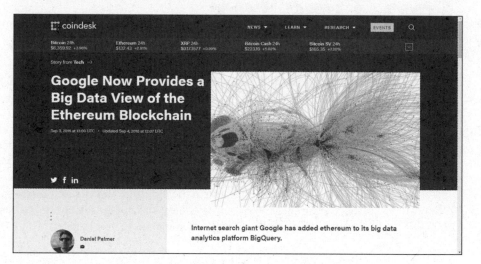

FIGURE 18-1:
Google's
BigQuery
visualization of
the Ethereum
blockchain.

You can read about BigQuery and its blockchain visualizations at www.coindesk. com/google-now-provides-a-big-data-view-of-the-ethereum-blockchain. Regardless of the source, taking time to look over how others have visualized their data can be both instructive and enlightening.

Leveraging the Community

Many analysts and data scientists of all skill levels are online and willing to help point aspiring data visualizers to the right datasets and tools. Stack Overflow, Reddit (and appropriate subreddits, such as www.reddit.com/r/dataviz/ or www.reddit.com/r/predictiveanalytics/), and Kaggle are all great places to network online, ask questions, and learn how to build first-rate visualizations quickly.

REMEMBER

Many of the tools you learn about in Chapter 17 have active communities. Don't ignore the value of asking questions of people who are more experienced than you. Chances are, they had lots of questions at some point in the past as well. User communities are great places to learn.

Figure 18-2 shows the results when I searched for *techniques for visualizing data* on Stack Overflow.

FIGURE 18-2:
Stack Overflow search results for *techniques for visualizing data*.

Figure 18-3 shows the community and subreddit results of searching for *visualizing data* on Reddit.

Figure 18-4 shows the Kaggle website. You'll find lots of resources on Stack Overflow, Reddit, and Kaggle, and all are worth bookmarking for later reference.

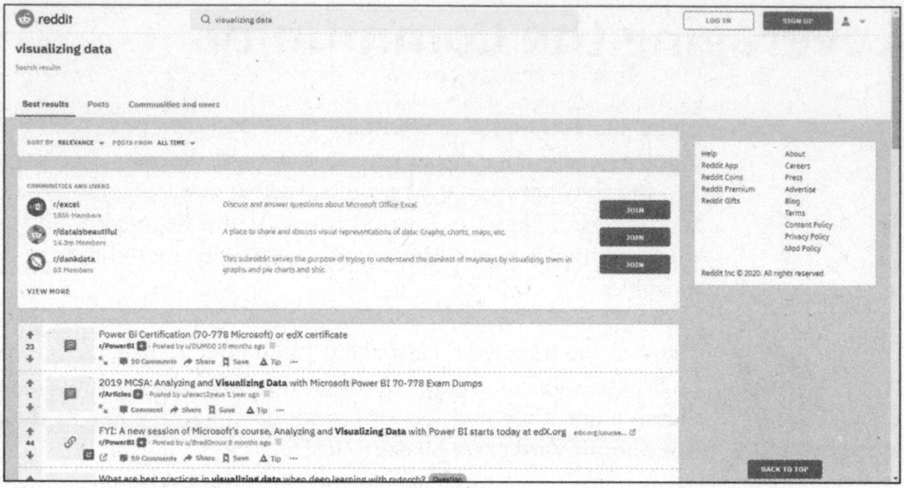

FIGURE 18-3:
Reddit search
results for
visualizing data.

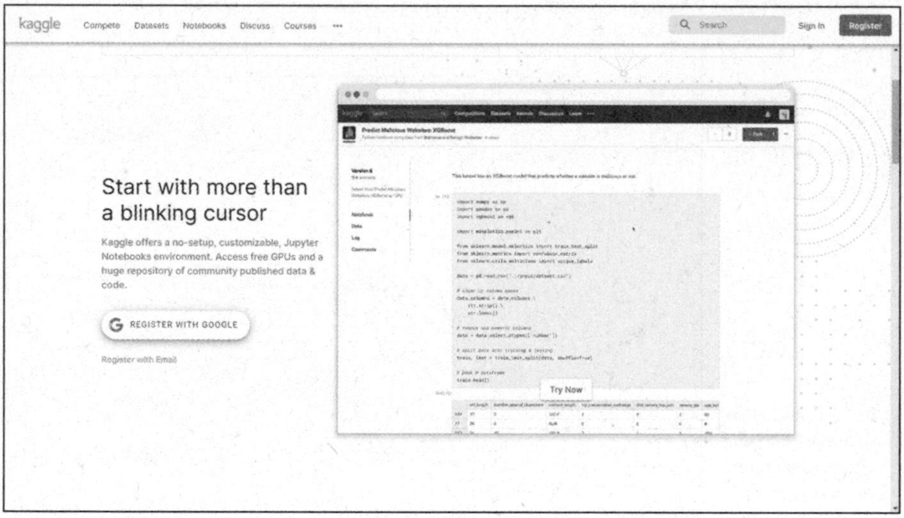

FIGURE 18-4:
The Kaggle
website.

Making Friends with Network Visualizations

One of the many data visualizations in computer science is the directed acyclic graph (DAG). DAGs have many uses and indications, and it's easy to dive deep in a short period of time. For our use, I'll stick with a simple explanation of DAGs. A DAG, also sometimes called a network graph, is a directed graph of vertices and edges. Vertices are generally states, and edges are transitions from one state to another.

If you're wondering how DAGs remotely relate to blockchain data, remember that blockchain technology excels at handling transfers of ownership. You can represent a blockchain transaction as two vertices (from account and to account), and an edge (amount of transfer). Using a DAG (network graph), you can visually show how assets are transferred from one account to another. Network graphs make it possible to visualize any transfer, such as in a supply chain blockchain.

Visualizing data using network graphs isn't new. For example, the GIGRAPH application (https://appsource.microsoft.com/en-us/product/office/WA10 4379873) makes it easy to turn spreadsheet data into a network graph. You could do the same thing with any type of blockchain data. Figure 18-5 shows an example of a network graph generated from tabular data in an Excel spreadsheet.

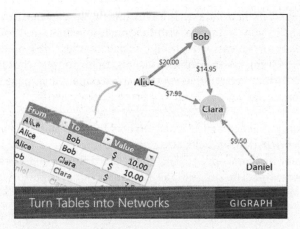

FIGURE 18-5:
GIGRAPH example of a network graph from Excel spreadsheet data.

Recognizing Subjectivity

Whenever you engage in cryptocurrency or other blockchain data analysis and visualizations, you should recognize that legacy systems often calculate value differently than new systems, especially new systems that incorporate cryptocurrency-based transactions. The value of transactions and the currency itself is subject to at least some degree of subjectivity. For instance, it's common to explain how blockchain transaction fees are far cheaper than the real-life processing fees they should replace. This may be true today, but if the value of cryptocurrency changes dramatically with respect to fiat currency, the relative values may change as well. A blockchain transaction fee today may seem very low, but worldwide financial turmoil coupled with a global strengthening of trust in cryptocurrency could invert today's value perception.

When you analyze and *especially* when you visualize, make sure you deal with any ambiguity that relative valuation may cause and communicate it clearly to the audience of your visualizations. Likewise, if your visualizations are built on any assumptions or constraints, be sure to note those as well. You want your visualizations to stand on their own as much as possible, not open to wildly different interpretations by the audience.

Using Scale, Text, and the Information You Need

Blockchain analysis is a data-rich environment, so you need to make sure you don't overwhelm your audience with too much information. Providing too many nodes or colors or excessively specific visual markers can make visualizations confusing, which misses the point of visuals. Determining what is "too much" is a bit of an art form. In general, use your best judgement and make sure you include only the information you need and are presenting it clearly.

Tableau Gurus published a nice article on how to avoid clutter in your visuals. The recommendations in this article, at https://tableaugurus.blogspot.com/2016/03/visualization-best-practises.html, are timeless and worth incorporating into your own work. The suggestions are simple but straightforward. Figure 18-6 shows an example suggestion from Tableau Gurus to simplify visualizations.

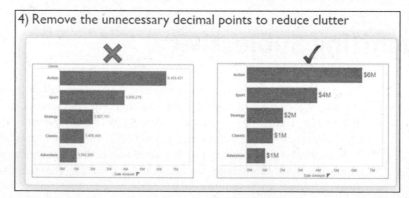

FIGURE 18-6: Visualization best practices example from Tableau Gurus.

If your data is either isolated to a narrow band in your visualization or varies widely, consider changing the scale. Decreasing the scale can cause narrowly depicted data to show more variance, and a log scale can show relative changes more clearly. If your data doesn't tell a story clearly, try changing its scale to see if that exposes interesting information.

Considering Frequent Updates for Volatile Blockchain Data

Although it's true that data in a blockchain block never changes, new blocks are added every few minutes or seconds. Regardless of when you execute an analytics model on blockchain data, the volatility of the blockchain makes your analysis stale almost immediately. New transactions are submitted in a nearly continuous stream, and any of those transactions could affect your models.

Your choice is to either frequently update your model and its associated datasets to be relatively current with the live blockchain or clearly state the highest block represented in your model. The latter approach tends to be easier but more confusing. Just reminding your audience that a model is based on outdated data generally doesn't communicate the potential risk of relying on old data. In most cases, frequent updates mean more accurate results.

To get an idea of the dynamic nature of blockchains, visit Ethviewer (http://ethviewer.live/), a real-time Ethereum blockchain monitor shown in Figure 18-7. You don't have to look at the Ethviewer web page long to get an appreciation of how quickly transactions are submitted and make it into a new block.

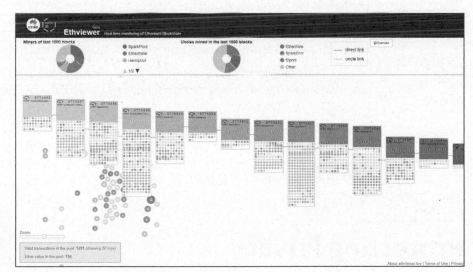

FIGURE 18-7: The Ethviewer real-time Ethereum blockchain monitor.

Getting Ready for Big Data

Blockchain analysis gives analysts access to massive amounts of information. If you want to successfully analyze and visualize large sets of data in compelling ways, both your visualization tools and the hardware that runs them must be capable of handling the load.

Hadoop is one of the most popular options for big-data analysis. On the visualization side, Jupyter, Tableau, D3.js, and Google Charts can help. A little research into the right tools goes a long way.

As far as hardware, make sure your CPU and memory are up to the task — you'll want at least a quad core CPU and 16 GB of RAM. You can run analytics on big data with less, but your performance might suffer.

Visit the following websites to get more information on visualization tools that are ready to handle big-data analysis:

>> **Jupyter** (https://jupyter.org/): I describe Jupyter in Chapter 17. This extremely useful toolset supports visualizations of datasets from small to extremely large. Learn about the products from the Jupyter Project; you'll be glad you did.

>> **Tableau** (https://www.tableau.com/): Tableau is a market leader in big data analysis and visualization. This product is mature and integrates with most large-scale data-handling and high-performance processing platforms. For an enterprise class analytics framework, Tableau is hard to beat.

>> **Google Charts** (https://developers.google.com/chart/): The Google Charts website says it all: "Google chart tools are powerful, simple to use, and free." It's from Google, and it's free.

>> **D3.js** (https://d3js.org/): The Data Driven Document JavaScript library (D3.js) provides the capability to visualize big data using many techniques in JavaScript programs. If you're using JavaScript to build analytics models, D3.js should be on your evaluation list.

Protecting Privacy

In today's hyper-regulated and privacy-sensitive business environment, you must ensure that you're using a large enough dataset or partitions to avoid the possibility of associating any unique individual with the data your audience views. To make matters worse, even large datasets or partitions may not be enough to protect privacy. Sophisticated reidentification capabilities can infer unique identities with what seems to be a minimal amount of data. In addition to taking care to preserve privacy when you build datasets, your models must also be built to preserve privacy in the results they produce.

Blockchain might seem immune to privacy issues because no real-life identities are associated with transactions. But Peter Szilagyi, a core Ethereum developer, has talked about various sites capable of creating links between a user's IP address and an Ethereum transaction address (www.coindesk.com/the-little-known-ways-ethereum-reveals-user-location-data). Although the ability he describes has generally been blocked in many apps, other attacks on privacy will arise. As with all data analysis and visualization efforts, it's better to be safe than sorry. Always pay attention to privacy as you build datasets and the models that analyze your data.

Telling Your Story

Any time you attempt to digest a large amount of data and present results, it's easy to overwhelm your audience with too much information and complex visualizations. Just as important as creating easy-to-understand visualizations is ensuring that they contribute to what you are trying to say. This point is true for any visualizations, not just those associated with blockchain. Keep in mind the big picture you're creating.

Go back to the beginning of your analytics project. Remind yourself of the original goals of the project. Then, as you work toward building visualizations for each model, revisit the goals for each model. As long as each visualization conveys the message you want to convey and meets one or more of the project's goals, you've created a useful visualization. Only include useful visuals. Extra visuals, no matter how flashy they may be, detract from the project's primary goal. Stay focused on what you've been asked to do.

Challenging Yourself!

Blockchain is an emerging technology and its uses are still being discovered and fleshed out. Keep up with the latest research, papers, and competitions on sites such as Kaggle to keep your analysis and visualization skills sharp. Take online courses on visualization topics and tools and just keep learning!

Remember that if a picture really is worth a thousand words, strive to use those thousand words better with each new project.

IN THIS CHAPTER

» **Examining financial transactions and product movement**

» **Bringing the Internet of Things together**

» **Making real-time predictions**

» **Sharing data**

» **Managing document integrity**

Chapter **19**

Ten Uses for Blockchain Analytics

A common question from management when first considering data analytics and again in the specific context of blockchain is "Why do we need this?" Your organization will have to answer that question in general, and you'll need to explain why building and executing analytics models on your blockchain data will benefit your organization. Without an expected ROI (return on investment), management probably won't authorize and fund any analytics efforts.

The good news is that you aren't the pioneer in blockchain analytics. Other organizations of all sizes have seen the value of formal analysis of blockchain data. Examining what other organizations have done can be encouraging and insightful. You'll probably find some fresh ideas as you familiarize yourself with what others have accomplished with their blockchain analytics projects.

In this chapter, you learn about ten ways in which blockchain analytics can be useful to today's (and tomorrow's) organizations. Blockchain analytics focuses on analyzing what happened in the past, explaining what's happening now, and even preparing for what's expected to come in the future. Analytics can help any organization react, understand, prepare, and lower overall risk.

Accessing Public Financial Transaction Data

The first blockchain implementation, Bitcoin, is all about cryptocurrency, so it stands to reason that examining financial transactions would be an obvious use of blockchain analytics. If tracking transactions was your first thought of how to use blockchain analytics, you'd be right. Bitcoin and other blockchain cryptocurrencies used to be viewed as completely anonymous methods of executing financial transactions. The flawed perception of complete anonymity enticed criminals to use the new type of currency to conduct illegal business. Since cryptocurrency accounts aren't directly associated with real-world identities (at least on the blockchain), any users who wanted to conduct secret business warmed up to Bitcoin and other cryptocurrencies.

When law enforcement noticed the growth in cryptocurrency transactions, they began looking for ways to reidentify transactions of interest. It turns out that with a little effort and proper legal authority, it isn't that hard to figure out who owns a cryptocurrency account. When a cryptocurrency account is converted and transferred to a traditional account, many criminals are unmasked. Law enforcement became an early adopter of blockchain analytics and still uses models today to help identify suspected criminal and fraudulent activity.

Chainalysis is a company that specializes in cryptocurrency investigations. Its product, Chainalysis Reactor (`https://www.chainalysis.com/chainalysis-reactor/`), allows users to conduct cryptocurrency forensics to connect transactions to real-world identities. Figure 19-1 shows the Chainalysis Reactor tool.

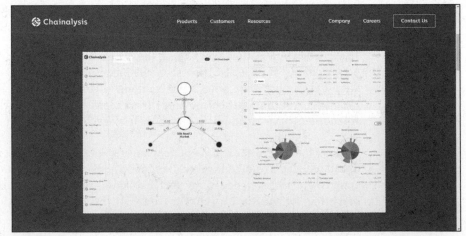

FIGURE 19-1: Chainalysis Reactor.

But blockchain technology isn't just for criminals, and blockchain analytics isn't just to catch bad guys. The growing popularity of blockchain and cryptocurrencies could lead to new ways to evaluate entire industries, P2P transactions, currency flow, the wealth of nation-states, and a variety of other market valuations with this new area of analysis. For example, Ethereum has emerged as a major avenue of fundraising for tech startups, and its analysis could lend a deeper look into the industry.

Connecting with the Internet of Things (IoT)

The *Internet of Things (IoT)* is loosely defined as the collection of devices of all sizes that are connected to the Internet and operate at some level with little human interaction. IoT devices include doorbell cameras, remote temperature sensors, undersea oil leak detectors, refrigerators, and vehicle components. The list is almost endless, as is the number of devices connecting to the Internet.

Each IoT device has a unique identity and produces and consumes data. All of these devices need some entity that manages data exchange and the device's operation. Although most IoT devices are autonomous (they operate without the need for external guidance), all devices eventually need to request or send data to someone. But that someone doesn't have to be a human.

Currently, the centralized nature of traditional IoT systems reduces their scalability and can create bottlenecks. A central management entity can handle only a limited number of devices. Many companies working in the IoT space are looking to leverage the smart contracts in blockchain networks to allow IoT devices to work more securely and autonomously. These smart contracts are becoming increasingly attractive as the number of IoT devices exceeds 20 billion worldwide in 2020.

Figure 19-2 shows how IoT has matured from a purely centralized network in the past to a distributed network (which still had some central hubs) to a vision of the future without the need for central managers.

The applications of IoT data are endless, and if the industry does shift in this direction, knowing and understanding blockchain analytics will be necessary to truly unlock its potential. Using blockchain technology to manage IoT devices is only the beginning. Without the application of analytics to really understand the huge volume of data IoT devices will be generating, much of the value of having so many autonomous devices will be lost.

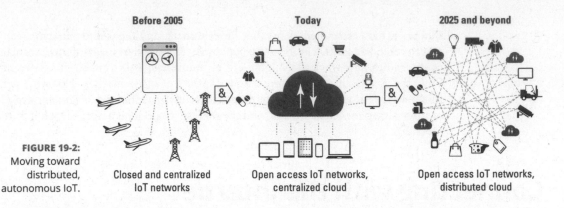

FIGURE 19-2:
Moving toward distributed, autonomous IoT.

Before 2005	Today	2025 and beyond
Closed and centralized IoT networks	Open access IoT networks, centralized cloud	Open access IoT networks, distributed cloud

Ensuring Data and Document Authenticity

The Lenovo Group is a multinational technology company that manufactures and distributes consumer electronics. During a business process review, Lenovo identified several areas of inefficiency in its supply chain. After analyzing the issues, Lenovo decided to incorporate blockchain technology to increase visibility, consistency, and autonomy, and to decrease waste and process delays. Lenovo published a paper, "Blockchain Technology for Business: A Lenovo Point of View" (https://lenovopress.com/lp1221.pdf), detailing its efforts and results.

In addition to describing its supply chain application of blockchain technology in its paper, Lenovo cited examples of how the *New York Times* uses blockchain to prove that photos are authentic. It also described how the city of Dubai is working to have all its government documents on blockchain by the end of 2020 in an effort to crack down on corruption and the misuse of funds.

In the era of deep fakes, manipulated photos and consistently evolving methods of corruption and misappropriation of funds, blockchain can help identify cases of data fraud and misuse. Blockchain's inherent transparency and immutability means that data cannot be retroactively manipulated to support a narrative. Facts in a blockchain are recorded as unchangeable facts. Analytics models can help researchers understand how data of any type originated, who the original owner was, how it gets amended over time, and if any amendments are coordinated.

Controlling Secure Document Integrity

As just mentioned, blockchain technology can be used to ensure document authenticity, but it can be used also to ensure document integrity. In areas where documents should not be able to be altered, such as in the legal and healthcare industries, blockchain can help make documents and changes to them transparent and immutable, as well as increase the power the owner of the data has to control and manage it.

Documents do not have to be stored in the blockchain to benefit from the technology. Documents can be stored in off-chain repositories, with a hash stored in a block on the blockchain. Each transaction (required to write to a new block) contains the owner's account and a timestamp of the action. The integrity of any document at a specific point in time can be validated simply by comparing the on-chain hash with the calculated hash value of the document. If the hash values match, the document has not changed since the blockchain transaction was created.

The company DocStamp (`https://docstamp.io/`) has implemented a novel use for blockchain document management. Using DocStamp, shown in Figure 19-3, anyone can self-notarize any document. The document owner maintains control of the document while storing a hash of the document on an Ethereum blockchain.

FIGURE 19-3: The DocStamp website.

WARNING

Services such as DocStamp provide the capability to ensure document integrity using blockchain technology. However, assessing document integrity and its use is up to analytics models. The DocStamp model is not generally recognized by courts of law to be as strong as a traditional notary. For that to change, analysts will need to provide model results that show how the approach works and how blockchain can help provide evidence that document integrity is ensured.

Tracking Supply Chain Items

In the Lenovo blockchain paper (mentioned in a previous section), the author described how Lenovo replaced printed paperwork in its supply chain with processes managed through smart contracts. The switch to blockchain-based process management greatly decreased the potential for human error and removed many human-related process delays. Replacing human interaction with electronic transaction increased auditability and gave all parties more transparency in the movement of goods. The Lenovo supply chain became more efficient and easier to investigate.

Blockchain-based supply chain solutions are one of the most popular ways to implement blockchain technology. Blockchain technology makes it easy to track items along the supply chain, both forward and backward. The capability to track an item makes it easy to determine where an item is and where that item has been. Tracing an item's provenance, or origin, makes root cause analysis possible. Because the blockchain keeps all history of movement through the supply chain, many types of analysis are easier than traditional data stores which can overwrite data.

The US Food and Drug Administration is working with several private firms to evaluate using blockchain technology supply chain applications to identify, track, and trace prescription drugs. Analysis of the blockchain data can provide evidence for identifying counterfeit drugs and delivery paths criminals use to get those drugs to market.

Empowering Predictive Analytics

In Chapters 10 and 11, you learn how to build several models that allow you to predict future behavior based on past observations. Predictive analytics is often one of the goals of an organization's analytics projects. Large organizations may already have a collection of data that supports prediction. Smaller organizations, however, probably lack enough data to make accurate predictions. Even large organizations would still benefit from datasets that extend beyond their own customers and partners.

In the past, a common approach to acquiring enough data for meaningful analysis was to purchase data from an aggregator. Each data acquisition request costs money, and the data you receive may still be limited in scope. The prospect of using public blockchains has the potential to change the way we all access public data. If a majority of supply chain interactions, for example, use a public blockchain, that data is available to anyone — for free.

As more organizations incorporate blockchains into their operations, analysts could leverage the additional data to empower more companies to use predictive analytics with less reliance on localized data.

Analyzing Real-Time Data

Blockchain transactions happen in real time, across intranational and international borders. Not only are banks and innovators in financial technology pursuing blockchain for the speed it offers to transactions, but data scientists and analysts are observing blockchain data changes and additions in real time, greatly increasing the potential for fast decision-making.

To view how dynamic blockchain data really is, visit the Ethviewer Ethereum blockchain monitor's website at `http://ethviewer.live`. Figure 19-4 shows the Ethviewer website.

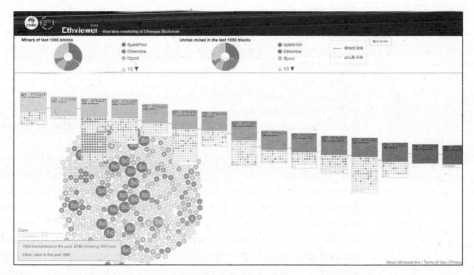

FIGURE 19-4:
Ethviewer Ethereum blockchain monitor.

Each small circle in the blob near the lower-left corner of the web page is a distinct transaction waiting to make it into a new block. You can see how dynamic the Ethereum blockchain is — it changes constantly. And when the blockchain changes, so does the blockchain data that your models use to provide accurate results.

Supercharging Business Strategy

Companies big and small — marketing firms, financial technology giants, small local retailers, and many more — can fine-tune their strategies to keep up with, and even get ahead of, shifts in the market, the economy, and their customer base. How? By utilizing the results of analytics models built on the organization's blockchain data.

The ultimate goal for any analytics project is to provide ROI for the sponsoring organization. Blockchain analytics projects provide a unique opportunity to provide value. New blockchain implementations are only recently becoming common in organizations, and now is the time to view those sources of data as new opportunities to provide value. Analytics can help identify potential sources of ROI.

Managing Data Sharing

Blockchain technology is often referred to as a disruptive technology, and there is some truth to that characterization. Blockchain does disrupt many things. In the context of data analytics, blockchain changes the way analysts acquire at least some of their data.

If a public or consortium blockchain is the source for an analytics model, it's a near certainty that the sponsoring organization does not own all the data. Much of the data in a non-private blockchain comes from other entities that decided to place the data in a shared repository, the blockchain.

Blockchain can aid in the storage of data in a distributed network and make that data easily accessible to project teams. Easy access to data makes the whole analytics process easier. There still may be a lot of work to do, but you can always count on the facts that blockchain data is accessible and it hasn't changed since it was written. Blockchain makes collaboration among data analysts and other data consumers easier than with more traditional data repositories.

Standardizing Collaboration Forms

Blockchain technology empowers analytics in more ways than just providing access to more data. Regardless of whether blockchain technology is deployed in the healthcare, legal, government, or other organizational domain, blockchain can lead to more efficient process automation. Also, blockchain's revolutionary approach to how data is generated and shared among parties can lead to better and greater standardization in how end users populate forms and how other data gets collected. Blockchains can help encourage adherence to agreed-upon standards for data handling.

The use of data-handling standards will greatly decrease the amount of time necessary for data cleaning and management. Because cleansing data commonly requires a large time investment in the analytics process, standardization through the use of blockchain can make it easier to build and modify models with a short time-to-market.

Index

A

ABI (application binary interface). *See* application binary interface (ABI)

access speed, 108–109

accessing
  Ethereum networks at scale, 289–290
  public financial transaction data, 306–307

Account/Balance model, 40

addParticipant() function, 102

addProduct() function, 102

Agile Project Management For Dummies, 2nd Edition (Layton and Ostermiller), 278

AI (artificial intelligence), 24

aligning
  analytics with business goals, 58–60
  features with business requirements, 31–35
  operations, 18
  personnel expertise with tasks, 250
  ROI with analytics currency, 146–147

alternative hypothesis, 133

Amazon, 8

Amazon Web Services (AWS), 145

AML (Anti-Money Laundering Act), 12–13

Anaconda
  about, 282–283
  adding to analytics lab, 84–92
  installing, 86–88

Anaconda Cloud, 88

analysis
  of blockchain data over time, 209–222
  data classification, 172–179
  of large datasets in Python, 290–291
  predictions, 190–203
  preserving artifacts for, 34, 35
  of real-time data, 311
  relationships, 190–203
  of time series data, 135–138

analysis datasets, building, 107–119

analytics
  about, 7–8
  aligning with business goals, 58–60
  assessing needs for, 268–273

analytics currency, aligning ROI with, 146–147

analytics lab
  adding Anaconda and Web3.js to, 84–92
  options for, 60–61
  reviewing, 80–81

analytics models
  developing, 282–283
  making decisions based on, 16
  prototyping, 284–285

analytics results recipients, as a category affecting compliance activities, 242

anonymous participants, 29–30

Anti-Money Laundering Act (AML), 12–13

Apache MXNet, 253, 260–261, 265

application binary interface (ABI)
  about, 48, 93–94
  finding for smart contracts, 94–100

application programming interface (API), interacting with blockchains with, 228–230

apriori algorithm, 129, 164–167

ARIMA (autoregressive integrated moving average) model, 211–214

artifacts, preserving for analysis, 34, 35

artificial intelligence (AI), 24

assessing
  analytics needs, 268–273
  data completeness, 110–111
  group membership, 126–129
  model effectiveness with diagnostics, 160, 167–168, 178–179, 201–203
  model quality as a team, 149–150
  results, 18
  smart contract event logs, 55

PoS (Proof of Stake) algorithm, 28, 30

post-operational models, managing, 247–248

PoW (Proof of Work) algorithm, 22, 24, 30

`predict()` method, 178, 204, 205

prediction analysis, 131

predictions

    analyzing, 190–203

    behavior, 14–16

    future outcomes with data, 13–16

    making, 130–135

predictive analytics

    about, 16, 133, 171

    challenges in, 17–18

    defining desired outcomes, 17

    empowering, 310–311

prescriptive analytics

    about, 16–17, 133

    challenges in, 17–18

    defining desired outcomes, 17

presence of protected data, as a category affecting compliance activities, 242

preserving

    artifacts for analysis, 34, 35

    privacy, 293–294

previous hash, in block headers, 45

primitives, 240

privacy

    exposing data without compromising, 34, 35

    protecting, 293–294, 302–303

privacy laws, 9, 12–13

private blockchain, 28

probability, calculating, 177

process, defining the, 270–271

process disintermediation, as a benefit of blockchain, 25

products, provenance of, 29

project management body of knowledge (PMBOK), 277–278

Project Management Institute (PMI), 277–278

Proof of Stake (PoS) algorithm, 28, 30

Proof of Work (PoW) algorithm, 22, 24, 30

protecting

    availability through redundancy, 34, 35

    privacy, 293–294, 302–303

prototyping analytics models, 284–285

provenance, of products, 29

pruning, in apriori algorithm, 165, 166

public blockchain, 27–28, 30

public financial transaction data, accessing, 306–307

punishing participants, 142–143

Python

    about, 83–84, 237

    analyzing large datasets in, 290–291

    checking installed version, 85

    implementing blockchain classification algorithms in, 179–188

    implementing blockchain clustering algorithms in, 160–163

    implementing regression algorithms in, 203–207

    implementing time series algorithms in, 216–221

    installing, 86

    versions, 84–85

    writing scripts to access blockchains, 92–100

Python Class, 84

`python` command, 85

Python For Data Science For Dummies, 2nd Edition (Mueller and Massaron), 155, 173, 212

PyTorch, 252, 256–258, 265

Q

quality

  of data, 150

  increasing, 244

R

R language, 285–287

randomness, as component of time series data, 220

ranking transaction/event data, 55

raw visualization, 137

`read_csv()` method, 181, 217–218

reading
  from blockchains, 230–234
  input data, 181–183
real-time data, analyzing, 311
receipt root, in block headers, 46
recommender engines, 130
recording transactions, 34, 35, 41–43
Reddit, 297
reducing costs, 32, 34, 35
redundancy, protecting availability through, 34, 35
registering smart contracts, 48
Registry of Open Data on Amazon Web Services (AWS), 115
regression algorithms
  determining uses for, 207–208
  implementing in Python, 203–207
regression line, 193, 195
regression models
  about, 15–16, 189–190
  for analyzing predictions and relationships, 190–203
  building datasets, 203
  developing code, 204–207
regulatory requirements, satisfying, 11–13
related data, identifying, 153–169
relationships
  analyzing, 190–203
  discovering among items, 129–130
Remember icon, 2
Remix IDE, 93
repeated analysis, compared with one-off analysis, 109–110
replication, increasing resilience through, 33
requestLoC( ) function, 55
residuals, 137, 195
resilience, increasing through replication, 33
resources
  Python, 84
  taking an inventory of, 271–273
results, assessing, 18

return on investment (ROI), aligning with analytics currency, 146–147
rewarding participants, 142–143
"right to be forgotten," 112
Rinkeby, 41
Ripple Transaction Protocol, 31
RocksDB, 52
ROI (return on investment), aligning with analytics currency, 146–147
root node, 174
Ropsten, 41
RStudio, 285–287

S

Sarbanes-Oxley (SOX) Act, 241
SAS Visual Investigator, 82
scalability
  for enterprises, 26–27
  third generation blockchain technology and, 24
  using, 300
scatterplot matrix, 160–161
scope creep, 245
score( ) method, 178, 201
seasonal trends
  as component of time series data, 220
  identifying, 130
seasonality visualization, 137
second generation, 23
semi-private blockchain, 29
sensitive information, 36
serializing transaction data, 49–50
SHA-3 standard, 44
shipProduct( ) function, 55
sigmoid function, 198
signature, in Ethereum transactions, 47
simple linear regression, 195
simulation, building models for, 17–18
sizes, of blockchains, 144
smart contract blockchains, 93, 101–102

About the Author

Michael G. Solomon, PhD, CISSP, PMP, CISM, PenTest+, is an author, educator, and consultant focusing on privacy, security, blockchain, and identity management. As an IT professional and consultant since 1987, Dr. Solomon has led project teams for many Fortune 500 companies and has authored and contributed to more than 25 books and numerous training courses. Dr. Solomon is a Professor of Cyber Security and Global Business with Blockchain Technology at the University of the Cumberlands, and holds a PhD in Computer Science and Informatics from Emory University.

Dedication

I want to thank God for blessing me so richly with such a wonderful family, and I want to thank my family for their support throughout the years. My best friend and wife of over three decades, Stacey, is my biggest cheerleader and supporter through many professional and academic projects. I would not be who I am without her.

And both our sons have always been sources of support and inspiration. To Noah, who still challenges me, keeps me sharp, and tries to keep me relevant, and Isaac, who left us far too early. We miss you, son.

Author's Acknowledgments

All quality projects of any size are team efforts. I greatly appreciate and value the input from this book's project team. Specifically, my technical editor, Andrew Hayward, provided valuable input to keep what you find in this book technically accurate, and the project editor, Susan Pink, did an astounding job throughout the project of keeping us all on track and making sure that I had what I needed to keep writing. Good PEs aren't as plentiful as you'd think.

Publisher's Acknowledgments

Executive Editor: Steve Hayes

Project Editor: Susan Pink

Copy Editor: Susan Pink

Technical Editor: Andrew Hayward

Proofreader: Debbye Butler

Sr. Editorial Assistant: Cherie Case

Production Editor: Mohammed Zafar Ali

Cover Image: © spainter_vfx/Shutterstock

Leverage the power

Dummies is the global leader in the reference category and one of the most trusted and highly regarded brands in the world. No longer just focused on books, customers now have access to the dummies content they need in the format they want. Together we'll craft a solution that engages your customers, stands out from the competition, and helps you meet your goals.

Advertising & Sponsorships

Connect with an engaged audience on a powerful multimedia site, and position your message alongside expert how-to content. Dummies.com is a one-stop shop for free, online information and know-how curated by a team of experts.

- Targeted ads
- Video
- Email Marketing

- Microsites
- Sweepstakes sponsorship

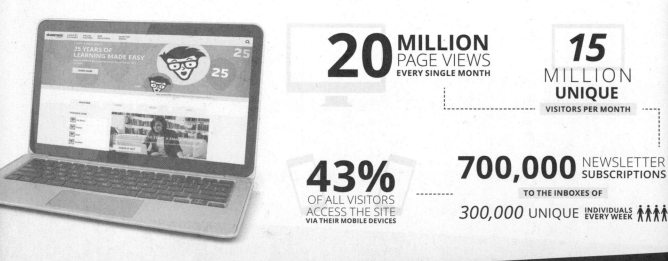

20 MILLION PAGE VIEWS EVERY SINGLE MONTH

15 MILLION UNIQUE VISITORS PER MONTH

43% OF ALL VISITORS ACCESS THE SITE VIA THEIR MOBILE DEVICES

700,000 NEWSLETTER SUBSCRIPTIONS TO THE INBOXES OF *300,000* UNIQUE INDIVIDUALS EVERY WEEK

# of dummies

Custom Publishing

Reach a global audience in any language by creating a solution that will differentiate you from competitors, amplify your message, and encourage customers to make a buying decision.

- Apps
- Books
- eBooks
- Video
- Audio
- Webinars

Brand Licensing & Content

Leverage the strength of the world's most popular reference brand to reach new audiences and channels of distribution.

For more information, visit dummies.com/biz

PERSONAL ENRICHMENT

Staying Sharp
9781119187790
USA $26.00
CAN $31.99
UK £19.99

Facebook
9781119179030
USA $21.99
CAN $25.99
UK £16.99

Guitar
9781119293354
USA $24.99
CAN $29.99
UK £17.99

Investing
9781119293347
USA $22.99
CAN $27.99
UK £16.99

Beekeeping
9781119310068
USA $22.99
CAN $27.99
UK £16.99

Digital Photography
9781119235606
USA $24.99
CAN $29.99
UK £17.99

Meditation
9781119251163
USA $24.99
CAN $29.99
UK £17.99

Pregnancy
9781119235491
USA $26.99
CAN $31.99
UK £19.99

Samsung Galaxy S7
9781119279952
USA $24.99
CAN $29.99
UK £17.99

iPhone
9781119283133
USA $24.99
CAN $29.99
UK £17.99

Crocheting
9781119287117
USA $24.99
CAN $29.99
UK £16.99

Nutrition
9781119130246
USA $22.99
CAN $27.99
UK £16.99

PROFESSIONAL DEVELOPMENT

Windows 10
9781119311041
USA $24.99
CAN $29.99
UK £17.99

AutoCAD
9781119255796
USA $39.99
CAN $47.99
UK £27.99

Excel 2016
9781119293439
USA $26.99
CAN $31.99
UK £19.99

QuickBooks 2017
9781119281467
USA $26.99
CAN $31.99
UK £19.99

macOS Sierra
9781119280651
USA $29.99
CAN $35.99
UK £21.99

LinkedIn
9781119251132
USA $24.99
CAN $29.99
UK £17.99

Windows 10
9781119310563
USA $34.00
CAN $41.99
UK £24.99

SharePoint 2016
9781119181705
USA $29.99
CAN $35.99
UK £21.99

Fundamental Analysis
9781119263593
USA $26.99
CAN $31.99
UK £19.99

Networking
9781119257769
USA $29.99
CAN $35.99
UK £21.99

Office 2016
9781119293477
USA $26.99
CAN $31.99
UK £19.99

Office 365
9781119265313
USA $24.99
CAN $29.99
UK £17.99

Salesforce.com
9781119239314
USA $29.99
CAN $35.99
UK £21.99

Coding
9781119293323
USA $29.99
CAN $35.99
UK £21.99

dummies.com

dummies
A Wiley Brand

Learning Made Easy

ACADEMIC

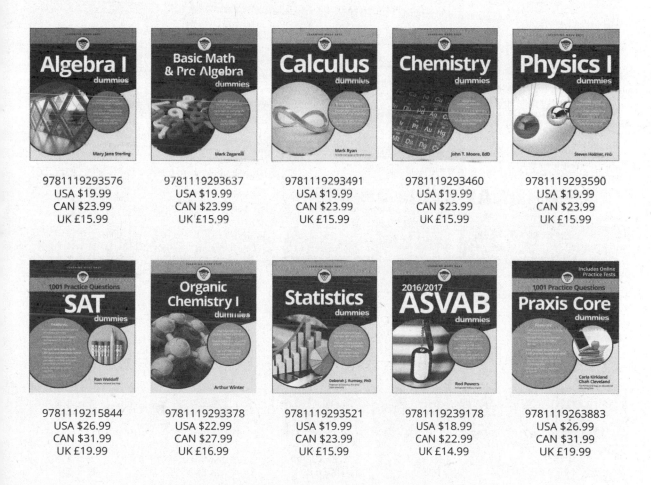

Algebra I
9781119293576
USA $19.99
CAN $23.99
UK £15.99
Mary Jane Sterling

Basic Math & Pre Algebra
9781119293637
USA $19.99
CAN $23.99
UK £15.99
Mark Zegarelli

Calculus
9781119293491
USA $19.99
CAN $23.99
UK £15.99
Mark Ryan

Chemistry
9781119293460
USA $19.99
CAN $23.99
UK £15.99
John T. Moore, EdD

Physics I
9781119293590
USA $19.99
CAN $23.99
UK £15.99
Steven Holzner, PhD

SAT 1,001 Practice Questions
9781119215844
USA $26.99
CAN $31.99
UK £19.99
Ron Woldoff

Organic Chemistry I
9781119293378
USA $22.99
CAN $27.99
UK £16.99
Arthur Winter

Statistics
9781119293521
USA $19.99
CAN $23.99
UK £15.99
Deborah J. Rumsey, PhD

2016/2017 ASVAB
9781119239178
USA $18.99
CAN $22.99
UK £14.99
Rod Powers

Praxis Core 1,001 Practice Questions
9781119263883
USA $26.99
CAN $31.99
UK £19.99
Carla Kirkland, Chah Cleveland

Available Everywhere Books Are Sold